Better Homes and Gardens®

Roses

Gardening Made Easy

Meredith® Consumer Marketing
Des Moines, Iowa

Roses

Gardening Made Easy

Pictured on the front cover:
Clockwise: New Dawn, Mr. Lincoln, split rail fence with old shrub rose.

Bailey Nurseries 155BL, 188BL; Louise Clements, Heirloom Roses 197BR, 215TL; Clemson University-USDA Cooperative Extension Slide Series, Bugwood.org 102TCR; Division of Plant Industry Archive, Florida Department of Agriculture & Consumer Services, Bugwood.org 104TR; Purdue University, Plant & Pest Diagnostic Lab 104TL; Robin Rosetta, Oregon State University 101TCR; Star® Roses and Plants/ Conard-Pyle 232TR; Ward Upham, Kansas State University 101TR; Carroll E. Younce, USDA Agricultural Research Service, Bugwood.org 102TR

First Edition.
Printed in the United States of America.
ISBN: 978-0-696-30150-6

All of us at Meredith® Consumer Marketing are dedicated to providing you with information and ideas to enhance your home. We welcome your comments and suggestions. Write to us at: Meredith Consumer Marketing, 1716 Locust St., Des Moines, IA 50309-3023.

Contents

Chapter 1

HISTORY AND DEVELOPMENT

Roses weren't always in the forms, shapes, and colors you see today. Learn how they evolved.

Chapter 2

ROSES FOR YOUR GARDEN

There's a rose right for every garden. Use these helpful guidelines when you buy them.

Chapter 3

LANDSCAPING WITH ROSES

Roses can beautify and solve problems in your yard. Be sure to cut some for bouquets.

Chapter 4

GARDEN PLANS

Create a beautiful rose garden using easy plans.

Chapter 5

ROSE CARE AND MAINTENANCE

To keep roses performing at their best, they need a little tender loving care.

Chapter 6

ROSE LIFESTYLE

Use fresh and dried roses, petals, and hips in bouquets, recipes, and crafts.

Chapter 7

ROSE GALLERY

Each of these roses is rated 7.5 or higher by the American Rose Society.

CHAPTER ONE

History and Development

A rose by any other name is just as fascinating. These beautiful blooms have been manipulated into a multitude of sizes, shapes, forms, and colors that continue to evolve and change.

From Wild to Wonderful

The first roses were called species roses. These plucky plants are the relatives of every type of rose planted in gardens today.

The earliest roses were wild. Botanists call them the species of the genus *Rosa*, part of the family Rosaceae. Taxonomists—specialists who classify roses—debate the issue, but they generally agree that 100 to 150 are true species. How the species evolved, possibly from one or two ancestors, can only be answered by extensive DNA analysis. Since that process is quite expensive, the answer is not likely to come soon.

Species roses thrive today

Most species roses originated in Asia and Europe; about a dozen are native to North America. Many species roses do very well in gardens today, displaying excellent blooms, hips, foliage, and thorns.

Rose hybridizers still rely on species roses as part of their breeding lines to improve disease resistance and cold hardiness. Virtually all species roses can still be purchased today.

Other roses appeared by about the first century, when classical writers mentioned specific roses, including three of the five old European rose families—gallicas, albas, and damasks. References to centifolias (also known as cabbage roses) emerged at the end of the 16th century.

About 100 years later, the centifolias mutated into moss roses. (The "moss" actually refers to the small growths on the sepals, the green, petal-like leaves at the base of each bud.)

Breeding hybrids begins

The first known rose hybridizing originated in Holland in the 18th century. Breeders planted roses close together, letting them naturally cross-pollinate, then harvested and propagated the seeds. Hybrid roses had been created this way in nature for thousands of years, but breeders used the same idea to speed up and improve the process.

opposite, above Champney's Pink Cluster, a soft pink noisette rose created in 1811 in South Carolina, is still available today. Other than wild roses, it's considered the first truly American rose. **opposite, below left** Madame Ferdinand Jamin, a hybrid perpetual bred in France, came to the United States in 1886 and was renamed American Beauty. **opposite, below right** The Apothecary's Rose, also called *Rosa gallica officinalis,* dates from before 1240 and is still a popular garden rose.

By the end of the 18th century, a watershed in rose development arrived with reblooming roses from China. They were originally called Chinas and tea-scented Chinas, and the latter became known as tea roses. While many of these first China roses were unsuited for gardens because they weren't cold-hardy, they turned out to be significant as parents. Their desirable reblooming genes were quickly blended with species and European roses.

Chinese roses become American

In 1811, the first crosses from Chinese roses created the noisette rose family. John Champneys of South Carolina produced Champneys' Pink Cluster from a cross between *Rosa moschata* (musk rose) and Parson's Pink China. While this can be considered the first truly American rose, the most famous is surely Harison's Yellow, created in 1824 from two other species. This beloved and tough rose was carried and planted by pioneers and settlers throughout the American West, where its small, fragrant flowers still bloom today.

In 1817, Parson's Pink China again played an important role. Paired with an unknown damask rose, it created a new hybrid to found the Bourbon family of roses. These large semiclimbing plants originated on Bourbon (now called Reunion), a French island in the Indian Ocean east of Madagascar.

Beginning in the 1830s, many types of roses made their way into the bloodlines of the hybrid perpetual family. Hybrid perpetuals—strong, upright plants with double, long-lasting but sparse repeat blooms— dominated rose breeding until the end of the 19th century.

American Beauty, immensely popular as a cut flower in the United States, is a hybrid perpetual hybridized by Henri Lédéchaux of France and originally named Madame Ferdinand Jamin.

From Wild to Wonderful

Modern roses are defined as any rose family created since the late 1800s. Hybrid teas, polyanthas, ramblers, and climbers are modern roses.

Hybrid tea roses are considered modern roses. The name implies that they're a cross between a hybrid perpetual and a tea, but so many rose families contributed to the earliest varieties that the original hybrid tea parentage will never be positively identified.

The American Rose Society has declared La France, a light pink rose created from a white tea and a red hybrid perpetual, to be the first.

In 1880, the Horticultural Society of Lyon, France, gave the moniker Hybrides de Thé (French for "hybrid tea") to roses created by English breeder Henry Bennett. The term came into general use about 10 years later.

Polyantha means "many flowers"

Polyantha (Greek for "many flowers") roses, a family of low-growing plants with a profusion of small flowers, have a more definitive history.

The first polyantha was the white Pâquerette, introduced by Guillot et Fils of Lyon, France, in 1875. Pâquerette was a seedling from a low growing *Rosa multiflora*, but unlike its parent, had a repeat-blooming habit.

Although polyanthas were all the rage around the turn of the 20th century, they've mostly fallen out of favor. However, some beloved varieties, such as The Fairy, are still available.

BHG TEST GARDEN TIP

HAVE NO FEAR!

Roses have a bad reputation with some people for being hard to grow. Not true! Many of the most recent and the very oldest roses are disease resistant. Check the tag for excellent disease resistance and repeat flowering, then water and feed these tough beauties for easy-care blooms throughout the growing season.

Ramblers and climbers appear

In 1880, Max Wichura sent a set of Japanese species plants to Europe, where they were promptly named *Rosa wichuriana* in his honor. These roses grew near to the ground with fairly long, creeping canes. While their small white blooms were unremarkable, their potential for breeding landscape plants was apparent. Among the first to take advantage of this potential were Americans Michael Horvath and Walter Van Fleet.

Horvath introduced Pink Roamer, a cross of *R. wichuriana* with the red China Cramoisi Supérieur in 1897. A year later, Van Fleet unveiled May Queen, a cross of *R. wichuriana* with Mrs. DeGraw, a pink Bourbon. These roses, with their long, flexible canes and masses of blooms, quickly became known as ramblers.

Ramblers were widely bred during the early 20th century. Although they don't rebloom, they are still popular, and many are available from mail-order sources.

Hybridizers in the early 20th century also wanted long-caned roses with a repeat blooming habit and larger flowers. Again, they enlisted a combination of species and hybrids. Many climbers were introduced although most are now long forgotten.

The first true large-flowered climber was New Dawn, a light pink, very fragrant variety introduced in 1930. New Dawn is a sport—a genetic mutation—of the rambler Dr. W. Van Fleet. It blooms recurrently, with one flush following another, rather than just once. New Dawn was the first rose to receive a plant patent in the United States.

opposite, left The reblooming qualities of its soft pink blooms make the large-flowered climber New Dawn a good choice for arbors. ***opposite, above right*** La Marne, a pink polyantha, should be protected for winter in cold areas of the country. ***opposite, middle right*** Cramoisi Supérieur, a climbing China rose, works well trained on a trellis or fence. ***opposite, below right*** La France is considered to be the first hybrid tea.

From Wild to Wonderful

New rose types continued to be introduced. Floribundas and grandifloras offer large and numerous blooms.

Searching for roses that bloomed in clusters like polyanthas but with larger flowers, breeders crossed polyanthas with hybrid teas and other large-flowered types to create what they initially called a hybrid polyantha.

The family name for this new rose changed from hybrid polyantha to floribunda in 1950. The first floribunda (Latin for "many flowers") is generally credited to Danish hybridizer Svend Poulsen. His Rödhätte (Danish for "Little Red Riding Hood"), a cherry red cross of a polyantha and a hybrid tea, debuted in 1911.

Floribundas flourish

World's Fair, a floribunda, was one of the first four roses honored in 1940 by All-America Rose Selections (a nonprofit association of growers and introducers), but the public tended to ignore floribundas until Fashion was introduced in 1949 and Vogue in 1951.

Both were hybridized by American Gene Boerner, who became known as "Papa Floribunda" during a 45-year career of breeding roses for the Jackson & Perkins Company.

Grandifloras arrive on the scene

Another American, Walter Lammerts, created the grandiflora (Latin for "large flowers") family. His Queen Elizabeth, introduced in 1954, was touted as the beginning of a new type of roses.

These large, robust plants combine the spray habit of floribundas with the large, fragrant blooms of hybrid teas. Few grandifloras approach the physical stature, bloom habit, and floral production of Queen Elizabeth, which was the second variety inducted into the World Rose Hall of Fame, in 1979. Peace, a hybrid tea, was the first, in 1976.

Smaller blooms suit other purposes

Miniature roses, with blooms about 1 to 1½ inches wide, originated from a dwarf China rose sent to England in the early 1800s. The rose was apparently lost, then rediscovered more than a century later and named Rouletii after its finder, a man named Roulet. Breeding started soon after its rediscovery. One of the first miniatures was the red Tom Thumb, bred in 1936 by Holland's Jan de Vink from Rouletii and a polyantha.

The first American hybridizer of minis, Ralph Moore, became known as the "King of the Miniatures" during more than 50 years of breeding hundreds of varieties. A little more than a decade ago, the rose world welcomed a new family called miniflora, consisting of small- to medium-size plants whose blooms boast the classic hybrid tea form and grow slightly larger than miniatures.

Which roses take the most work?

ANSWER: The bigger they are, the more work. Miniatures generally need less tender loving care than large-flowered climbers.

opposite, above The well-named Brass Band, a floribunda, grows large sprays of luscious blooms with tones of orange, apricot, and melon. ***opposite, below*** Miniature roses perform well in containers and in the garden.

From Wild to Wonderful

New roses were developed to look like old roses, but exhibited important differences such as a reblooming habits and wonderful fragrance.

Thanks to their easy-going, disease-resistant qualities, shrub roses have made a big splash with gardeners in the past 25 years.

Botanically, all roses are shrubs because they fit this definition: a woody plant of relatively low height with several stems arising from the base. However, the American Rose Society calls any rose a "shrub" if it doesn't fit easily into one of the other classes.

Shrubs break down into four subfamilies: hybrid kordesii, hybrid musk, hybrid rugosa, and hybrid moyesii. However, many varieties are simply generically called shrubs.

This incredibly diverse class includes large spreading plants as well as low-growing groundcover types and everything in between.

David Austin roses: Old with new

Among shrubs, the first significant development began nearly 50 years ago with the introduction of David Austin's Constance Spry. This pink cross of an Old Garden Rose with a floribunda was the first of hundreds of Austin roses that he dubbed "English Roses."

Austin roses combine the flower forms and fragrance of Old Garden Roses with the reblooming habit and wider color palette of modern roses. They're available in many plant sizes and growth habits, and in an equally large series of colors, bloom habits, and aromas.

Most Austin varieties have reasonably good disease resistance; some are exceptional.

Rugosas and other tough contenders

Rugosa shrub roses (technically "hybrid rugosas") are super winter-hardy with extremely disease-resistant foliage and very fragrant blooms. The downside is a rather sparse bloom habit. The plants, most introduced a century ago, can grow quite large, 7 to 8 feet tall.

In the mid-1980s, low-growing rugosas about 3 to 4 feet tall with a moderate spreading habit came on the market. This family of 24 to 36 low-growing varieties usually carries the word "Pavement" or "Roadrunner" in the name.

In 1990, the extremely disease-resistant Flower Carpet series emerged. Touted as groundcover roses, Flower Carpets often grow more upright than spreading. They reach about 3 feet tall and wide and are available in nine color varieties. Unlike low-growing rugosas, most Flower Carpet blooms have slight aromas.

The roses in the newest groundcover family, Drift, are crosses between full-size groundcover roses and miniatures, making them ideal for small gardens. Drift roses come in seven colors.

Knock Out roses introduced

The Knock Out series, which began in 2000, represents the most significant recent addition to shrub roses. The original cherry red Knock Out grows 4 to 5 feet tall and blooms from spring until frost. It's touted as one of the most disease-resistant roses and is the most widely sold rose in North America. The series currently includes seven roses in a range of colors and flower forms.

Knock Out and Rainbow Knock Out earned All-America Rose Selections awards, and the original also received an American Rose Society's Members' Choice award. They're widely available at nurseries and garden stores, and by mail order.

Exciting upgrades in the future

What will the future bring for rose development and evolution?

Hybridizers around the world seek two qualities: improved disease resistance and more fragrance—ideally both in the same variety.

Some hope for a blue or black rose, but it remains to be seen whether genetic engineering can bring either of these chimeras to reality.

Whatever happens in the next 10, 20, or 50 years, one thing is sure: There will be intriguing and thrilling additions to the millennia-long story of the world's favorite flower.

BHG TEST GARDEN TIP

MAKE A TOUGH CHOICE

There's an apparent genetic link between fragrance and disease problems in roses. The more fragrant the blooms, the more disease-prone the plants can be. Gardeners often have to choose between fragrance and a clean, disease-resistant plant.

left The multiple petals and rich fragrance of Prospero characterize the qualities of most David Austin English roses. ***above right*** Cherry red blooms and incredible disease resistance make Knock Out a garden winner. ***below right*** Rainbow Knock Out's floral display of coral-pink blooms with yellow centers lasts the entire growing season.

CHAPTER TWO

Roses for Your Garden

Every rose is perfect for someone, but no rose is perfect for everyone. Identify the right rose and plant it in the right spot, and you'll love the results.

Choosing Roses

Success with roses begins with picking the right ones for your garden or landscape. Size, type, and quality matter.

Avoid buying blooming roses on impulse at the garden center—do some research first! Roses that perform well in Southern California won't necessarily act the same in Maine or Kansas. Favorable reviews from producers don't always mean their roses will grow well everywhere.

Untold numbers of enthusiastic gardeners get discouraged with growing roses simply because they make poor choices. With a little guidance, it's easy to make a good pick.

Become a savvy shopper

Buy your roses by following some critical steps that are somewhat akin to buying a new car—but without the hassle of negotiating a price.

Decide your wants for color, shape, and use.

Calculate your needs for your garden.

Determine how much time and energy you want to devote to care; some roses are easier to maintain than others.

Choose whether to use fungicides, insecticides, and miticides, or whether to take a purely organic approach.

Check the marketplace—local and mail order—to compare when shopping for varieties.

Identify your local USDA plant hardiness zone (see map, page 115) to see which rose types grow best where you live.

While this may seem like a daunting list, it's easier than it looks. As you follow each step, selecting a rose becomes an exciting and much-anticipated process that will beautify your garden.

Select your priorities

Remember: There is no perfect rose. No single variety will offer every desirable bloom quality, such as beauty, size, fragrance, long vase life, and long stems. Nor is there a single rose variety with vigor, heavy bloom, quick repeat bloom, winter hardiness, disease and insect resistance, and a neat upright habit.

You'll need to compromise. As the song performed by the rock group Poison suggests, "Every Rose Has Its Thorn." It helps to make a prioritized list for bloom and bush.

Although fragrance is often a priority, remember that many very good to excellent roses carry little to no fragrance. You may have to make a tough choice between disease resistance and fragrance.

Why is bloom color so variable?

ANSWER: Weather plays a significant role in rose bloom colors. Some varieties stay more colorfast in heat while others fade. Ask a local Consulting Rosarian (www.ars.org, "Need Advice?") what works best for your area.

opposite Check the plant tag for notes on disease resistance, sun requirements, and other helpful information. If possible, select a rose that's not yet blooming. That means the bush is spending most of its energy growing good roots instead of flowers.

Color, Shape, And Forms

Roses grow in almost every color and come in a variety of bloom shapes and habits to fit any garden.

Color your garden

Roses grow in almost every color other than blue, black, or green. Blooms appear as solids or blends, from bright to pastel. Some roses have different colors on the tops and bottoms of their petals. Others can be striped or mottled.

Choose bloom shape

Bloom shape is described by the number of petals and overall appearance. Here are petal definitions:

Single: A "single" is often defined as a rose with five-petal blooms, but the American Rose Society's definition is five to eight petals.

Semidouble: A semidouble rose has 8 to 16 petals, usually noted when the rose is at its peak and bloom stamens are visible.

Double: Doubles may contain 16 to 60 petals. Hybrid teas, grandifloras, miniatures, minifloras, and floribundas are often said to have classic form. When viewed from the top, a classic double resembles a perfect bull's-eye with a tight or pinpoint center around which the petals unfurl evenly to a nearly horizontal level. Other doubles are called informal; they include anything that doesn't look classic.

Very double: Very double roses, including many of the Old Garden Roses and the David Austin English roses, have more than 60 petals.

Select for bloom habit

Bloom habit refers to the various ways a rose bush and its flowers behave or look. Despite what the plant tag states about when and how often the plant will bloom, your climate will influence the number of flowers produced and the time between bloom cycles.

Some roses, such as hybrid teas, miniatures, and minifloras, generally produce one bloom per stem. Others, such as floribundas and many varieties of shrubs, climbers, and Old Garden Roses, produce sprays of roses.

Some roses work best for specific purposes. For cutting or exhibiting at flower shows, choose a hybrid tea or a miniature.

For landscaping, varieties with flowers that grow in sprays are good choices. Some types, such as hybrid teas, offer a combination of both spray and one-bloom-per-stem habits.

BLOOM COLOR

1 Angel Face, a floribunda, grows with purple-pink sprays. ***2*** Scentimental, a floribunda, shows unusual red-and-white candy-striped petals. ***3*** Octoberfest, a grandiflora, displays brilliant orange classic blooms. ***4*** Black Jade, a miniature rose, is one of the darkest roses available.

BLOOM SHAPE

***1* Single bloom,** Flower Carpet Coral ***2* Semidouble,** Playboy ***3* Double Classic,** Voluptuous! ***4* Double Informal,** Livin' Easy ***5* Very Double,** Königen van Dänemark

BLOOM HABIT

***1* Spray Roses,** Trumpeter ***2* One Bloom Per Stem,** St. Patrick ***3* Fully Open,** Cupcake ***4* Quartered,** Tournament of Roses

BHG ASK THE GARDEN DOCTOR

What is a fully open or quartered rose?

ANSWER: A rose bloom can be described as fully open or quartered. A fully open rose is a double or very double bloom open to the point that the stamens are visible. A quartered rose is a very double bloom that appears segmented into four sections.

Fragrance

Roses have a subliminal allure beyond their great looks: scent. As with flower forms, there are numerous scents to enjoy.

If beauty is in the eye of the beholder, fragrance is in the nose of the sniffer. Fragrance is extremely difficult to quantify or describe, and its effect can vary significantly from one person to the next.

Olfactory experts have identified about 40 distinct rose fragrances. Rose breeder Henri Delbard says the first fragrance noticed in roses—called the head—is a citrus scent (such as lemon and mandarin) or an aromatic (such as lavender and citronella). This is followed by the heart—a longer-lasting floral scent (such as lilac), a fruity aroma (raspberry), or a spicy scent (nutmeg). Sometimes fragrance relies on the cumulative presence of many blooms, such as the ones covering the shrub Westerland or many of the Old Garden Roses. Because fragrance is subjective, visit rose shows and rose gardens to find which varieties seem pleasingly aromatic to you.

Which roses are most fragrant?

It's difficult to find objective evaluations of rose fragrance. The aroma of any variety can vary from one geographical area to another and can depend on climate and other factors.

The All-America Rose Selections (AARS), a nonprofit association of rose growers and introducers, evaluates new roses on about a dozen criteria, including fragrance. If a rose has earned an AARS award, its background information will include details about its scent (if any).

Hybrid teas, grandifloras, and many of the David Austin English roses are quite fragrant. Nearly all purple roses are moderately to highly fragrant.

Perdita, Molineux, Sceptered Isle, and Teasing Georgia have won fragrance awards in the United Kingdom. Although many overseas rose trials make fragrance awards each year, the only trial in the United States that rewards roses for fragrance is at the Rose Hills Pageant of Roses Garden in Whittier, California.

opposite Molineux, a shrub rose from English breeder David Austin, is highly fragrant, like many of the Austin roses.

THE SWEETEST SCENTS

Many roses are sweetly fragrant, but some are simply standouts in the world of fragrance. If you want flowers that are as sumptuous smelling as they are beautiful, try these varieties.

FRAGRANT CLOUD
Captivating fragrance from big coral red blooms. Fragrant Cloud is a vigorous hybrid tea with a lot of flower power.

FRAGRANT PLUM
Noteworthy for its lavender blushing hue and its sweet scent, which is rich and plumlike, Fragrant Plum is a hybrid tea that bears almost perfectly shaped flowers.

AMERICA
Strongly scented coral pink flowers bloom all summer long. America is disease resistant, so you can count on it to look good at the end of the season.

RADIANT PERFUME
This grandiflora rose's name says it all! The big, golden yellow blooms bear a wonderfully intense citrus scent. Thanks to their long stems, the flowers are perfect for cutting.

MISTER LINCOLN
An award-winning rose introduced in 1965 that's just as popular today, it features rich, velvety red flowers packed with a strong fragrance.

Rose Bush Habits

For peace of mind and the overall appearance of your garden, choose the right rose plant size and shape.

Shrub

Shrub roses take the best of the hardiest rose species and combine those traits with modern repeat blooming and diverse flower forms, colors, and fragrances. Some shrub roses may grow tall, with vigorous, far-reaching canes; others stay compact. Recent rose breeding has focused on developing hardier shrub roses for landscaping that need little to no maintenance. Shrub roses usually grow as wide as they do tall—often 3 to 6 feet—and have an attractive bushy growth habit.

The shrub family includes roses of all shapes and sizes. This leads to some confusion because rose producers sometimes come up with their own descriptive names such as groundcover, shrublet, and Flower Carpet for plants of a certain size and habit of shrub rose.

Rose hybridizers have different view of what constitutes a shrub. For example, David Austin's English roses range from short floribunda-like plants such as Bredon to virtual climbers such as Abraham Darby, but Austin has chosen to classify them all as shrubs.

To better define shrubs, mostly for exhibition purposes, the American Rose Society has designated four subfamilies of shrubs: hybrid kordesii, hybrid rugosa, hybrid musk, and hybrid moyesii.

Some shrubs roses become known by a specific name. These often represent the output of a single hybridizer; many were bred for a special purpose, such as cold hardiness. These include Buck, David Austin, Earth-Kind, Easy Elegance, Explorer, Knock Out, Morden, and Romantica. Shrub roses to try include Autumn Sunset (right), Pink Knock Out, and Chuckles.

SHRUB ROSES

Among the hardiest of rose species, shrub roses also offer many beautiful traits: repeat blooming, diverse flower forms and colors, and lovely fragrance. Easy-care shrub roses are popular in landscapes and gardens alike.

REQUIREMENTS, CHARACTERISTICS, AND USES

LIGHT: Sun

ZONES: 3–10

PLANT HEIGHT: 1–5 feet tall or taller

PLANT WIDTH: To 3 feet wide

LANDSCAPE USES: Containers, beds & borders, slopes

FEATURES: Attractive foliage, fragrant, winter interest, cut flowers, attracts birds, easy to grow

Rose Bush Habits

Hybrid Tea

Hybrid teas traditionally produce the showiest blooms. In fact, most roses at florist shops are hybrid tea varieties. The form of a hybrid tea rose is tall and upright, with sparse foliage toward the base. Hybrid teas grow fairly upright and can reach 6 feet tall in the right conditions. The lower canes can appear leggy.

Today's rose breeding emphasizes fragrance as well as plant vigor. The blooms develop singly on long stems, and the buds are often as elegant as the open blooms. The flower and bud of the hybrid tea is the classic shape most often thought of as the rose flower.

Hybrid tea rose bushes rarely need support to withstand rain and wind. The foliage normally begins 1 or 2 feet above ground level, often giving hybrid teas a bare-legged look that some gardeners prefer to screen with companion plants such as catmint (*Nepeta*) or low-growing roses. Gemini and Elina are good hybrid teas for nearly every climate.

Hybrid teas require careful pruning while still dormant in early spring to ensure good air circulation through the plant and development of vigorous, healthy canes. A sunny location with well-drained, fertile soil and rose food applied at least three times a season will guarantee abundant flowers to enjoy in a vase. Protect roses in climates colder than Zone 6 with heavy mulching around the base of the plant.

Classic hybrid teas to try in your garden are Kardinal (right), Irish Elegance, and Touch of Class.

BHG TEST GARDEN TIP

ROSE FRAGRANCE

The fragrance of a garden rose is enhanced by mild humidity and warmth, but not excessive heat. Depending upon your climate, mornings and mid or late afternoons are the best times to enjoy the fragrances of your roses.

CLASSIC HYBRID TEAS

The quintessential rose flower shape, the hybrid tea is the flower of choice for bouquets and flower arrangements. In the garden or a vase, this classic rose offers velvety petals and frequently a lovely fragrance.

REQUIREMENTS, CHARACTERISTICS, AND USES

LIGHT: Sun

ZONES: 5–9

PLANT HEIGHT: 4–6 feet tall

PLANT WIDTH: 2–3 feet wide

LANDSCAPE USES: Containers, beds & borders

FEATURES: Attractive foliage, fragrant, cut flowers, easy to grow

Rose Bush Habits

Groundcover

A new breed of landscaping roses came about with the advent of shrub roses, which offer beautiful ways to fill in borders and cover bare earth. These low-growing groundcover roses are useful for mass planting in a border or under a tree and to mix colorfully with perennials or shrubs, line a path, cover a slope, or plant in hanging baskets or window boxes for a bloom-spilling display.

Most are quite disease resistant and attractive, but they must be planted close together for a true groundcover effect. To reinvigorate groundcover roses each year, cut back the plants by two-thirds while they are still dormant in early spring.

Varieties touted as groundcover roses are usually low-growing, somewhat bushy shrubs that don't actually spread and cover the ground. Some of the best groundcover roses include Sea Foam, a white variety often described as a trailing climber; some of the Meidiland series including White Meidiland; the Blanket and Ribbon varieties; and the Flower Carpet roses (right), which come in a variety of colors (Scarlet, Red, Yellow, Amber, Coral, Pink, Pink Supreme).

Carpet of Color demonstrates how groundcover roses blanket the garden.

GRAND GROUNDCOVER

Low-growing groundcover roses are ideal for massing together in a bed, border, or hedgerow to create a continuous line of bountiful blooms.

REQUIREMENTS, CHARACTERISTICS, AND USES

LIGHT: Sun, part sun

ZONES: 5–9

PLANT HEIGHT: 1–3 feet tall

PLANT WIDTH: To 4 feet wide

LANDSCAPE USES: Containers, beds & borders, slopes

SPECIAL FEATURES: Attractive foliage, attracts birds, easy to grow

Rose Bush Habits

Rambler

Ramblers, which only bloom once a year, are the giants of the rose world, sometimes reaching 30 feet tall.

The now-unofficial name "rambler" is still useful when describing once-blooming roses with very long, flexible canes. The rose does indeed ramble. But this rose class was abolished by the American Rose Society in 1999. Most ramblers were reclassified as hybrid wichurianas or hybrid multifloras.

In general, ramblers are heavy bloomers and are perfect for training along a fence, scrambling across a wall, or climbing up and over an outbuilding. Because ramblers bloom only once, it's a good idea to interplant them with other recurrent-blooming roses.

Another charm of ramblers is that they are highly fragrant. Many varieties are available to buy in garden centers or to order online.

Ramblers to try include Lavender Lassie (right), Paul's Himalayan Musk, and Albéric Barbier.

Ramblin' Red, a large-flowered climber, can grow massive enough to cover an entire house wall.

ROVING RAMBLERS

The long canes of rambling roses can easily cover an arbor, creating a bower of bloom. Plant a rambler on each side of an arbor or trellis and train them to the structure as they climb upward.

REQUIREMENTS, CHARACTERISTICS, AND USES

LIGHT: Sun, part sun

ZONES: 5–10

PLANT HEIGHT: 6–30 feet tall, depending on variety

PLANT WIDTH: To 6 feet wide, depending on variety

LANDSCAPE USES: Beds & borders, privacy

FEATURES: Attractive foliage, fragrant, winter interest, attracts birds, deer resistant, easy to grow

Rose Bush Habits

Miniature

Gardeners who have limited space can enjoy all the fun and fragrance of rose growing by cultivating miniature roses in small beds or containers. They make excellent flowerbed edgers, blooming boldly in the front of the border with perennials and annuals. They make colorful low hedges too. And they can even be grown in window boxes. Miniature roses are so versatile, they can grow anywhere.

Most miniatures can be thought of as scaled-down hybrid teas. A few bear the heavy bloom habit of floribundas. Irresistible is an example of a hybrid tea type of miniature; Anytime has a floribunda style.

Miniature roses first came into being in the early 1930s as an accidental result of rose hybridizing. Since then, master miniaturists have created many jewel-like varieties featuring perfectly shaped tiny blooms on clean, healthy plants that generally stay under 2 feet.

Miniature roses respond to all the care basics of regular-size roses, which means deep irrigation, sunshine, and regular fertilizing. Because their foliage is close to the soil, miniature roses are particularly susceptible to spider mites. They also need extra winter protection in colder climates. To ensure the plant doesn't die back to the roots, in Zone 5 and below, bury the rose plant in a mound of soil.

Miniature roses bloom in all the same colors as larger roses, so you can match them to any garden color theme. Clip them for small bouquets; many are richly fragrant. Try Jilly Jewel (right), Giggles, and Jean Kenneally in beds, borders, and container gardens.

GREAT IN GROUPS

Because miniature roses are so small, they look best when planted in groups. Pair them in containers or add them in groups of three in a small garden bed. If you use miniatures as edging plants, line them up to enjoy their diminutive blooms in mixed perennial borders. Like their larger cousins, miniature roses will continue to bloom if they are deadheaded, so clip off dead and fading flowers often to keep plants in top blooming form.

ADORABLE MINIS

Small in stature, miniature roses make excellent edging plants for rose or perennial gardens. They bloom in a wide range of flower colors and have a variety of foliage types. They make great cut flowers too.

REQUIREMENTS, CHARACTERISTICS, AND USES

LIGHT: Sun, part sun

ZONES: 4–11

PLANT HEIGHT: 1–3 feet tall

PLANT WIDTH: To 2 feet wide

LANDSCAPE USES: Containers, beds & borders

FEATURES: Attractive foliage, fragrant, cut flowers, easy to grow

Rose Bush Habits

Standard

Standards are often dubbed tree roses, and they can be created from many modern rose families. To make a standard, a bud from a hybrid rose is grafted onto a wild rose cane that's 1½ to 3 feet tall, giving it the look of a small tree. Standards are frequently staked to help prevent damage from heavy winds and rain. Because of their shape, they are somewhat top-heavy, so they should be planted in a heavy container.

A standard can make a stunning focal point in a garden. Some nurseries offer "weeping" standards created from lax-caned varieties that give a cascading effect.

Double-budded standards offer even more drama. A double-budded standard has two different varieties grafted on opposite sides, creating a plant that can produce two colors and types of flowers.

Because standards are more susceptible to winter damage than their bush counterparts, they're recommended only for warmer climates. In cold areas, a standard can be overwintered in a pot if it is kept where the roots won't freeze.

Northern Encore is a good standard for cold climates because it is an own-root rose.

STELLAR STANDARDS

These lollipop-shape plants are also called tree roses and come in a variety of sizes. They excel in containers and look lovely in pairs to flank a doorway or garden entryway. Almost any rose can be trained as a standard.

REQUIREMENTS, CHARACTERISTICS, AND USES

LIGHT: Sun, part sun

ZONES: 5–10

PLANT HEIGHT: 2–5 feet tall

PLANT WIDTH: 1–2 feet wide

LANDSCAPE USES: Beds & borders, containers

FEATURES: Attractive foliage, fragrant, easy to grow

Rose Bush Habits

Climber

The acrobats of the rose world, climbing varieties develop long canes well adapted to training on pillars, fences, arbors, outbuildings, and gazebos.

Most climbing roses are mutations or variations of bush-type varieties. They develop either large single flowers or clustered blooms on a stem. Climbers may bloom once a season or continually, depending on the variety.

Climbers can be trained to bloom more heavily by leading their canes in a horizontal direction. Loose anchoring to a support will encourage young plants to climb. Climbing roses can be trained horizontally and vertically. Wait a year after planting a climbing rose to train it to a structure; it will have more cane growth and be easier to train. Canes can be threaded through appropriate structures or tied loosely to a structure.

Climbers come in many sizes, including miniatures that reach 6 feet and large-flowered climbers up to 30 feet. Climbers to try include Dr. W. Van Fleet (right), Dream Weaver, and Don Juan.

BHG ASK THE GARDEN DOCTOR

What is a rose sport?

ANSWER: In rose terminology, a "sport" is a genetic mutation. But this is not necessarily a bad thing. There are two kinds of sports: color and climbing. Color sports are when the bloom color changes but all the characteristics of the plant remain the same. For example, Blushing Knock Out is a sport of the original Knock Out rose. Climbing sports happen when bush varieties develop longer canes. An example is Climbing Peace, a sport of the famous hybrid tea rose Peace. Most rose sports are unstable and revert to their original form, making them not commercially viable.

PERFUMED CLIMBERS

Climbing roses offer flowers and fragrance overhead. And what a beautiful way to greet visitors to your home. Plant a pair of the same climber for a continuous arc of color, or mix two climbing roses to intermingle colors.

REQUIREMENTS, CHARACTERISTICS, AND USES

LIGHT: Sun, part sun

ZONES: 4–11

PLANT HEIGHT: 6–30 feet tall, depending on variety

PLANT WIDTH: To 6 feet wide, depending on variety

LANDSCAPE USES: Containers, beds & borders, privacy, slopes

FEATURES: Attractive foliage, fragrant, winter interest, attracts birds, deer resistant, easy to grow

Rose Bush Habits

Pillar

Any long-caned rose that is trained to grow straight up can be called a pillar rose. These roses have moderately long canes and can be grown onto a pillar or vertical rose structure. Roses grown as pillars need support to prevent them from collapsing.

The structures that pillar roses grow on can vary. Some are simple pedestals; others have domed tops. The structure beneath gives shape to the overall growth of the pillar rose. In addition to wooden and metal structures, rose pillars can also be made from stone. Whatever the material, the design of the pillar is functional in giving shape and structure to a rose that grows upward.

Pillar roses make strong vertical accents for garden focal points. They can be centered in a round or square bed or grown in the back of a border. In a large garden, use a series of pillar roses to flank a walkway or create a backdrop.

Pillar roses to try include Pierre de Ronsard (right), Altissimo, and American Pillar (below).

American Pillar is a classic pillar rose with soft pink petals and a white eye.

VERTICAL PILLARS

Pillar roses make excellent additions to formal rose gardens. They add vertical accents to beds and borders. Pillar roses also make gorgeous backdrops in large landscape situations.

REQUIREMENTS, CHARACTERISTICS, AND USES

LIGHT: Sun, part sun

ZONES: 5–10

PLANT HEIGHT: 6–10 feet tall, depending on variety

PLANT WIDTH: To 6 feet wide, depending on variety

LANDSCAPE USES: Beds & borders, privacy

FEATURES: Attractive foliage, fragrant, winter interest, attracts birds, deer-resistant, easy to grow

Rose Families

Roses have a long family history. Understanding the different lineages will help you get to know the types of roses to plant in your yard.

Each of the rose families offers special qualities you may want in a garden. The American Rose Society (ARS) recognizes 37 different classes (or families) of roses. On the following pages, you'll meet the 11 most commonly grown rose families designated by ARS, the international registration authority for roses. All rose families other than species and Old Garden Roses are considered modern roses.

BHG TEST GARDEN TIP

LEARN ABOUT THE AMERICAN ROSE SOCIETY

The American Rose Society (ARS) is the largest rose organization in the world and one of the largest plant societies in the United States. Most ARS members are home gardeners who enjoy growing roses and want to expand their knowledge.

Headquartered in Shreveport, Louisiana, the ARS includes some 11,000 members in more than 300 affiliated societies. For inspiration, visit the ARS American Rose Center gardens at 8877 Jefferson Paige Road.

The ARS also offers free advice to all gardeners through the Consulting Rosarian program. To locate a Consulting Rosarian in your area, go to the ARS website at www.ars.org.

Hybrid tea

Hybrid teas come from a very uniform family. They normally grow 4 to 6 feet tall with fairly strong canes. The blooms, generally the largest of any rose family, are borne singly or in clusters.

Shown: Bewitched

Blooms: Perfect flowers with reliable repeating; deadhead for repeat bloom

Fragrance: Many varieties

Hardiness: Requires heavy winter protection in Zone 5 and colder

Disease: Some varieties are susceptible to black spot.

Comments: Most popular type of rose; rather bare on lower canes

Miniature

Miniatures grow with an upright to bushy habit, usually 1 to 2½ feet tall, although some reach as tall as 4 feet. The blooms tend to be smaller than 1½ inches in diameter and, like those of hybrid teas, are borne singly or in small clusters.

Shown: Sun Sprinkles

Blooms: Most usually have tiny blooms; part of their charm

Fragrance: Little fragrance

Hardiness: Grown on own roots, so more hardy

Disease: Susceptible to black spot and spider mites

Comments: Excellent for small-space gardens; perfect for containers

Floribunda

Floribundas produce an abundance of blooms. They range from about 2 to 5 feet tall, and all have a bushy habit. Their canes range from strong in some varieties to rather thin in others, such as Iceberg. While floribundas can hold themselves erect in dry weather, the canes can collapse under the weight of heavy blooms after a rain. Consider adding support for floribundas if you live in a wet climate.

Shown: French Lace

Blooms: Nonstop bloom with large trusses of many flowers; deadhead for repeat bloom

Fragrance: Many varieties

Hardiness: Winter hardiness varies by variety

Disease: Some varieties are susceptible to black spot.

Comments: Easy to grow; suitable for wet climates; attractively bushy; smaller blooms than hybrid teas

Miniflora

Most minifloras in the United States have been bred for exhibition and have a classic bloom form and are held singly on their stalks. Plants grow up to 4 feet tall with blooms as wide as 3 inches—larger than miniatures but smaller than floribundas. This is a relatively new class designated by the American Rose Society in 1999. Most miniflora varieties are available only through mail order.

Shown: Olympic Gold

Blooms: Most usually have tiny blooms; part of their charm

Fragrant: Little fragrance

Hardiness: Grown on own roots, so more hardy

Disease: Susceptible to black spot and spider mites

Comments: Excellent for small-space gardens; perfect for containers

CHOREOGRAPH BLOOMS

Each rose type has a specific size bloom, but you can get bigger or more well-spaced blooms per plant by some judicious pruning.

GET BIGGER BLOOMS: To get large, one-bloom-per-stem hybrid teas, remove all the buds on a stem except the one on the end, which is the first one to emerge.

GET CONSISTENT BLOOMS: To get consistent, well-spaced blooms in a floribunda or other spray rose, do the opposite. Take out the terminal (end) bud and let the side buds develop into blooms.

Rose Families

Grandiflora

An idealized combination of hybrid teas and floribundas, grandifloras will sometimes grow 7 to 8 feet tall. Most have an upright plant habit, with large blooms borne either singly or in sprays. Grandifloras work well in the background of a rose bed or a mixed flower border.

Shown: Strike It Rich

Blooms: Reliable repeat bloomers if deadheaded

Fragrance: Many varieties

Hardiness: Winter hardiness varies by variety.

Disease: Some varieties are susceptible to black spot.

Comments: Smaller blooms than hybrid teas

Large-flowered climber

There are two types of reblooming, large-flowered climbers that grow with long canes.

The first type has stiff canes held mostly upright that reach 8 to 12 feet tall. It has a spreading habit and can be trained onto a support when the canes are young and still somewhat flexible.

The second type features thin, flexible canes that reach up to 16 feet but are more easily trained due to their suppleness. There's little difference in habit between large-flowered climbers and large shrub roses.

Shown: Fourth of July

Blooms: Ramblers bloom only once. Both types come in many flower forms and colors.

Fragrance: Varies

Hardiness: Some not winter hardy in Zone 5 and colder

Disease: Varies, but often disease resistant

Comments: Useful for adding vertical color in the landscape or disguising unattractive structures

Polyantha

Polyanthas are low-growing plants—about 3 feet tall—bearing small blooms in very large clusters. Over time, many polyantha varieties have turned into climbing forms, bearing lax canes up to 10 feet long that can be readily trained. Although few polyanthas are hybridized today, several older varieties are still available.

Shown: Lovely Fairy

Blooms: Small flowers grow in large clusters with nonstop bloom.

Fragrance: Some varieties

Hardiness: Winter hardiness varies by variety.

Disease: Good disease resistance, but some varieties highly susceptible to black spot

Comments: Low-growing; excellent container roses; attractive foliage

Old Garden Rose

An Old Garden Rose is a specific term used by the ARS to denote members of any rose class existing prior to 1867, when the first hybrid tea was introduced. There are 22 different kinds of Old Garden Roses, including hybrid gallicas. Since hybrid gallicas existed before 1867, any roses bred in the 20th century with a hybrid gallica parent can be registered as hybrid gallicas and be considered Old Garden Roses. Many rosarians disagree with this definition, so there are many synonyms for 18th- and 19th-century roses: heritage roses, heirloom roses, old roses, and others.

Shown: Complicata

Blooms: Some repeat but others bloom only once.

Fragrance: Varies

Hardiness: There's a type to suit nearly any hardiness zone.

Disease: Some varieties are prone to mildew.

Comments: Versatile landscape roses; offer a connection to the past; some spread problematically through suckering

Noisette

Noisette roses are truly American. Although it's not known exactly when this family originated, experts lean toward 1811 as the date when John Champneys, a Charleston, South Carolina, rice farmer, received a Parson's Pink China from Philippe Noisette, his neighbor, and crossed it with a species musk rose. His Champneys' Pink Cluster resulted in a new class of Old Garden Roses.

Noisettes became known for their vigorous and abundant repeat bloom. Although at one time there were about 250 varieties in South Carolina, only 75 to 80 still exist today.

Shown: Alister Stella Gray

Blooms: Repeat bloom in spring and fall

Fragrance: Some varieties

Hardiness: Winter hardiness varies by variety. Tea-Noisettes are less hardy.

Disease: Varies, but often disease resistant

Comments: Good roses for southern gardens

Portland

Portland roses, a relatively small Old Garden Rose classification originating in the late 1700s, were named for the English Duchess of Portland. Medium size, tidy plants can fit easily into almost any garden and produce lovely hips. The original Portland, a scarlet rose named Duchess of Portland, is still available today.

Shown: Comte de Chambord

Blooms: Repeat bloom

Fragrance: Very fragrant

Hardiness: Winter hardiness varies by variety.

Disease: Varies

Comments: Flowers are usually pink in hue. Plants are slow growing.

Hybrid wichuriana

Hybrid wichuriana is the official class for virtually all varieties formerly known as ramblers. It includes any very long-caned, once-blooming roses.

Shown: Albertine

Blooms: Some repeat but others bloom only once.

Fragrance: Some varieties

Hardiness: Winter hardiness varies by variety.

Disease: Varies, but often disease-resistant

Comments: Large flowers

BHG ASK THE GARDEN DOCTOR

What is a good rose to help attract wildlife?

ANSWER: Try species roses. If you favor a slightly wilder style in your garden, look to the ancestors of roses you grow and enjoy for many of the same admirable qualities. Most species roses can tolerate extreme weather conditions, and, because of their colorful hips (fruit), they are good choices for attracting birds and other wildlife to the garden. The canes are often vigorous and arching. Stems may be highly colored but are almost always thorny, making large species good candidates for privacy hedging and deer-frequented areas. Most species roses offer small blooms, and they usually appear only once a season, but their landscaping benefits make them worthwhile to include in borders and background plantings.

Roses by Region

Northwest

Almost all rose families and varieties grow well in the generally temperate area west of the Rockies. The Northwest is a rose grower's heaven.

States covered

This area covers Northern California, Oregon, Washington, and western Idaho.

USDA Zones

This region generally includes USDA Zones 7 to 9.

Which roses to plant

In the Northwest, own-root and budded plants on Dr. Huey or multiflora rootstocks do well. Before buying a rose, check the rootstock.

Once-blooming "cool-weather" Old Garden Roses, including hybrid gallicas, albas, damasks, centifolias, and mosses, plus Bourbons, hybrid perpetuals, and Portlands, grow especially well here. Avoid the reblooming families of teas, Chinas, and noisettes because they need more heat for best performance.

Floribundas and other spray roses do very well throughout a Northwest growing season.

Things to watch for

Black spot is a problem in rainy areas, so plant disease-resistant varieties.

1. **BEGINNERS** Hansa hybrid rugosa
2. **HYBRID TEA** Olympiad
3. **FLORIBUNDA** Livin' Easy
4. **GRANDIFLORA** Fame!
5. **MINIATURE** Gourmet Popcorn
6. **OLD GARDEN ROSE** Stanwell Perpetual
7. **SHRUB** Sally Holmes
8. **CLIMBER/RAMBLER** Compassion

Roses by Region

Midwest and Plains

This is one of the coldest areas of the United States, so choose roses that can withstand hard winters.

States covered

This large territory covers Minnesota, Wisconsin, Michigan, Ohio, Indiana, Illinois, Iowa, North Dakota, South Dakota, Nebraska, Wyoming, Montana, and eastern Idaho.

USDA Zones

This region generally includes USDA Zones 3 to 6.

Which roses to plant

Cool-weather Old Garden Roses grown on their own roots, such as hybrid gallicas, albas, damasks, centifolias, mosses, Bourbons, hybrid perpetuals, and Portlands, are good choices for this area. Avoid the reblooming families of teas, Chinas, and noisettes that need more heat for best performance.

Hardy shrubs such as rugosas, Explorers, Bucks, Knock Outs, Easy Elegance, and Mordens do well in chilly Midwestern winters.

Things to watch for

Midwestern and Plains states gardeners growing hybrid teas and other modern roses should select plants grown on their own roots and provide extensive winter protection. During winter, roses grown in pots should be moved to a greenhouse, garage, or other space that doesn't freeze, so the roots will survive.

1. **BEGINNERS** Carefree Beauty shrub rose
2. **HYBRID TEA** Elina
3. **FLORIBUNDA** Eyepaint
4. **GRANDIFLORA** Earth Song
5. **MINIATURE** Hot Tamale
6. **OLD GARDEN ROSE** R. gallica versicolor
7. **SHRUB** Graham Thomas
8. **CLIMBER/RAMBLER** Royal Sunset

Roses by Region

Northeast

While often not as cold as the Upper Midwest, conditions in the Northeast still require gardeners to plant hardy varieties and provide winter protection.

States covered

This region runs from Maine south through New Hampshire, Vermont, New York, Pennsylvania, West Virginia, and the Atlantic seaboard states.

USDA Zones

This region generally covers USDA Zones 3 to 7.

Which roses to plant

Nearly all shrub families do well in the Northeast, as do most cool-weather Old Garden Roses, including hybrid gallicas, albas, damasks, centifolias, mosses, Bourbons, hybrid perpetuals, and Portlands. Avoid the reblooming families of teas, Chinas, and noisettes because they need more heat for best performance.

Roses enjoy the adequate rain and snowfall common to this region.

Things to watch for

Modern roses, either budded or on their own root, do best with winter protection because this region has four distinct seasons and potentially severe winters.

BEST ROSES FOR THE NORTHEAST

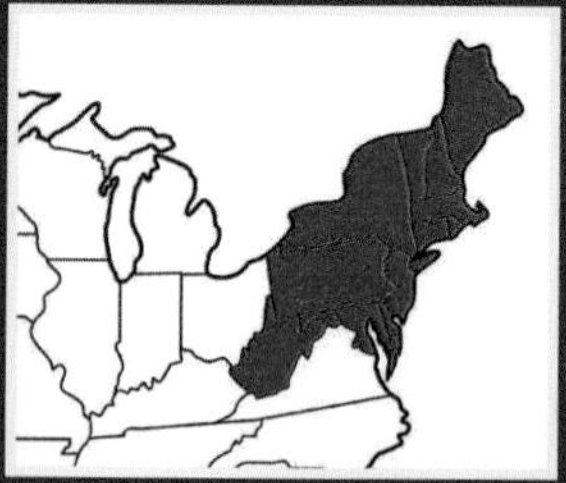

1. **BEGINNERS** Double Knock Out shrub
2. **HYBRID TEA** Gemini
3. **FLORIBUNDA** Betty Prior
4. **GRANDIFLORA** Queen Elizabeth
5. **MINIATURE** Irresistible
6. **OLD GARDEN ROSE** Mme Hardy
7. **SHRUB** Robusta
8. **CLIMBER/RAMBLER** New Dawn

Roses by Region

Southeast

The warm, wet weather in most of the Southeast provides ideal growing conditions for many kinds of roses.

States covered

The Southeast includes Alabama, Mississippi, Louisiana, Georgia, and Florida in the south and ranges north to Kentucky and Virginia.

USDA Zones

This region generally includes USDA Zones 6 to 10.

Which roses to plant

All repeat-blooming Old Garden Roses perform well in the Southeast, particularly teas, Chinas, and noisettes. The Earth-Kind roses and most shrub families are good choices. Grow minis and minifloras on their own roots and modern roses on Fortuniana rootstock.

Gardeners along the coastline should test their soil for salt content. Ask a local extension service which soil amendments are best for growing roses.

Things to watch for

The moist conditions of this region are ideal for spawning black spot, so choose disease-resistant varieties.

1. **BEGINNERS** Mlle Cécile Brünner polyantha
2. **HYBRID TEA** Moonstone
3. **FLORIBUNDA** Lavaglut
4. **GRANDIFLORA** Melody Parfumée
5. **MINIATURE** Bees Knees
6. **OLD GARDEN ROSE** Champneys' Pink Cluster
7. **SHRUB** Abraham Darby
8. **CLIMBER/RAMBLER** Pierre de Ronsard

Roses by Region

South Central and Lower Midwest

Extreme summer heat often followed by very cold winters makes this region a challenging one in which to grow roses.

States covered

This region covers Eastern Colorado, Kansas, Missouri, and Oklahoma and heads south to the tip of Texas.

USDA Zones

This region generally covers USDA Zones 5 to 10.

Which roses to plant

The Earth-Kind family of roses does very well in the lower Midwest and Texas as do repeat-blooming Old Garden Roses that like more heat: noisettes, Chinas, and teas.

Modern roses growing on Fortuniana rootstock are preferred by many rosarians.

Some gardeners in this region avoid the David Austin English roses, believing they are less well suited to the heat.

Things to watch for

Hot, humid conditions promote black spot and other fungal diseases. Water the roots, not the foliage, and plant disease-resistant varieties to win the battle.

BEST ROSES FOR THE SOUTH CENTRAL STATES

1. **BEGINNERS** Belinda's Dream shrub rose
2. **HYBRID TEA** St. Patrick
3. **FLORIBUNDA** Playgirl
4. **GRANDIFLORA** Tournament of Roses
5. **MINIATURE** My Sunshine
6. **OLD GARDEN ROSE** Mutabilis
7. **SHRUB** Sea Foam
8. **CLIMBER/RAMBLER** America

Roses by Region

Southwest and Southern California

Often considered the prime rose-growing area of the country, the Southwest—with warm summers and temperate winters—allows nearly all rose families to flourish.

States covered

This region stretches from central and southern California, Nevada, and Utah to western Colorado, Arizona, and New Mexico.

USDA Zones

This region generally covers USDA Zones 5 to 10.

Which roses to plant

Modern roses growing on Dr. Huey and Fortuniana rootstocks do well. Most Old Garden Roses, miniatures, minifloras, and shrubs perform nicely. Heat may bring more saturated colors to the blooms and darker colors to leaves.

Things to watch for

High temperatures, especially in desert regions, also mean roses will require daily or even twice-daily watering. To prevent fungal diseases always water the roots, not the foliage.

In most areas, amending the soil with plenty of organic material, such as compost, and mulching will improve water retention.

1. **BEGINNERS** Julia Child floribunda
2. **HYBRID TEA** Marilyn Monroe
3. **FLORIBUNDA** Hot Cocoa
4. **GRANDIFLORA** Gold Medal
5. **MINIATURE** Baby Grand
6. **OLD GARDEN ROSE** Rose de Rescht
7. **SHRUB** Sally Holmes
8. **CLIMBER/RAMBLER** Fourth of July

DayDream™

Buying Roses

Once you've decided what kind and color of roses you like and what will work best in your yard, the next choice is where to buy and in what form.

First, choose between a budded or an own-root rose. Each has its advantages.

Budded roses

Budding is a type of grafting that creates a stronger rose. A bud (called the scion) from a hybrid rose is inserted into a cutting of a vigorous wild or nearly wild rose (called the rootstock or understock). This gives the hybrid scion hardiness it might not get on its own roots because the rootstock is usually stronger than the scion.

The rootstocks grow in a field at a nursery for as long as a year before they are grafted (budded). The newly grafted plant stays in the field for another year before it is harvested, put into cold storage, and shipped to retailers. Most budded roses are 2-year-old plants.

Budded roses are graded by a system from the American Association of Nurserymen. A number 1 grade plant must have at least three canes, one of which must be at least $^{5}/_{8}$ inch in diameter. A number 1½ grade plant must have two "reasonably sized" canes, while number 2 grade plants are essentially throwaways.

Own-root roses

Roses can also be started as cuttings. Because it's considerably less expensive to produce a plant on its own root than by budding, most mail-order outlets use this method. Own-root roses are generally propagated in a greenhouse and occasionally replanted outdoors.

Own-root roses are not subject to a grading system. Mail-order nurseries may send anything from a 4- to 6-month-old greenhouse plant to a field-grown rose more than a year old. It's a good idea to contact the company before you order to discover the age and size of the plants.

Decide which is best

Despite claims to the contrary, there is no inherent superiority of own-root over budded roses, or vice versa.

Own-root plants have the advantage of being more winter-hardy than budded ones because they will grow back true to their variety if the plant is killed to the ground, while budded roses will revert back to their rootstock. You'll find a wider range of rose cultivars sold as own-root plants.

The major disadvantage of own-root roses is that they're often sold as younger plants than budded roses. Because own-root roses need more time to reach productive maturity, they're not as good a value.

Rootstocks vary by climate

Owners of budded roses should learn what rootstock their plant has. The overwhelming majority of budded roses in the United States is grown in southern California or Arizona on a rootstock called Dr. Huey, a near-species variety. This rootstock is used primarily because it's compatible with the soil in those areas and works well with most hybrid scions.

However, Dr. Huey doesn't perform well everywhere in the United States. Gardeners in the South or Southeast should seek roses budded on a Fortuniana rootstock. This is a near-wild species much better suited to southern soils and climate.

Likewise, gardeners in the northern United States and southern Canada will do better with budded plants on a strain of *Rosa multiflora*, suited for colder areas. Roses purchased from a Canadian company (there are no importation problems) will be budded primarily on this tougher rootstock.

opposite, left This healthy bare-root rose arrived in good condition with large canes and strong roots. Prune off any extra-long roots, and soak the rose overnight before planting. ***opposite, above*** Read the plant tag carefully to determine what kind of rose you're buying and what kind of care it will take. ***opposite, middle*** This Knock Out rose shows good form. If possible, buy plants that are not in bloom, or completely remove all blooms after planting so the rose can direct its energy into getting established. ***opposite, below right*** You can see the bud union—the knobby scar where the grafted parts meet—on the stem just above the fingers holding this bare-root rose.

Buying Roses

The next big decision is where to buy roses. Purchase by mail or locally? From an independent garden center or a big box store? Each choice has its advantages and disadvantages.

Mail order

Mail-order companies offer the greatest selection of varieties and rootstocks. Even the largest local nursery cannot begin to carry the array of roses found online or in catalogs.

Another advantage: Budding propagators ship bare-root plants with well-established root systems 1 foot long or longer, something not usually available from a local nursery or big box store.

The obvious disadvantage of mail order: not being able to inspect the plants prior to sending money.

Bagged plants

The most common way to package rose plants for sale at big retail outlets is in plastic bags, often with wax-sealed canes. Both of these features are designed to keep moisture in the plant during shipping and display. The disadvantage of bagged plants is the unknown amount of time they are out of water and the fact that they are often not number 1 grade. The advantage: They're usually inexpensive.

If you buy a bagged plant, remove the bag and submerge the entire plant in water for a couple of days to rehydrate it before planting. Many rosarians also advise cutting off the waxed canes entirely, allowing the plant to start over with new, healthy canes. All in all, bagged plants are the lowest quality.

Local nurseries and garden centers

Almost all nurseries sell roses in peat or plastic pots, a practice that also cannot be termed bare-root. The reason for potting the plants is economic: Too many careless buyers seek refunds after their bare-root plants dry out and die from lack of prompt planting or rehydration by soaking. Potting provides a source of moisture and nutrients for the roots.

opposite In recent years, online ordering has become even easier than ordering from a catalog. Check the reviews of any mail-order source before you order.

BUYING FROM LOCAL NURSERIES

Should you buy your roses locally or from a mail-order source? It depends on your priorities. Consider these advantages and disadvantages of buying locally.

ADVANTAGES:

In-person selection of plants allows you to see exactly what you are purchasing.

Access to rose advice from a trained nursery staff person.

Easy return or exchange of damaged or otherwise low-quality plants.

DISADVANTAGES:

Limited selection of varieties.

Added expense for the cost of the pot, the potting soil, and the labor.

Short roots that have been trimmed to fit into the pot. The more and longer the roots, the better start a plant gets.

HOW ROSES ARE SOLD

Roses are generally sold in three ways: bare-root, container, and bagged. Although the most attractive choice is a blooming container, starting as a bare-root plant gets the rose off to a better start.

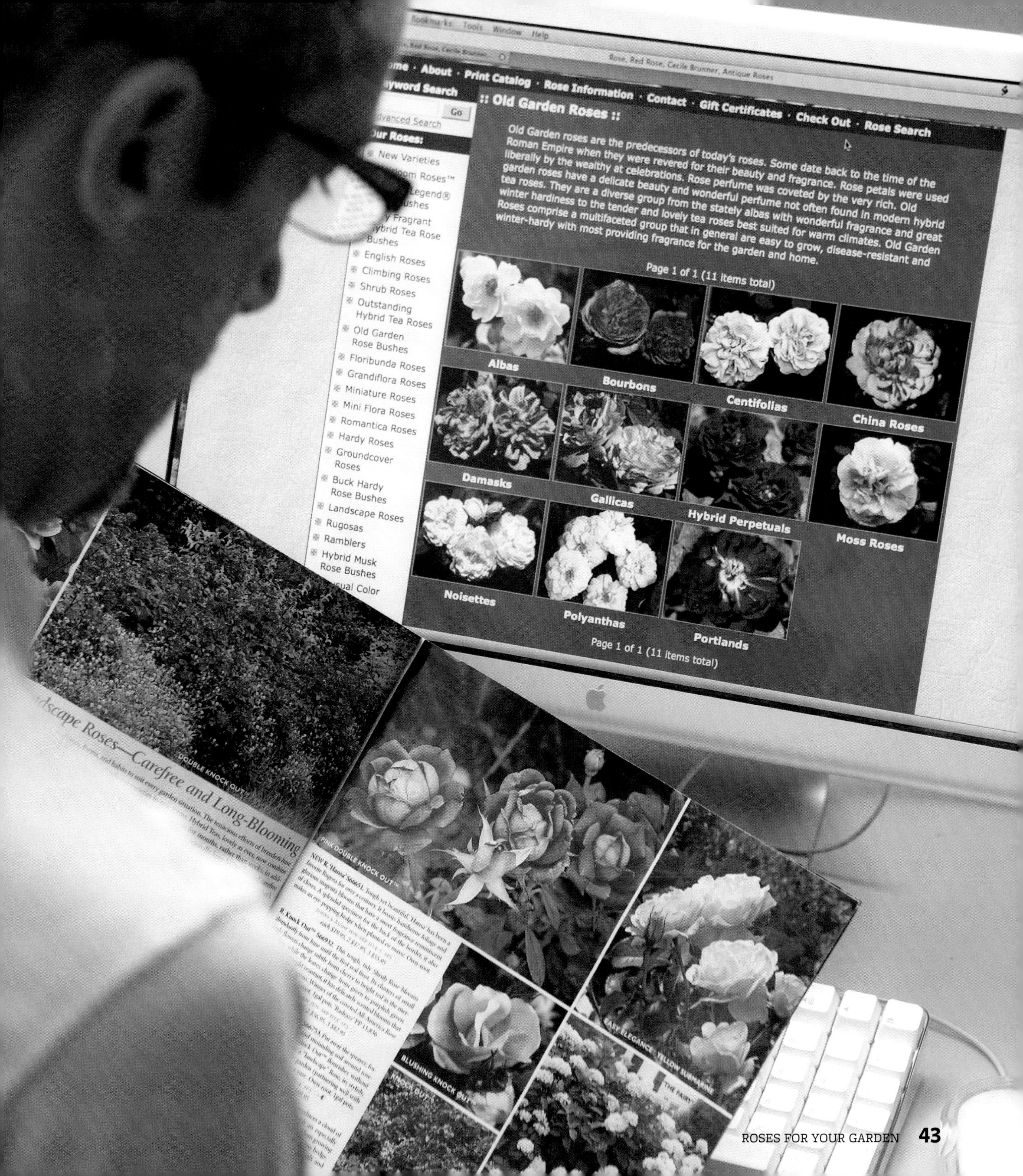

Bookmarks Tools Window Help
Rose, Red Rose, Cecile Brunner, Antique Roses
About · Print Catalog · Rose Information · Contact · Gift Certificates · Check Out · Rose Search
Go
:: Old Garden Roses ::
Old Garden roses are the predecessors of today's roses. Some date back to the time of the Roman Empire when they were revered for their beauty and fragrance. Rose petals were used liberally by the wealthy at celebrations. Rose perfume was coveted by the very rich. Old garden roses have a delicate beauty and wonderful perfume not often found in modern hybrid tea roses. They are a diverse group from the stately albas with wonderful fragrance and great winter hardiness to the tender and lovely tea roses best suited for warm climates. Old Garden Roses comprise a multifaceted group that in general are easy to grow, disease-resistant and winter-hardy with most providing fragrance for the garden and home.
Page 1 of 1 (11 items total)
New Varieties
English Roses
Climbing Roses
Shrub Roses
Outstanding Hybrid Tea Roses
Old Garden Rose Bushes
Floribunda Roses
Grandiflora Roses
Miniature Roses
Mini Flora Roses
Romantica Roses
Hardy Roses
Groundcover Roses
Buck Hardy Rose Bushes
Landscape Roses
Rugosas
Ramblers
Hybrid Musk Rose Bushes
Albas
Bourbons
Centifolias
China Roses
Damasks
Gallicas
Hybrid Perpetuals
Moss Roses
Noisettes
Polyanthas
Portlands
Page 1 of 1 (11 items total)
Carefree and Long-Blooming
DOUBLE KNOCK OUT
PINK DOUBLE KNOCK OUT
BLUSHING KNOCK OUT
EASY ELEGANCE
YELLOW SUBMARINE
THE FAIRY

CHAPTER THREE

Landscaping With Roses

Roses can solve many landscaping dilemmas in such a beautiful way. They tame slopes, hide foundations, and add color and fragrance.

left Large urns planted with miniature or miniflora roses next to columns draped with large-flowered climbers create a classic formal look. ***above*** Neatly clipped, curved boxwood borders provide distinctive edges for a formal design. ***below*** Pebble pathways serve as the borders in this formal design. Massing roses in single colors packs a punch.

Formal Gardens

Roses have many personalities, but they really show off their high-toned, sophisticated side when exhibited in formal gardens.

The traditional image of a formal rose garden is one with a geometric layout, usually containing hybrid teas or grandifloras and surrounded by a low boxwood hedge. However, any planting devoted entirely to roses can be considered a formal rose garden, whether bordered by boxwood or not. The design can be a series of simple rectangles or something more intricate.

One of the reasons that roses are frequently planted in formal gardens is that this reflects a tradition dating back hundreds of years. Formal gardens, resplendent with roses, grace grand European estates and castles.

Design considerations

When designing a layout for a formal rose garden:

Plant hybrid teas and grandifloras about 3 feet apart to give them room to grow and allow for easier maintenance.

Install soaker hoses or allocate space to move hoses because roses usually need extra water.

Add pathways to allow you and visitors to cut or smell the blooms. Avoid walking directly on the beds, which compacts the soil and affects roots.

Create parallel lines of roses, the most efficient planting scheme for maintenance. Rows can be straight or curved, but the denser the plantings, the harder they are to maintain.

Exquisite gardens of any kind require an immense amount of work. Many large gardens have paid or volunteer staffs to keep them looking good. Consider how to allocate time, energy, and finances to maintain the garden, not just install it. Think and plan realistically.

Formal garden ideas

Enhance the geometric or linear patterns of a formal rose garden by adding focal points that draw your eye to the center or to the corners. In warm areas of the country, standards (also called tree roses) can serve as visual anchors.

Instead of edging a rose garden with traditional boxwood, use low-growing floribundas, polyanthas, or shrubs to add color and to camouflage the lower parts of hybrid teas and grandifloras.

Place a gazebo or other circular structure at the center of a circular formal garden, training large-flowered climbers (using one or more varieties) vertically along the columns.

When planning a formal rose garden, think about the architectural maxim "form follows function." A formal garden can provide bouquets, serve as a peaceful place of repose, offer fragrance, and more. Knowing how you'll use the garden will dictate some of its design. A cutting garden may be strictly functional, but a sanctuary garden should include benches.

Finally, don't be constrained by what books say a formal rose garden should look like. Be creative when conjuring up your dream garden. Do what serves your needs and makes you happy.

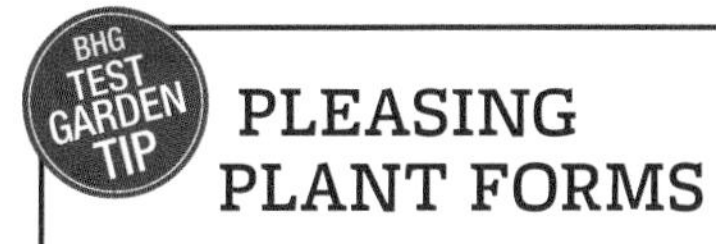

PLEASING PLANT FORMS

Plant roses in pairs or groups to give a sense of solidity and avoid the disorganized look of single-variety plantings.

above Pink shrub roses provide height and color that balance the yellows, blues, and whites along this garden path. ***left*** Pink Knock Out shrub roses pair beautifully with blue catmint (*Nepeta*).

Mixed Flower Gardens

Roses are easy mixers in less-formal beds and borders. In fact, one of the hallmarks of a cottage garden is roses blooming amid other perennials.

The English cottage garden, a seemingly unplanned, riotous mixture of plants of all types that spill over and crowd one another in a "natural" setting, is a rose-laden landscape most gardeners seem to love.

Don't be fooled! The English cottage garden is as deliberately designed and planned as any other landscaping approach, and woe to the gardener who simply adds plants willy-nilly without careful consideration.

Friends or foes

Roses play well with most other plants and can add blooms and fragrance to the mixed garden in a way that no other plant family can match.

When choosing partners for a cottage garden, remember that some plants should not be partnered directly with roses:

Tall plants that may block the sun.

Plants with invasive root systems, including most groundcover plants, that can rob a rose of food and water. Some plants formerly common in mixed gardens, such as purple loosestrife (*Lythrum salicaria*), should be avoided entirely because of their invasive habits.

Acid-loving azaleas and hydrangeas that need a different soil pH from roses. (Roses prefer a soil pH of 6.0 to 7.0.)

Shade-loving annuals and perennials are not apt partners because roses require at least 6 to 8 hours of sun per day.

Carefully consider the needs of your garden's rose companions: heights; widths; blooming seasons; and needs for water, food, and other cultural necessities. Unlike some landscape plants, roses need regular care such as pruning, fertilizing, watering, and winter protection in many areas.

These tasks are difficult when roses and other plants are placed close together. Plan carefully before you install the garden to ensure there will be sufficient access to your roses to perform essential chores, such as pruning and deadheading, throughout the season.

Mixing it up

Caveats aside, a mixed garden can be a glorious display, offering opportunities well beyond what roses alone can provide. Creative gardeners can:

Produce a four-season garden, packed with plants that bloom at different times and foliage that changes colors with the passing seasons.

Use plants with a variety of textures and colors. For example, the bright pink single flowers of *Rosa rubrifolia* (also known as redleaf rose or *R. glauca*) grace the landscape for two months, and the blue-gray foliage with reddish overtones provides a unique color much of the year. It's a tough plant that can hold its own in a cottage garden.

Employ other flowers to compensate for the lack of blue (and black) in rose blooms. Most blue-flowered plants mix well with roses, including catmint (*Nepeta*), 'Rozanne' hardy geranium, and delphiniums.

Appear to paint the garden with pastel shades of blues, pinks, and whites—almost required in mixed garden plantings.

BHG ASK THE GARDEN DOCTOR

What goes in a mixed border?

ANSWER: A mixed border cries out for both horizontal and vertical accents. Add foxgloves, delphiniums, and similar spiky plants to create upright interest. Spreading groundcover roses give a horizontal dimension to the palette. For an unusual focal point, consider growing *R. sericea pteracantha* (right) for its huge red, translucent thorns.

Solving Slopes

In addition to being beautiful, roses can show their hardworking side when planted as groundcovers in hard-to-plant areas.

A slope, even a moderately steep one, need not be a problem planting area. If attractively terraced, it can be an ideal location for almost any kind of rose. A slope provides ready-made drainage, and walls or embankments are perfect places to fill with improved soil.

Some yards have spots you'd want to cover with attractive plantings—and then basically ignore. With a little advance planning, you can use roses to fulfill this purpose admirably.

Groundcover roses

Most roses touted as groundcovers do not truly fit that definition. Some are simply low-growing shrubs, others are very upright, and some grow with a slight spreading habit. To allow them to cover the ground, they must be planted very close together—1 foot apart or less. Most of the Flower Carpet varieties fall into this category.

Low-growing rugosas are even more suitable as groundcovers. If grown on their own roots, rugosas have a tendency to sucker and spread into unfilled areas, eventually presenting a mass of color on a low-maintenance plant.

A few rose varieties grow long, low-growing, relatively lax canes that can truly be considered groundcovers. These include Sea Foam, with white blooms on canes that can reach 6 feet or more, and Red Ribbons, with lax canes between 4 and 6 feet. The next best: Max Graf, a once-blooming rugosa hybrid with single pink blooms, and Nozomi, a miniature with 3- to 4-foot-long lax canes. Many of the ramblers can also be used effectively as groundcovers.

Making more plants

To cover a larger area, gardeners can propagate more plants using a process known as layering, similar to creating new strawberry plants from runners.

About 3 feet or farther from the mother plant, pin one of the long canes to the ground with a piece of strong wire, such as coat hanger wire, being careful not to cut into the bark. Cover the pinned spot with a little soil. Within a few months, new roots will form where the cane meets the soil. Once the new plant gets established, remove the pin and cut the cane between the new growth and the mother plant.

Care for groundcover roses

Although many groundcover roses are touted as care-free, they produce more flowers when spent blooms are removed (deadheading.) This is especially true for low-growing rugosas. Avoid thinking of them as plants that can thrive without any attention. They grow best with fertilizer once or twice in the spring and summer plus they need watering even after they are established. Many are winter hardy to Zones 4 or 5 with little to no winter protection.

opposite, left Raised beds offer better drainage and the opportunity to amend and improve the soil. ***opposite, above right*** Use the many heights and sizes of roses to create layers of color within sloped and terraced beds. ***opposite, middle right*** Red Ribbons, a highly rated shrub rose, grows with canes long enough to let them flop and cover the ground. ***opposite, below right*** Groundcover roses stabilize and beautify a sunny hillside.

Creating Hedges

What's more beautiful than a running line of blooming roses alongside a fence or property line?

Nothing catches the eye of a garden visitor like a mass planting of one rose variety. That bright wall of color makes a focal point like no other. Mass plantings can include tight groupings of three plants, a linear hedge, or a border of dozens of plants. Generally, the more plants used, the greater the visual impact.

For best effect, choose a variety that grows no taller than about 4 feet. The best selections for mass plantings include heavy-blooming floribundas, polyanthas, and shrubs. Walls, other structures, or evergreens serve as effective backdrops to set off the brilliant colors.

Close neighbors require care

When designing a mass planting, check the plant tag to see how wide the rose bush grows. Roses in a mass display should be planted about 1 foot apart for the best blooming display. However, planting roses close together makes it more difficult to care for them.

Use these guidelines when massing roses:

Plant no more than two bushes wide when making a border or a hedge, so plants can be approached from either side.

Keep tight circles of bushes no larger than 3 feet wide to allow access to all plants from the outside. A larger arrangement creates a hard-to-reach area inside.

Choose disease-resistant varieties for mass plantings because problems will spread more quickly than among wider-spaced plants.

opposite Plant tough shrub roses next to a see-through fence, such as split rail or ornamental iron, for an extra decorative effect. ***above right*** Use color as a mass planting opportunity. The yellow Behold miniature rose shields the leggy lower portions of the St. Patrick hybrid tea. ***below right*** Spaced close together, Martha's Vineyard shrub roses make an effective and beautiful hedge.

Roses as hedges

An old adage claims that fences make good neighbors. Using roses to create a hedge or fill a border is a most beautiful fulfillment of this promise. A rose hedge can fill the role of a living fence, serve as a visual privacy hedge, or simply create a garden room. If you want privacy, however, remember that roses drop their leaves for winter in most areas of the country.

Decide how tall you want your hedge to be, choose an attractive variety, then determine its spreading habit to decide how closely to plant the bushes. The closer they are planted to one another, the more quickly a hedge will fill out.

Varieties touted as hedge roses often are not the best choice for this purpose. Shrubs work well, as do hybrid rugosas, which can reach up to 6 feet tall. Rugosas can be pruned lower, if needed, require no spraying and little water, and display attractive hips and varying foliage colors in autumn. Most shrubs and all rugosas are generally hardy in most areas of the country.

above Use cloth or soft plastic ties (shown in green) to keep climbing roses attached to pergolas and other structures. ***left*** To grow climbing roses on structures, attach a trellis, then train the roses to grow in the right direction. Use a climber or rambler with the longest possible canes.

Vertical Accents

Climbing roses grow up and away, and over arbors and trellises, offering gorgeous blooms and fragrance from overhead.

Many rose varieties grow very tall and, if trained to do so, very wide. In a garden, blooming roses in all their glory can grace arches, trellises, pergolas, columns, gazebos, and other structures. Roses can also screen or decorate buildings, trees, fences, and other structures.

Choose climbers with recurrent bloom for the best effect. The beautiful cascading roses in pictures of Giverny, Bagatelle, and other French rose gardens are primarily planted with once-blooming ramblers that look spectacular for about two months but less than wonderful the rest of the year.

How to train long-caned roses

Climbing, rambling, and shrub roses with long canes cannot attach themselves to supports. They must be trained in the desired direction, then manually attached to the supporting structure. Latticework is especially convenient because the openings make it easy to attach the ties.

Training is an apt word: It happens over time. Begin by attaching growing young canes to the support with a material that will not cut into the canes when they're blown about by the wind. Avoid twist-ties with wire centers or hard plastic ties. Soft plastic or cloth ties are just as durable but gentler to the plant.

In a couple weeks, continue training. Move the canes a little farther along the structure and secure them again. Repeat this process as often as necessary. By the time the canes grow to their full lengths, they should need no further training.

Be gentle with tender new canes. If forced too far, they have a tendency to break. Most long-caned roses grow canes one year and bloom on them the following year.

TRAINING ROSE CANES

Climbing roses look stunning scrambling along the top of a fence or a wall. Get the heaviest bloom possible from long-caned roses by training the canes as close to horizontal as possible. Training rose canes horizontally forces the plant to bloom along the top of the canes by removing the plant's apical dominance, a botanical process that inhibits the growth of side shoots or buds on a stem.

New Dawn, a rose that earned the first plant patent in 1930, is hardy in Zones 4 to 9a. It tolerates poor soil and partial shade. Give it strong support, such as an iron fence, for its heavy canes.

Water-Wise Roses

Low-maintenance roses are ideal in any landscape, but for areas with water restrictions, they're a must.

Water restrictions exist in many parts of the country. An eco-conscious gardener who wants to wisely use the Earth will want to consider growing roses that need fewer resources, including water.

For best performance, most roses need moderate but dependable amounts of water, usually 1 to 2 inches per week. However, some varieties adapt nicely to arid conditions and are especially recommended for drier regions of the country.

Seek out Earth-Kind varieties

The easiest way to know which roses thrive in dry climates is to check for an Earth-Kind designation. Earth-Kind rose trials began about a decade ago at the Texas AgriLife Extension Service in College Station. Plants were given a minimum of food and water. There was no insecticidal or fungicidal spraying. After years of scientific testing, 15 varieties earned the Earth-Kind designation for pest tolerance and outstanding landscape performance. The list has now expanded to 21.

The group includes Old Garden Roses, shrubs, polyanthas, floribundas, and climbers—but no hybrid teas.

Not all vendors label these high performers as Earth-Kind, so take a list of names when shopping for roses. Some are not hardy in northern climates; research the care requirements first.

Earth-Kind expands

The Texas program inspired six other universities (Colorado State, Iowa State, Kansas State, Louisiana State, University of Minnesota, and University of Nebraska) to institute similar research. Earth-Kind designations for other areas of the country are planned in the future.

In addition to providing water resource suggestions, the Earth-Kind website advocates other environmental practices, such as growing roses in clay or loam soils using compost and organic mulches to eliminate the need for commercial synthetic or organic fertilizers.

EARTH-KIND CULTIVARS

These varieties have been scientifically proven to use less fertilizer, pesticide, and water. Gardeners, especially those in the South, should consider growing these environmentally friendly roses.

DWARF SHRUBS
The Fairy (*shown*)
Marie Daly
Souvenir de St. Anne's

SMALL SHRUBS
Caldwell Pink
Mlle Cécile Brünner (*shown*)
Perle d'Or

MEDIUM SHRUBS
Belinda's Dream
Carefree Beauty (*shown*)
Ducher
Duchesse de Brabant
Else Poulsen
Georgetown Tea
Knock Out
La Marne
Mme Antoine Mari

MANNERLY CLIMBERS
Climbing Pinkie
Sea Foam (*shown*)

VIGOROUS CLIMBERS
New Dawn (*shown*)
Rêve d'Or

left Small shrubs or miniature roses blend well with annuals in large containers. Because containers can dry out quickly, monitor the soil—but avoid overwatering. ***above*** A pair of standard roses in containers flanks a garden path. Begonias or other annuals are natural companions to add color at the base. ***below*** Even if you don't have room for a full rose garden, cluster groups of containers and cut roses together to achieve this look.

Containers

Place roses anywhere you need a dose of color and fragrance. It's easy when you grow them in containers.

Any rose can be grown in a pot or other container. You just need a container with enough room to allow the roots to expand. The bigger the mature plant, the bigger container it needs.

Hybrid teas, grandifloras, and floribundas can be grown in 10- to 15-gallon containers. Miniatures, minifloras, and small shrubs take 3-gallon or larger pots. Shrubs and large climbers require at least a 15-gallon container.

Selecting a container

All kinds of containers can be used for growing roses. A classic concrete urn is appropriate for a formal garden, while a pot that resembles a giant head reflects a sense of whimsy. Wooden half barrels suit rustic gardens. Southwestern-style terra-cotta pots easily house a collection of miniatures. Ceramic or metal work well almost anywhere.

While container gardens generally add beauty to a garden, some rose enthusiasts have even been known to grow entire rose gardens in trimmed plastic garbage cans mounted on dollies or casters.

Advantages of containers

Potted roses offer gardeners the best of all possible worlds, with virtually unlimited designs and a wide range of roses.

Place containers virtually anywhere in the landscape without worrying about soil conditions or drainage.

Station pots in the sunniest spots, moving them during the growing season to follow the sun's changing position.

Shoehorn a series of small to medium containers into tiny spaces, such as apartment balconies and on patios.

Set pots on tables, benches, or other elevated surfaces so you don't need to bend or kneel. This makes it easy for people with physical limitations to grow roses.

How to grow container roses

The basics of growing successful container roses are much the same as for any other plant: good potting soil, good drainage, and a nearly continuous supply of water during warm summer months.

Roses destined to stay in pots should be repotted periodically as their size increases. Plants that will stay in one container need to have their potting soil changed or replenished every couple years.

Other cultural considerations, such as disease and insect control, fertilizing, and pruning, are virtually the same as for roses in the ground.

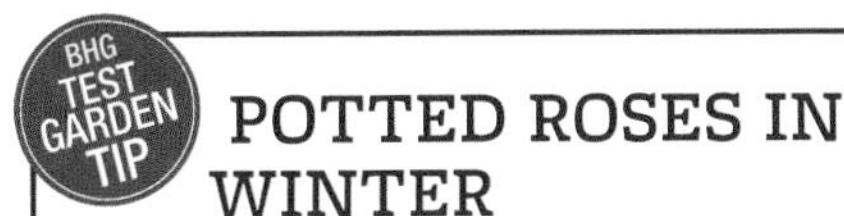

POTTED ROSES IN WINTER

In northern climates, move container roses to a sheltered space or garage to avoid winterkill. Avoid planting in clay pots, which crack when the soil goes through freeze-and-thaw cycles.

Rose Container Companions

Roses look stunning in containers when paired with other sun-loving plants. You can mix small rose bushes with perennials or annuals.

Long-lived perennials

Since roses and perennials return year after year (even in containers) they make ideal planting companions. Try these perennials:

Perennial geranium

The single-petaled flowers of perennial geranium add bright spots of jewel tone color intermixed with rose flowers and foliage. Plus, perennial geraniums are one of the longest-blooming perennials.

Catmint

Easy-care catmint also features airy blue flowers and gray-green foliage. Add shorter-growing varieties such as 'Blue Wonder' to the base of containers planted with tree roses. The blue flowers look great with white- or pink-flowering roses.

Lavender

Clump-growing, densely branched lavender bears gray-green foliage and is topped with spires of fragrant lavender-blue flowers. Lavender and roses are a classic combination and both can be use to make scented sachets.

Bright annuals

Annuals add colorful accents to containers planted with roses. Choose annual flowers in colors that complement the roses you select. Try these annuals:

Petunias

This trailing annual comes in a wide range of pastel colors (pink, yellow, white) as well as darker colors such as fuchsia. It looks lovely spilling over the sides of a container packed with flowering roses.

Lobelia

Electric blue lobelia looks stunning planted with white or pink roses. This low-growing annual produces waves of blue blooms. There are mounding and edging forms.

Mandevilla

This tropical vining plant grows well in a container and easily scrambles upward onto a pot-sized trellis. Mandevillas bloom in lipstick shades of red, pink, and white. Mix mandevilla and climbing roses together in a large container for a big bold look.

BHG TEST GARDEN TIP

WATERING CONTAINERS

Roses planted in containers require watering more often than those planted in the ground. Make sure the container has adequate drainage—check for holes in the bottom so that the plant's roots don't sit in water.

opposite, left Roses love to rub shoulders in containers with easy-care annuals and perennials such as bacopa, ivy, and verbena. It's like a cottage garden in a container. ***opposite, above right*** Catmint, with its lavender-blue flowers and gray-green foliage, is an ideal planting companion with groundcover roses. ***opposite, below right*** Fragrant and full, a window box is packed with lavender, miniature roses, and variegated ivy.

CHAPTER FOUR

Rose Garden Plans

As easy as plant-by-number, rose garden plans mix roses with perennials, shrubs, climbers, and annuals to create solutions for a variety of landscapes.

Cascading Entryway

Pair climbing roses with upwardly mobile perennials, such as clematis, to double your pleasure on arbors and trellises.

Combine Climbers and Clematis

The perfect pair: climbing roses and vining clematis. Together they intertwine, bloom, and prove that when it comes to flowers, more is definitely better!

Like champagne and strawberries, climbing roses and clematis are an elegant, classic combo that has stood the test of time. For centuries gardeners have enjoyed planting the two together to watch the spectacular relationship grow and flower.

Climbing roses are rambling woody plants that need support to sprawl on. Clematis, on the other hand, have nimble, flexible stems that need a support to climb. Roses, with their many branches, give the clematis excellent purchase to scramble skyward. But unlike some vines, which can be rampant, clematis are moderate growers that will not smother roses. Instead, most clematis have sparse enough foliage to allow in enough sunlight for the roses to thrive.

Some climbing roses and clematis bloom at the same time. If the two are of contrasting colors, such as a pink rose with a purple clematis or a red rose with a white clematis, the sight can be breathtaking. Other pairings of climbing roses and clematis can extend the blooming season. For example, pair an early-summer blooming climbing rose with a late-summer blooming clematis, and you'll be treated to a few weeks of bloom from the rose and then a few weeks of bloom from the clematis.

In this garden, repeat-blooming New Dawn climbing roses intertwine with deep purple Jackman clematis to embellish a classic white arbor and picket fence, the destination of a gently rising walk. The walk is flanked with low-maintenance red barberries, junipers, and delicate pink The Fairy roses, which are easy to grow.

left An arbor dripping with roses, clematis, and perennials extends the perfect welcome.

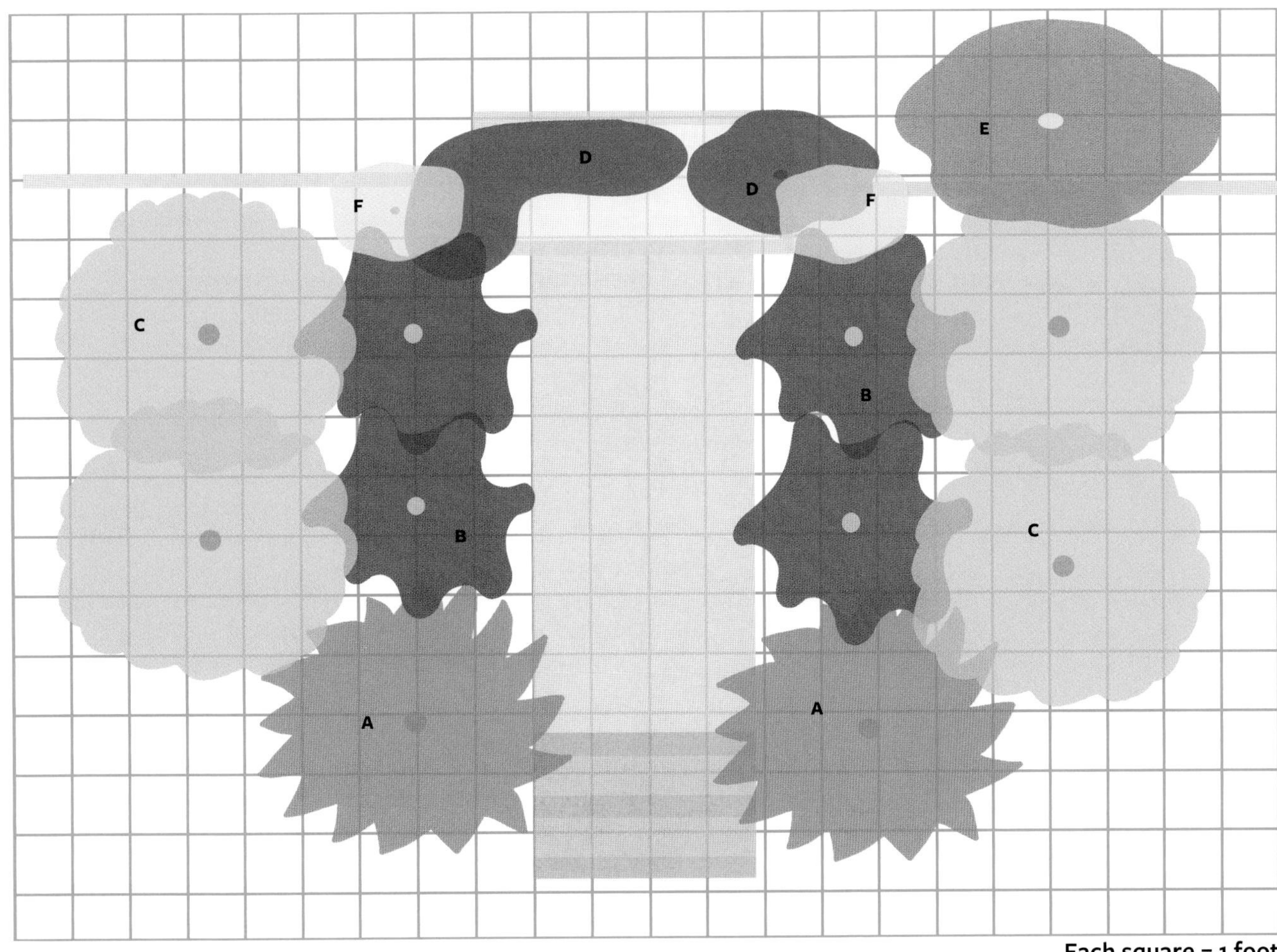

Each square = 1 foot

Plant List

A. 2 Creeping junipers
(*Juniperus horizontalis* Bar Harbor)
Zones 5–9

B. 4 Red Japanese barberries
(*Berberis thunbergii* Atropurpurea)
Zones 5–8

C. 4 The Fairy roses
Zones 5–9

D. 2 New Dawn climbing roses
Zones 5–9

E. 1 Constance Spry shrub rose
Zones 5–9

F. 2 Jackman clematises
(*Clematis* Jackmanii)
Zones 4–8

MATCH THE CLEMATIS WITH THE ROSE

It's important to choose the right size clematis so that it doesn't overwhelm or get lost in the rose.

Rambling roses, which can sprawl 40 feet, combine well with sweet autumn clematis (*Clematis terniflora*), which grows to 20 feet.

For most climbing roses, which range in size from 10 to 20 feet, choose large-flowered clematises, most of which become no taller than 10 to 15 feet.

Pair shrub roses with one of the small clematises, such as Durand's clematis (*Clematis* × *durandii*), alpine clematis (*C. alpina*), or Italian clematis (*C. viticella*), that climb no more than 4 or 5 feet high.

New Dawn rose and Jackmanii clematis

Floral Walkway

Welcome visitors to your front door with a petal-packed pathway of hybrid tea, antique, and fragrant landscape roses.

A Rosy Outlook

Line a walk with a variety of roses edged in boxwood for a time-honored display of flowers and an undulating ribbon of foliage.

It's an elegant look: a gently curved sidewalk flanked with boxwood and roses. The plan can be adapted to nearly any stretch of sunny path.

This walk is lined primarily with hybrid tea roses. It's a showy way to display a collection of hybrid teas and display the breadth of their color range. Choose roses that offer different charms:

Hybrid teas are a smart selection for a rose planting that also serves as an excellent source of cut flowers to bring indoors. The more flowers you cut, the more roses are produced. That's because the goal of any flowering plant is to set seed and reproduce. By constantly trimming off flowers, either for cut flower arrangements or by deadheading spent blooms, the plant's attempt to set seed is circumvented. This makes it go into flowering double-time in an attempt to produce more flowers that have a higher chance to set seed.

Landscape roses would be a lower-maintenance choice for this rose-lined front path. Make the planting more cold-hardy and less work by planting a row of Knock Out, Flower Carpet, or Easy Elegance Series roses, which are among the most cold-hardy and disease-resistant roses. They also need minimal pruning.

Antique rose fanciers could also use this general design to show off a collection of old roses. Or adapt the plan to a particular color theme, such as a garden entirely of red roses or entirely of white roses.

left Grow fragrant roses where they'll best be enjoyed. The heights of these hybrid teas invite a sniffing of their fragrance.

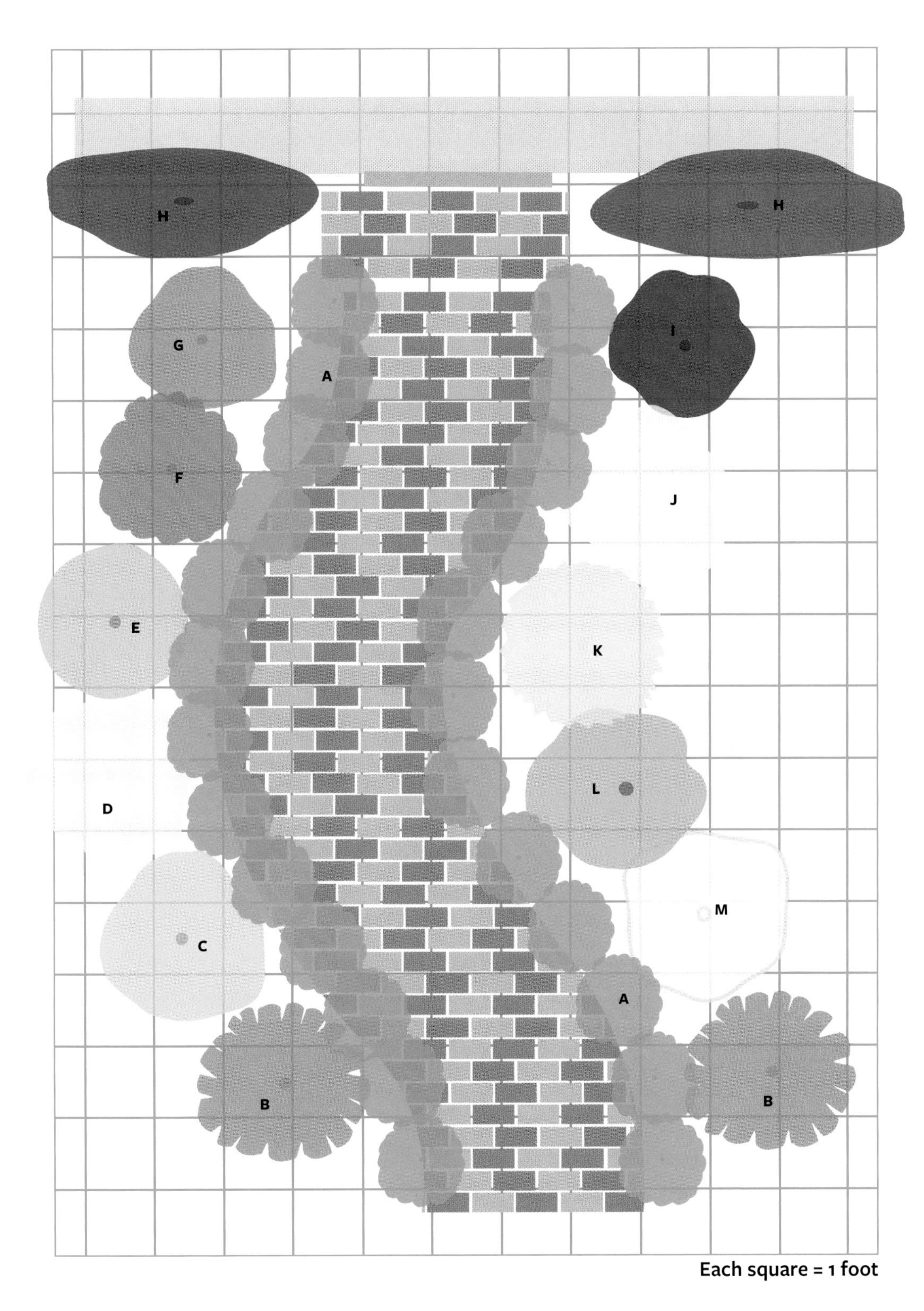

Plant List

A. 25 Boxwoods
(*Buxus* Green Gem)
Zones 5–9

B. 2 Carefree Wonder roses
Zones 5–9

C. 1 Gold Medal rose
Zones 5–9

D. 1 Perfume Delight rose
Zones 5–9

E. 1 Queen Elizabeth rose
Zones 5–9

F. 1 Royal Highness rose
Zones 5–9

G. 1 Rio Samba rose
Zones 5–9

H. 2 Blaze climbing roses
Zones 5–9

I. 1 Mister Lincoln rose
Zones 5–9

J. 1 Sunbright rose
Zones 5–9

K. 1 Sexy Rexy rose
Zones 5–9

L. 1 Playboy rose
Zones 5–9

M. 1 John F. Kennedy rose
Zones 5–9

Rosy Ring

Create a garden focal point in a front yard or a backyard with a circular bed packed with roses and other bold bloomers.

above A vertical element that centers a circular bed adds dimension and impact. Center the bed with a wooden tuteur like this one or an elegant wrought-iron structure.

Fantastic Focal Point

An easy-care circular bed with French country charm suits nearly any sunny landscape. Extend the French theme with a tuteur (which means "guardian" or "support") and a load of Romantica roses, bred in Provence by the famed House of Meilland. The Romanticas, a series of hybrid teas that resemble the many-petaled English roses, are named for famous authors, painters, and other artistic figures.

Like other hybrid teas, Romanticas must be tended with extra care for best performance, but they reward with blooms that beg to be cut and brought into the house. Shrubs or polyanthas can be substituted in northern gardens, but the effect won't be quite the same.

Climbing Structure

A tuteur is a classic structure for a garden, but you can add any tall object to the middle of a round bed. Train climbing roses to scramble up and over. Erect a freestanding trellis or arbor, or use a piece of found art such as a column salvaged from a home.

Fill out the rosy ring with low-maintenance perennials such as lamb's ears, sedum, perennial salvia, and chrysanthemum. Their colors will complement almost any color of rose you choose. All of the plants require a mininum of six hours of sun per day for best performance. Prune any spent blooms from the salvia so they will rebloom.

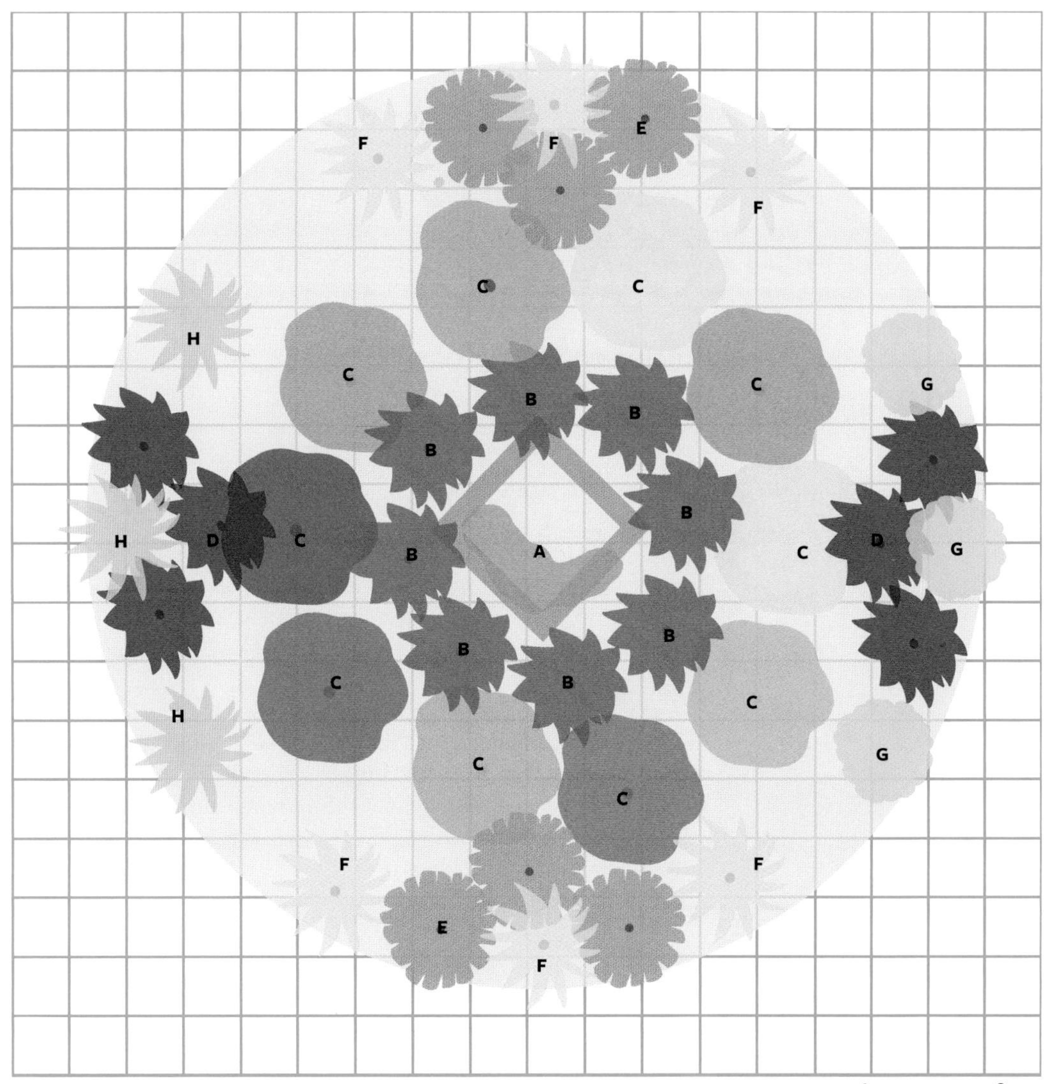

Plant List

A. 1 **Climbing rose** such as Colette
Zones 5–9

B. 8 **Chrysanthemums**
(*Chrysanthemum × morifolium*)
Zones 5–10

C. 10 **Romantica shrub roses**
such as Auguste Renoir,
Comtesse de Provence,
Francois Rabelais,
Guy de Maupassant,
Johann Strauss, Tchaikovski,
Yves Piaget, and Peter Mayle
Zones 5–9

D. 6 **Miniature roses** such as Alfie,
Baby Paradise, and Rainbow's End
Zones 5–9

E. 6 **Tall sedums** such as Autumn Fire
(*Sedum spectabile*)
Zones 4–9

F. 6 **Perennial salvias**
(*Salvia × sylvestris* May Night)
Zones 5–9

G. 3 **Lady's mantles**
(*Alchemilla mollis*)
Zones 4–7

H. 3 **Lamb's ears**
(*Stachys byzantina* Silver Carpet)
Zones 4–8

PLANT SUPERSTAR: ROMANTICA ROSES

Call them English roses with a French accent. Similar to David Austin roses, which are also known as English roses, Romantica roses are modern roses that have been crossed with antique roses in an effort to capture the best characteristics of both. They were bred in Provence by the famed House of Meilland, which is known for producing tough, beautiful roses.

David Austin roses also are valued for their cold hardiness (to Zone 5), but they often do not bloom well in warmer climates. Romantica roses, on the other hand, do better in the heat, bearing larger flowers in hotter regions of the country.

David Austin rose bushes have a shrubby, full shape. Romantica roses tend to be smaller but upright, like floribunda and hybrid tea roses. The Romantica flower form is similar to that of a hybrid tea rose; David Austin roses have a fuller, rounded, old-fashioned flower form.

David Austin roses are renowned for their fragrance. Most, but not all, Romantica roses have a notable fragrance.

Jean Giaono Romantica rose

Romantic Gateway

A rose-swathed arbor creates a beautiful entrance to a side yard or backyard. Climbing roses and mixed perennials make a welcome view.

above Keep roses and other perennials mulched to conserve moisture. Use plant-based organic mulches, which will break down and improve the soil. Expand your planting from a couple of climbing roses on an arbor to a simple but elegant rose garden by adding a few easy-care perennials and shrubs.

Arbor Entryway

This pleasant mix of perennials and roses is sure to set off any arbor. Imagine this picture without the roses. It just doesn't look right, does it? Roses add the romance that kicks up this garden entry from merely pretty to spectacular. Luckily, it's an easy project that can be completed in just a few hours of time and will look beautiful for years to come.

On each side of a garden gate (or welcoming arbor), plant a New Dawn climbing rose. This tough rose (it's even earned an Earth-Kind designation for being eco-friendly) will bloom once in spring and again throughout the growing season. Extend the delicate color theme with a Ballerina shrub rose, which produces fluffy pink clouds of pink single roses that resemble apple blossoms.

On the opposite side of the arbor, the Annabelle smooth hydrangea grows about the same height as Ballerina, providing balance. This easy-care hydrangea likes partial shade, but needs about the same amount of water as roses.

Colorful Edgers

Low-growing, long-blooming perennials such as pinks and perennial verbenas add color throughout the growing season. These low-growers will spill over the pathway edge, softening the look of the angular landscape. Other good perennial edgers include short varieties of catmint and moss phlox.

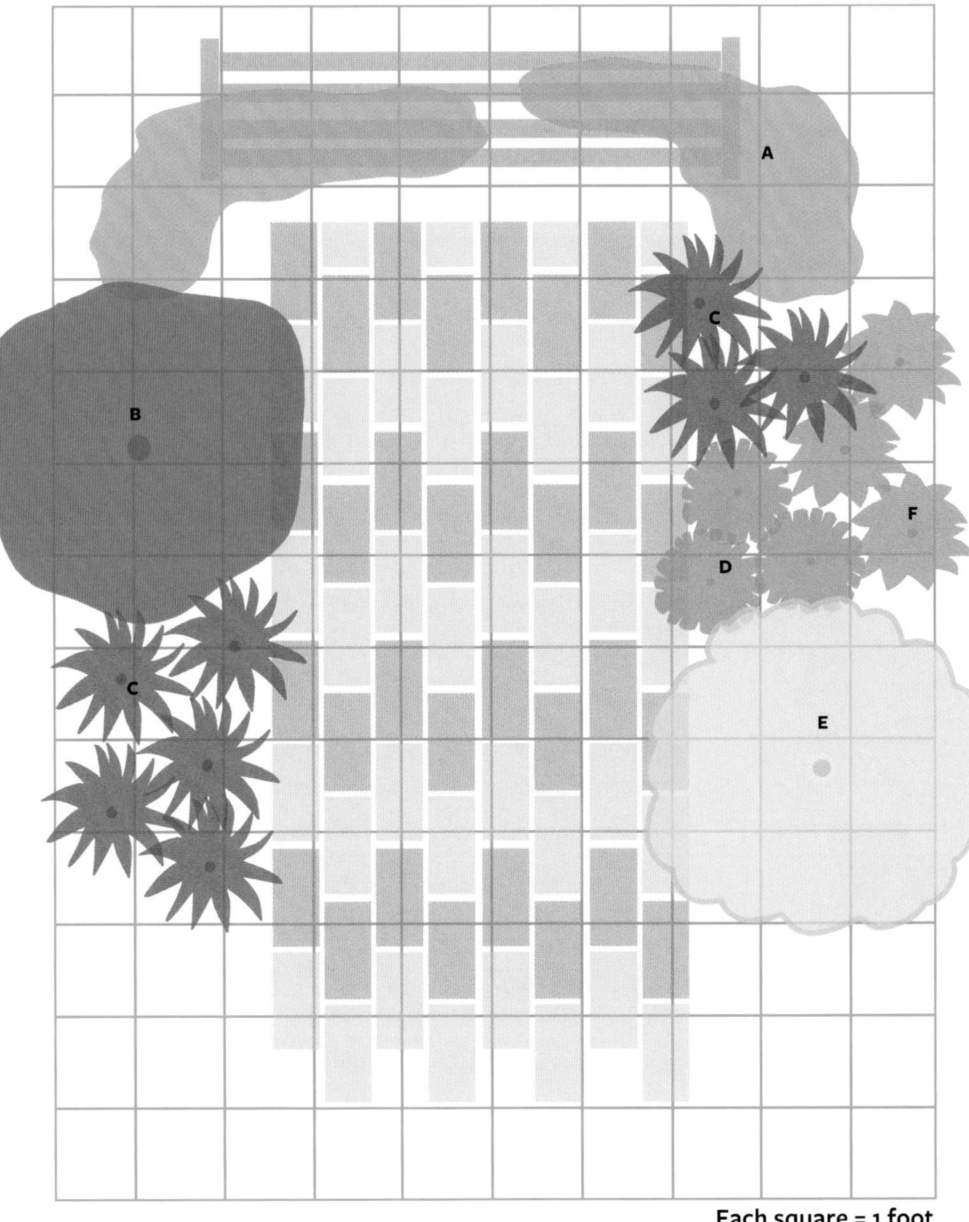

Plant List

A. 2 New Dawn climbing roses
Zones 5–9

B. 1 Ballerina rose
Zones 5–9

C. 8 Rose verbenas
(*Verbena canadensis*)
Zones 4–8

D. 3 Pinks
(*Dianthus* spp.)
Zones 3–10

E. 1 Annabelle smooth hydrangea
(*Hydrangea arborescens* Annabelle)
Zones 4–9

F. 3 Foxgloves
(*Digitalis purpurea*)
Zones 4–8

WHEN TO PLANT ROSES

As a general rule, plant container-grown roses any time of year except during temperature extremes. Avoid periods when hard freezes (below 25°F) or extended heat (above 90°F) are likely. In most regions this means planting container-grown roses from early spring through autumn. In warmer climates plant them from fall through late winter.

Bare-root roses have a narrower window for planting. They need temperate, moist conditions to get established. Plant bare-root roses in spring about the same time that other plants are leafing out, but before daytime temperatures regularly climb into the 80s. In the southern region of the United States, you can also plant them in fall and winter.

In Zone 6 and colder, it's best to avoid planting container-grown roses in the fall. They don't have enough time to get established before winter cold hits, and their chances of dying are much higher.

Fragrant Slope

Tame a slope with roses and other fragrant beauties for a garden that's spectacular from top to bottom.

Slope Solution

Landscaping a hillside can be a daunting task, but this plan breaks it down and makes it easy. An array of beautiful low-maintenance roses combined with fragrant annual and perennial flowers turns even the most forlorn slope into a showstopper. Partnering reblooming roses with nonstop bloomers such as pincushion flower and alyssum ensures a dramatic show. Anchoring the base of the slope with railroad ties raises the garden for better viewing and creates a strong contrast to billowy mounds of flowers.

The plan lists specific easy-care shrub roses in pink and white, but you can substitute your favorites or what your local garden center has in stock. Choose low-maintenance landscape roses such as those in the Knock Out, Flower Carpet, or Easy Elegance series. This is especially important in Zones 5 and colder, where winter protection is an issue. 'Polar Joy' is a good substitute for the 'Iceberg' standard (tree rose) in these colder regions.

Design Tips for Slopes

Control erosion. Avoid working the soil excessively. Make narrow, deep planting holes to minimize disturbing the surface soil.

Terrace to tame a slope. In addition to landscape timbers, you can use flagstones or paving stones stacked two or three high to create a short wall. Make a solid base for the wall and bury the first layer in soil.

Opt for shrubs and perennials. Their extensive root systems better anchor the soil. Also, you don't have to dig up the soil each year as you would with annual flowers.

Choose heavy mulch. Mulch prevents erosion, but light mulches, such as pine needles or cocoa hulls, wash away easily. Choose nugget-size chunks of bark that are more likely to remain in place.

Consider containers. Potted plants add interest. Slightly bury the base into a slope for stability.

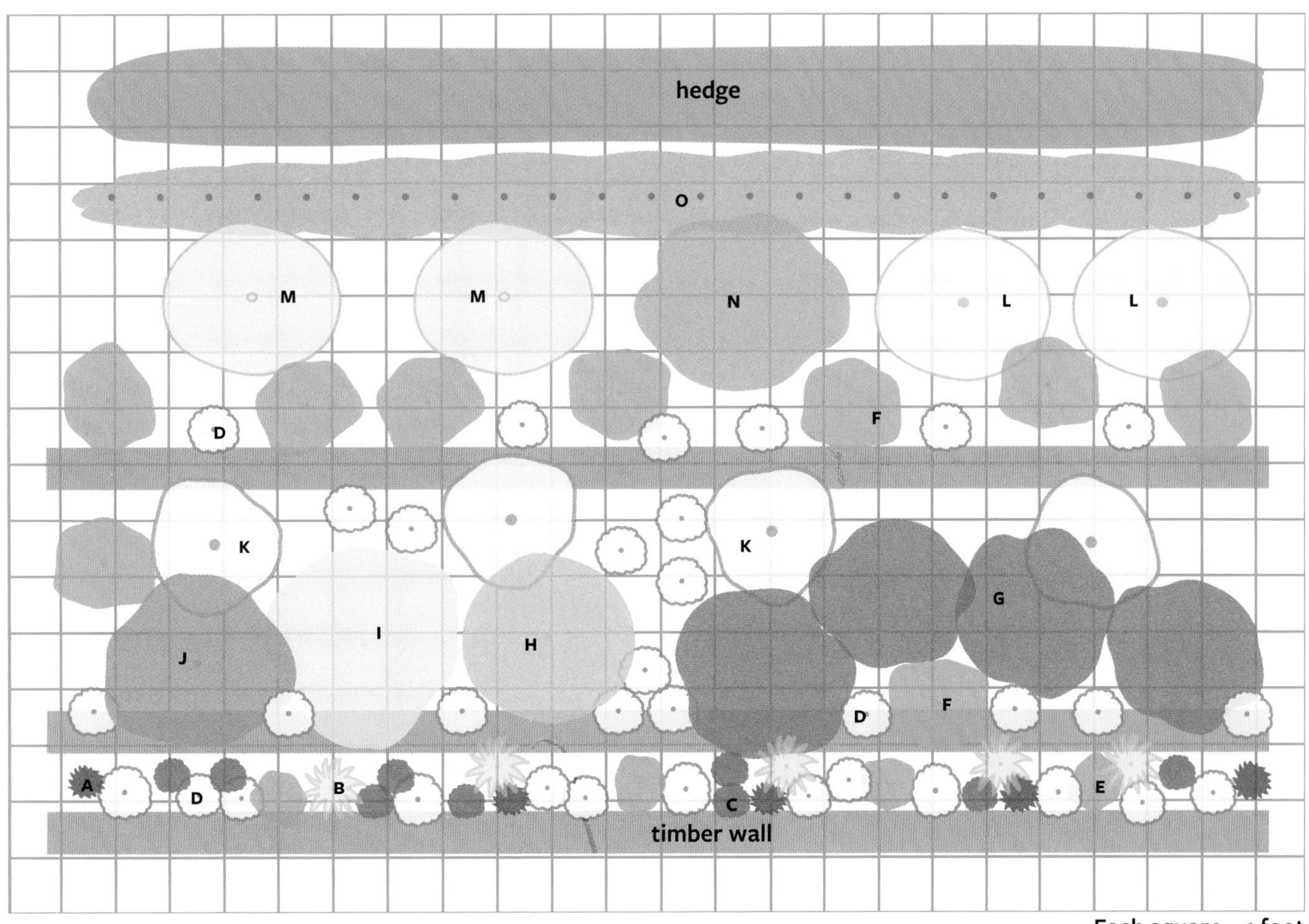

Plant List

A. 5 Pink or red annual phloxes
(*Phlox drummondii*) Annual

B. 5 Flowering tobaccos
(*Nicotiana × sanderae*) Annual

C. 9 Blue or purple violas
(*Viola tricolor*) Annual

D. 34 Sweet alyssums
(*Lobularia maritima*) Annual

E. 4 Edging lobelias
(*Lobelia erinus*) Annual

F. 9 Pink or blue pincushion flowers
(*Scabiosa columbaria*)
Zones 3–9

G. 4 Pink shrub roses such as
Gertrude Jekyll
Zones 5–9

H. 1 Pink shrub rose such as Heritage
Zones 5–9

I. 1 Soft pink shrub rose such as
Katherine Morely
Zones 5–9

J. 1 Apricot-color shrub rose such as
Abraham Darby
Zones 4–9

K. 4 Iceberg or other white tree roses
Zones 6–9

L. 2 White floribunda roses such as
Margaret Merril
Zones 5–10

M. 2 Soft pink shrub roses such as
Sheer Bliss
Zones 6–10

N. 1 Pink shrub rose such as Hero
Zones 4–9

O. 24 Foxgloves (*Digitalis purpurea*)
Zones 4–8

BHG TEST GARDEN TIP

DO IT YOURSELF?

When landscaping a slope, it can be tricky to figure out whether you should create the terraces or low retaining walls yourself or have a pro do it. If the walls will be no more than a foot tall, you're probably safe. Otherwise, hire a professional to prevent frustrating erosion or a potentially dangerous collapse.

Carefree Rose Border

Unfussy shrub roses are the antidote for a lackluster landscape. These bold bloomers add color and flowers for bouquets all summer.

Easy-Care Blooms All Season

This rose bed may look high-maintenance, but it takes less care than a bed of annual flowers. The bonus: It comes back year after year!

Are you a beginning rose gardener? This combination bed is great for a novice.

It consists of a few easy-care roses, rimmed with lady's mantle, a low edging plant that's a classic with roses. Its pretty green foliage and chartreuse flowers blend easily with nearly any kind of rose.

A climbing rose in the back, New Dawn, is fairly cold-hardy and tough. It adds a helpful vertical element to the planting, integrating it with whatever may be in the background. Train this climber up a gazebo, as shown, or grow it along a fence or hedge (with the help of a trellis to give it some support).

The other roses are among the lowest-maintenance roses available, and most will bloom heavily in late spring with light flowering until frost. Follow this plan exactly or substitute other easy roses that you can find at your local garden center. It's pretty to try a mix of colors—red, pink, and white—though you could also create a planting of solely one spectacular variety.

Be sure to plant any rose bed in full sun—at least 8 hours of direct, unfiltered light. This bed will also appreciate a sprinkling of a granular, balanced slow-release fertilizer once in the spring and a good inch or two of mulch. Otherwise it needs little care.

left Tuck this semicircular bed into a sunny spot in your landscape, by the driveway, or in a corner of the yard. It's quick to plant and is filled with no-fuss roses and perennials.

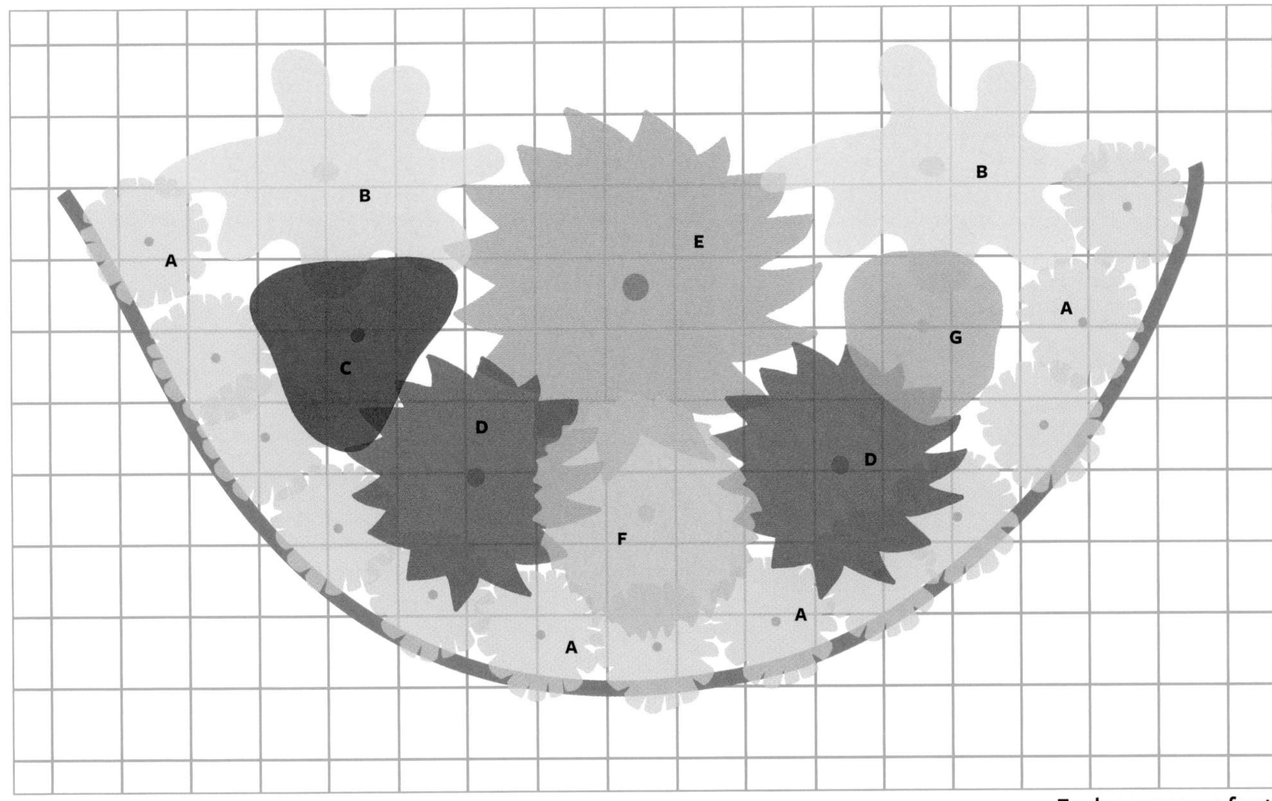

Plant List

A. 13 Lady's mantle
(*Alchemilla mollis*)
Zones 4–8

B. 2 Light pink climbing roses such as New Dawn
Zones 5–9

C. 1 Red shrub rose such as La Sevillana
Zones 4–10

D. 2 Red shrub roses such as Knock Out
Zones 4–10

E. 1 Deep pink shrub rose such as William Baffin*
Zones 3–8

F. 1 Light pink shrub rose such as The Fairy
Zones 4–9

G. 1 Apricot-pink shrub rose such as Perdita
Zones 4–9

* Climbing form also available

PLANT SUPERSTAR: TREE ROSES

In this or other rose plantings, consider using tree roses. Tree roses are lovely accents for the landscape, but in Zones 6 and colder, they need extensive winter protection. Many gardeners resort to partially digging them up, tipping them over into a trench, and burying them each winter to protect them from the cold. That's because most tree roses are grafted onto a trunk that is very tender and can be killed by winter cold.

Polar Joy is a particularly cold-hardy variety that is shaped into a tree form without the extra step of grafting. That means it can grow in Zones 4 and warmer with no winter protection. It has 2-inch-diameter soft pink flowers. The plant will grow 5 to 6 feet tall although it can be pruned shorter if desired.

Polar Joy

Formal Flower Circle

A round garden bed is a classic choice for yards of all sizes. Adjust the size of the circle and the number of plants to fit the space.

A Subtle Circle

Small and simple, this garden in blues and shimmering whites is ideal for the middle of a small lawn or other sunny spot.

This formal design is easy to create. It's one of those gardens you can dig and plant in an afternoon.

Simply use a stake with a string on it to mark out the perimeter. (Put the stake in the middle and rotate the string around to mark the edge). Remove the sod from the circle. Then add plenty of soil amendments, such as compost. Fill the container with top-quality potting soil. Then plant it with a boxwood.

Choose small shrub roses for the garden. 'Iceberg' is a classic, but any rose that remains under 3 or 4 feet tall and wide will do. (Hard pruning in spring helps control the size.)

For early spring color, consider tucking in white daffodils among the mealycup sage. About the time the daffodil foliage is fading, the annuals will cover the browning bulb leaves with their new foliage.

BHG TEST GARDEN TIP

ADD SOME COLOR

The mealycup sage in this plan provides a bolt of deep blue throughout the growing season. Consider substituting catmint or perennial sage (such as May Night). These perennials cost a little more up front but save money and time in replanting.

left Like so many formal gardens, this one starts with a focal point—in this case, a nicely shaped pot. It's then ringed in understated white roses and silvery-leaved mealycup sage with blue flowers.

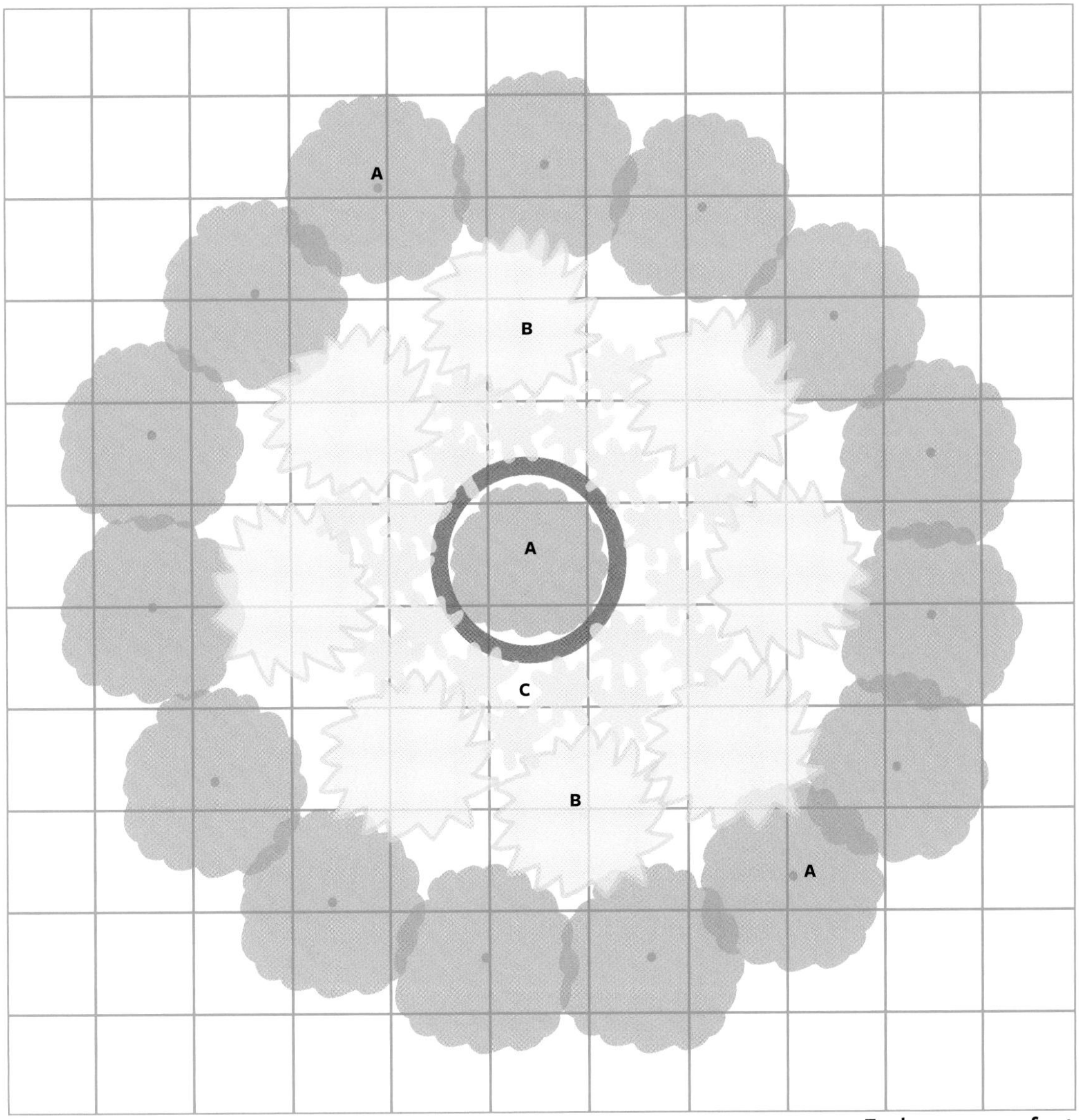

Each square = 1 foot

Plant List

A. **16 Dwarf boxwoods*** such as Green Gem (*Buxus* spp.) Zones 4–7

B. **8 Small white shrub roses** such as Iceberg Zones 5–9

C. **20 Mealycup sages** such as Victoria Blue (*Salvia farinacea*) Annual

* In Zones 4 to 5, wrap boxwood in burlap for winter protection.

Rose-Filled Corner

A bold shrub rose creates a flowering backdrop for a trio of bloom-busting containers.

above In this design, sophisticated urns and a muted planter play strong supporting roles. They team beautifully with their detailing of swags and garlands, mimicking the look of classical iron and lead containers.

A Regal Composition

Elegant containers and classic plants combine to create a planting with timeless beauty.

You don't have to pay a king's ransom for such containers. Instead, purchase containers made of fiberglass or other composites that give the look, but not the price tag—or the weight—of heavy stone or metal pots.

These containers are filled with billowy pink hydrangeas, spiky silver spear, mounded succulents, trailing wandering Jews, and purple Rex begonias. A rose bush planted in the ground behind the containers becomes a natural part of the composition. These plants thrive in full sun to light shade.

If you love the plants more than the containers in this design, change the look by substituting two large glazed ceramic pots for the urns and a complementary ceramic trough garden for the long planter. Or grow the hydrangeas in large square wooden planters and pair them with a wooden window box.

BHG TEST GARDEN TIP

SAVE ON SOIL

Many people dump their containers each year so they don't have to deal with old roots entangled in the soil and old plant debris that may harbor disease. But if you've grown healthy plants, you can easily reuse potting soil for several years. Mix in some new potting soil to help rejuvenate a depleted potting mix. After several years, dump the old soil into a flowerbed and start over fresh.

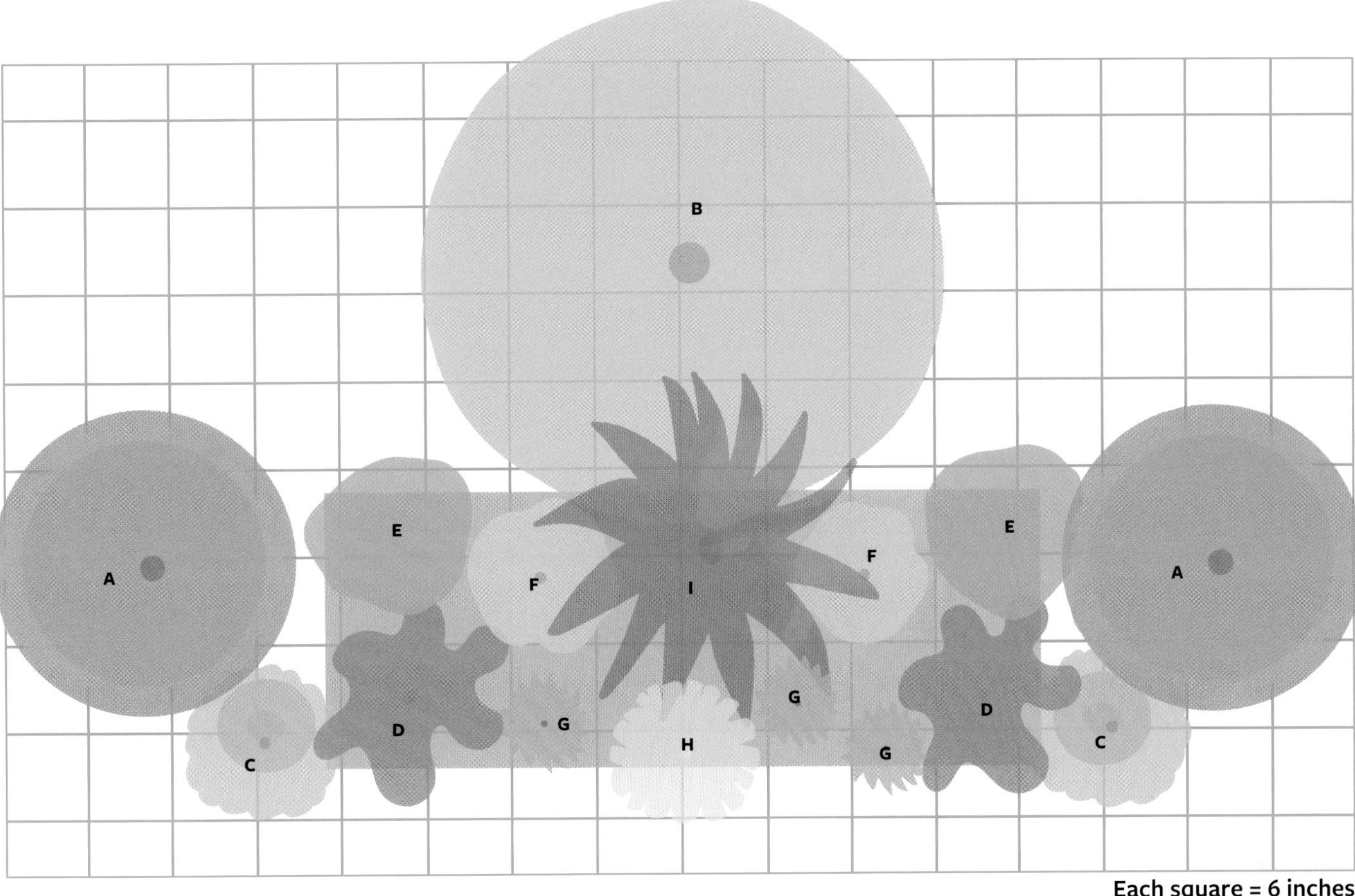

Each square = 6 inches

Plant List

A. **2 Bigleaf hydrangeas** such as Pia (*Hydrangea macrophylla*) Zones 6–9

B. **1 Shrub rose** such as Anne Boleyn or other David Austin Series rose Zones 5–9

C. **2 Geraniums** (*Pelargonium* spp.) Zones 10–11, annual elsewhere

D. **2 Wandering Jews** (*Tradescantia zebrina*) Zones 10–11, annual elsewhere

E. **2 Low-growing sedums** such as *Sedum sieboldii* Zones 5–9

F. **2 Rex begonias** such as Pink Minx (*Begonia rex-cultorum*) Zones 10–11, annual elsewhere

G. **3 Hens-and-chicks** (*Sempervivum tectorum*) Zones 4–9

H. **1 Dichondra** (*Dichondra argentea* Silver Falls) Zones 9–11, annual elsewhere

I. **1 Silver spear** (*Astelia chathamica*) Zones 9–11, annual elsewhere

WINTERIZING SHRUBS IN CONTAINERS

You can plant shrubs (such as roses and hydrangeas) and perennials (such as sedum, hens-and-chicks, and silver spear) in containers, but come late fall in colder regions of the country, you'll need to move them to a protected spot to overwinter them.

In Zones 7 and colder (roughly the northern two-thirds of the United States), place them in a cool (below 40°F) garage so that the plants go dormant. However, the space should remain warm enough (only occasionally dipping below freezing) so that the soil doesn't freeze solid.

In Zones 8 and warmer (roughly the southern third of the United States as well as areas of the coastal Pacific Northwest), you can leave the containers outdoors unprotected.

Cutting Garden

If you love fresh flowers for your home, plant a garden full of snippable roses and perennials for bouquets all season long.

Grow Your Own Bouquets

Enjoy flowers indoors and out with this formal cutting garden.

Even if you never pluck a single posy from this garden, it's so attractive you could plant it just to gaze at from afar. And that's an accomplishment, because too often, cutting gardens look like utilitarian mini farms rather than attractive landscaping.

This design is an exception. It's no plant-it-all-in-rows cutting garden. Instead, flowers are planted in relaxed drifts here and there so this garden is as pretty to look at as the arrangements you'll create from it.

Two pots, filled with annuals for cutting, make cheerful sentries at the entrance. A spectacular crape myrtle adds a vertical element, as do the two climbing roses scaling the back wall.

Since there are no paths for easy access into the beds, you may want to strategically place stepping-stones, pavers, or flagstones to give you a handy landing pad as you snip plants.

And while the garden shown is backed by a wall, you could easily adapt the design by extending the low hedge around the back and adding two more pots. Plant shrub roses instead of climbers, and you'll be set for armloads of flowers spring through fall.

BHG TEST GARDEN TIP

COLD-HARDY CHOICES

In colder regions, substitute dwarf Korean lilac for the camellia and saucer magnolia for the crape myrtle. Both are hardy through Zone 4.

left Create an outline with low-growing boxwood and then fill this garden with a rainbow of flowers you can cut all growing season long.

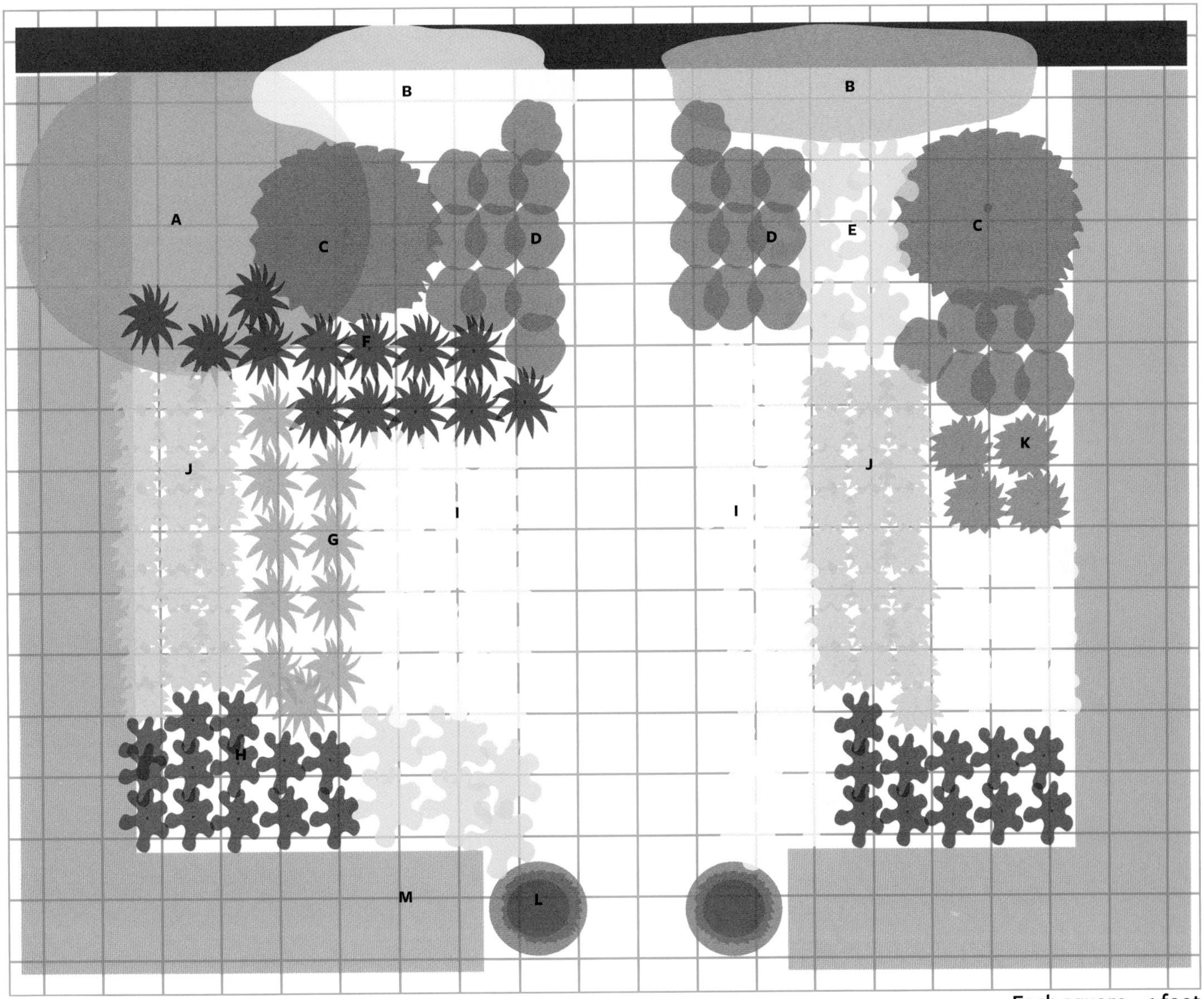

Each square = 1 foot

Plant List

A. 1 Crape myrtle
(*Lagerstroemia indica*)
Zones 7–9

B. 2 Climbing roses
(*Rosa* hybrids)
Zones 5–10

C. 2 Camellias
(*Camellia japonica*)
Zones 6–8

D. 28 Tall zinnias
(*Zinnia elegans*)
Annual

E. 12 Black-eyed susans
(*Rudbeckia fulgida*)
Zones 4–9

F. 13 Red Asiatic lilies
(*Lilium* hybrids)
Zones 4–9

G. 10 Yellow Asiatic lilies
(*Lilium* hybrids)
Zones 4–9

H. 24 Stocks (*Matthiola incana*) or snapdragons (*Antirrhinum majus*) or a mix
Annuals

I. 39 Shasta daisies
(*Leucanthemum × superbum*) or ox-eye daisies (*L. vulgare*)
Zones 4–8

J. 50 Cosmos
(*Cosmos bipinnatus*)
Annual

K. 4 Gloriosa daisies
(*Rudbeckia hirta*)
Zones 3–7

L. 8 Martha Washington geraniums
(*Pelargonium × domesticum*)
Annual

M. 22 Dwarf boxwoods
(*Buxus* spp.)
Zones 5–8*

* In Zone 5, choose a cold-hardy cultivar such as Green Gem and wrap in burlap for winter protection.

Flowering Foundation

Add a flower-filled garden of perennials and shrubs snugged up next to your house to hide an unsightly foundation.

Foundation Fix Up

Forget ordinary and go for extraordinary! This front-yard planting will be the talk of the neighborhood.

The job of a foundation planting is to integrate the house with the landscape so that the two blend seamlessly, creating a welcoming, harmonious look. Without a foundation planting, a house looks stark, as though it rises directly from the ground.

Instead of the usual row of evergreens, this foundation planting features low-maintenance shrub roses, fronted by neat rows of perennials and backed by sprawling clematis—a romantic touch that is the hallmark of cottage style.

If you don't have three windows along the front, simply plant clematis on either side of a larger window or smaller multiple windows. Choose large-flowered clematis, which grow about 6 to 12 feet tall, just the right size for this scheme. Provide the clematis with a trellis for support. Inexpensive prefabricated types from the garden center will do fine. Just make sure the trellis is at least 6 to 8 feet tall. If possible, anchor the top to the house to prevent tipping outward.

Go Longer or Shorter

To adapt this plan (or to create a lush border alongside a driveway), it's a simple matter to shorten it or extend it as far as needed. Just add or subtract daylilies, salvias, and shrub roses. The shrubs provide anchor plantings.

left Most foundation plantings are nothing more than some evergreens and a tree. Get adventurous and add in a mix of colorful roses.

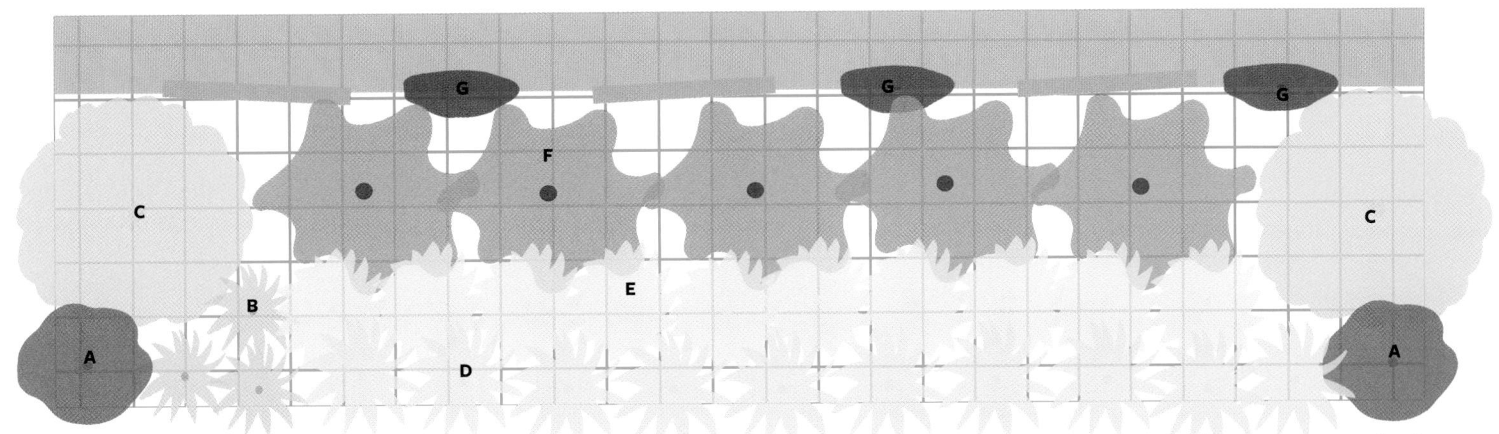

Plant List

A. 2 **Miniature roses**
Zones 5–9

B. 3 **Dwarf Asiatic lilies** such as Lollipop
(*Lilium* hybrids)
Zones 3–8

C. 2 **Indian hawthorns**
(*Raphiolepis indica*)
Zones 8–10*

D. 10 **Miniature daylilies** such as
Stella de Oro
(*Hemerocallis* hybrids)
Zones 3–10

E. 10 **Perennial sages**
(*Salvia* × *sylvestris* May Night)
Zones 4–8

F. 5 **Shrub roses** such as Betty Prior
Zones 5–9

G. 3 **Large-flowered clematises** such
as Jackmanii (*Clematis* hybrids) and
Henryi
Zones 4–9

* In colder regions, substitute dwarf
Korean lilacs (*Syringa meyeri*)

SHRUB ROSES

When landscaping around your home, choose shrub roses as preferred foundation plantings. On sunny sides of the house, these long-blooming and easy-care roses add a combination of structure, color, and fragrance. Shrub roses are low-maintenance choices that mix well with flowering perennials, ornamental grasses, and shrubs. Roses are also a nice complement to flowering shrubs such as lilacs.

CHAPTER FIVE

Rose Care and Maintenance

Get your roses off to a good start with proper care: food, water, protection, and an occasional haircut. Add sunlight and you're set!

left A raised bed protects roses from neighboring tree roots, and a fence or wall provides support. ***above*** Roses, especially hybrid teas, grandifloras, and floribundas, grow best in full sun—at least six hours every day. ***below*** Raised beds are ideal for roses. You can add the right soil and amendments for good drainage and to allow roots to grow deep.

Site Preparation

You'll succeed with roses if you plant them where and how they like to grow. Choose the right site and you'll have success!

Choose the right site and prepare the soil properly so roses have everything they need to grow like weeds—figuratively speaking, of course!

Keep on the sunny side

To perform at its best, a rose needs at least six hours of sunshine a day—preferably more. Without sunlight to promote photosynthesis, the plant cannot make the food it needs to thrive. If there's a choice, place a rose where it gets morning sun to help overnight rain or dew dry off the foliage quickly, which helps suppress fungal growths such as black spot.

Hybrid teas, grandifloras, and floribundas need the most sun. Miniatures also require at least a half-day of sun; when planted in pots, they can be moved to better sun locations as the growing season progresses.

Some types of roses can grow in less than a half-day of sun, though they'll thrive with more. These include large, vigorous types that can grow tall enough to find sunlight and perform well, such as shrubs, climbers, and some Old Garden Roses. If they're planted in a shady area, these roses require fertilizer and good air circulation around the plants to get them off to a good start.

Root for good roots

Roses' extensive root systems produce thousands of root hairs to feed the plants. Once established, these roots can coexist with many annual and perennial plants. However, the invasive roots of nearby large trees and shrubs can rob a rose of water and nutrients, leading to its decline and eventual death.

Check for roots in the planting area before placing a rose near a tree or large shrub. Remember that the TLC you give a rose—good soil, water, fertilizer—may also attract other roots to the site.

Some gardeners grow roses in raised beds 6 to 12 inches deep to solve two critical needs: good soil and good drainage. You can add the ideal soil mix into the beds. And the combination of great soil and height helps the water hydrate then drain away.

You can also grow roses in large pots or other containers. Use pedestals or stumps to raise the containers a few inches off the ground to allow drainage and avoid invading roots from neighboring trees.

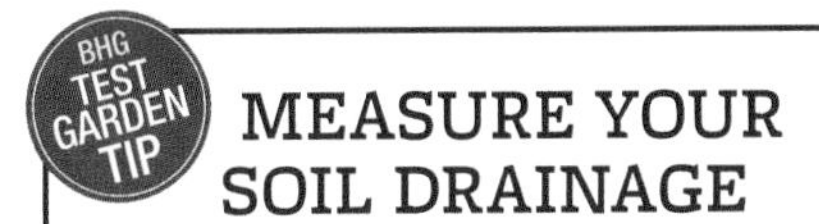

MEASURE YOUR SOIL DRAINAGE

To find out how well your soil drains, dig a straight-sided hole 12 inches deep. Fill the hole with water, let it drain completely, then refill with water. Wait one hour. Use a ruler to measure how far below the soil line the water dropped. Less than 1/2 inch indicates poor drainage; 1/2 to 2 inches is moderate; a 2- to 6-inch drop is good; more than 6 inches indicates rapid drainage.

POTTING SOIL

pH
4.0
Very Acidic
5.0
Very Acidic
6.0
Acidic
7.0
Neutral
8.0
Alkaline
9.0
Very Alkaline

Soil

Roses need well-aerated, organically rich soil with a pH range of 6.2 to 6.8. Test your soil's pH and amend it if needed.

To determine soil pH, take a sample to your local extension service office or buy a home kit. If possible, prepare an entire bed rather than just a planting hole for your roses.

You can remove sod and dig up the ground to make a new bed; however there are two easier ways:

Spray the existing lawn carefully with an herbicide containing glyphosate, following label directions. Use a spray with droplets rather than a mist, which can drift and kill nearby plants. These herbicides don't leave residual chemicals in the soil, so the bed can be prepped as soon as one day later. You don't need to wait for the grass to completely die; the spray is already killing the grass tissues.

An excellent chemical-free alternative is to place several thicknesses of newspapers over the planned planting area, and cover them with compost or mulch. By the time the newspapers decompose, the grass will be dead and compost or mulch can be tilled in.

When to dig

Many home lots have been graded to remove all but a thin covering of topsoil, leaving only impenetrable clay or hardpan. In these cases, fill a raised bed with a commercial 3- or 5-way soil mix. These mixes contain variable amounts of soil, sand, sawdust, and manure. For best results, amend the soil mix with another 10 to 15 percent of organic material such as compost.

Amend soil only when it is fairly dry and loose to the touch. If you try to work with soil that's too wet, you risk ruining the soil structure. Test a handful of soil; if it clings together in a ball and won't come apart when prodded with a finger, it's too wet to work. Wait a few days for the soil to dry before working in amendments.

opposite, above A spading fork is useful for incorporating organic amendments such as compost and peat. ***opposite, below left*** Properly prepared soil should be rich and crumbly, allowing both good drainage and water retention. ***opposite, below middle*** Place several layers of newspapers on the ground and cover with mulch to make a new bed. ***opposite, below right*** Use a soil testing kit before you plant your garden to learn which amendments to add.

Traditional digging—or an easier way

There are two schools of thought about how to amend soil. The traditional method is to dig the bed at least 18 inches deep, then work in about 25 percent compost or other organic material. Because this process raises the soil level 6 to 12 inches, it's best done a few months before planting to allow soil to settle.

A more contemporary method is to plant a rose bush in natural, nonamended soil, then topdress the planting area with about 6 inches of organic mulch—compost, well-rotted manure, and wood chips—every year. Nutrients from the decaying mulch leach into the soil, sustaining biotic activity and making the labor-intensive work of amending the soil unnecessary. The Earth-Kind rose trials in Texas, as well as a growing number of gardening and landscaping experts, use this approach.

Whichever method you choose, continually add organic material into the soil for healthy and vigorous rose growth and production. Buy or build a container to make your own handy source of compost, and seek local sources for well-aged animal manure or other materials.

BHG TEST GARDEN TIP

WATER, BUT PROVIDE GOOD DRAINAGE

Roses need water (at least 1 inch per week) but they don't like wet feet, so avoid planting roses in a low area of your yard or garden. Heavy clay soil that doesn't drain well can cause problems. Amend the soil with compost and other organic material. Water that doesn't drain away causes roots to rot.

Rose Planting

Proper planting gives your roses a foundation that protects against setbacks in coming years.

The better health a rose bush has, the better it can ward off pests and diseases, stretch out its roots to find food and water, and produce more leaves that allow the plant to convert sunlight into food.

When to plant

A rose bush can be planted or transplanted whenever the soil is workable. The best time is late fall to early spring when plants are dormant. Although most nurseries won't ship plants in the fall, autumn-planted bushes develop roots over the winter. Local nurseries sell potted plants at the appropriate planting time for your area.

Preparing bare-root roses

Bare-root roses often arrive with longer and more canes than the roots can feed. Choose three to six of the best canes spread in all directions, then cut them back with pruners to a length of 4 to 8 inches, snipping just above outward-facing buds.

Snip about ½ inch off the tips of the larger roots. A fresh, clean cut helps by stimulating the root end to make a callus, which causes the plant to form nutrient-seeking hair roots.

Some types of roses, such as hybrid teas, come grafted onto sturdier rootstocks. The roots of a rose grown on a Dr. Huey rootstock tend to naturally spread horizontally, while those of multifloras twist downward. Fortuniana roots are shallow and spreading.

PRUNE BEFORE PLANTING

Roses often need a little pruning before planting. Remove old, dead wood. On bare-root plants, trim canes to the length of the roots. Prune the tips of bare-root roses to encourage the growth of root hairs, which feed the bush.

Preparing potted or boxed roses

Always assume a potted or boxed rose is dehydrated. Remove all packaging and soil from a boxed rose, and completely submerge it in a bucket of water for at least one day to rehydrate.

Avoid planting it encased in a box or peat pot. Although the container will eventually decompose, it severely restricts a plant's roots, resulting in a small and unhealthy root system.

Water potted roses for one or two days before planting. Remove damaged stems. Prune buds and flowers so the plant will put its energy into establishing its roots before developing new stems and flowers.

To remove the rose from its pot, place the container sideways on the ground, then gently press your foot on the pot so you can ease the rose from its container.

BHG TEST GARDEN TIP

BARE ROOTS ARE BEST

Roses thrive when started as bare-root plants. Because the roots of a container rose may not wish to venture out from the potting medium, shake off some of the soil or rough up the root ball before planting.

opposite A spading fork is useful for incorporating organic amendments such as compost and peat.

Rose Planting

Proper planting is like serving a balanced breakfast to your child. It gets your rose off to a good start.

Although it's tempting to buy a rose bush already in bloom, if a plant is growing vigorously and buds or flowers have already formed, the transplant shock can be severe. Instead of putting it into the ground right away, repot a blooming rose into a larger pot, keeping the root ball intact, and maintain it through the growing season. Plant it in the ground in the fall, when the plant is naturally beginning to go dormant.

How deep to plant

How deep to plant a rose varies according to geographical location.

In cold areas of the country, position the bud union (the swollen area where a grafted rose meets the rootstock) 2 to 3 inches below ground level. On an own-root rose, the crown (the area where the roots fan out) should be used as the guideline. Placing the bud union or crown below the soil gives it more winter protection. In milder regions, the bud union should be planted at or slightly above the surface of the soil.

Dig the hole

When you plant roses, give the roots a firm soil base. Dig a hole about 2 feet wide by 1 foot deep, amending the soil with compost. To support bare roots, pack some soil into a small, firm cone and position the plant so it is firmly anchored. Spread out the roots in all directions. Potted roses should be positioned so the bud union is placed in the correct position.

Avoid adding any chemical fertilizer containing nitrogen to the planting hole because it burns the plant's roots. New rose bushes develop slowly from food stored in their canes and need no fertilizer at the time of planting.

The only fertilizer that should be placed in the planting hole is phosphorus, in either organic or chemical form. Because phosphorus moves very slowly through the soil, adding it to the soil in the planting hole makes it more available to the plant than applying it at the soil surface. Phosphorus will not burn the tender plant roots.

Fill the hole

Once the plant is positioned, half-fill the hole with soil, then add water, using a hose or watering can. Once the water has drained, completely fill the hole with soil to ground level; water well again.

Avoid firming the soil around the plant with your foot or a shovel; this compacts the soil too much.

If you plant during cool weather, mound up enough soil over the canes so about 1 inch of the tips is visible. This protects the canes from drying out in wind and cold temperatures. Once the weather warms and the plant starts to sprout, gently wash the mounded soil away.

BHG ASK THE GARDEN DOCTOR

How do I move a rose?

ANSWER: When transplanting a rose bush, the guideline is to balance the length of the root system with the length of the canes the rose needs to feed. Cut back canes to the length of the roots. Because it takes time for a rose's roots to get established and start feeding, any long canes left unpruned will probably die.

opposite, above Use a tool handle across the hole to see where to place the bud union of a hybrid tea. In warm areas, set it above the soil line, as shown. In colder areas, plant it 2 to 3 inches below the soil line. ***opposite, below left*** Inspect and loosen any circling roots before planting a container rose. ***opposite, below right*** Carefully water the entire root area of a newly planted rose.

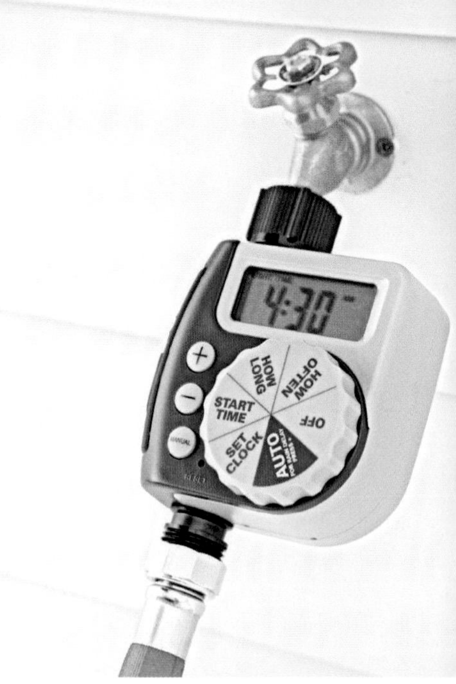

left A soaker hose allows a slow, steady application of water, sending it to the roots instead of the foliage. ***above right*** A programmable water timer automates watering chores. ***above*** Single watering sources can be laid below individual plants.

Watering

While the image of a gardener watering roses with a watering can seems charming, hand watering is a labor-intensive and inefficient practice.

Roses need regular, deep watering during hot weather; watering by hand is simply not very practical. The kind of watering system you use depends upon the layout of the garden, the number of roses, and factors such as water pressure and time availability.

Water slowly

Watering slowly allows moisture to percolate down to the deep roots and prevents wasteful runoff. Large rose gardens generally require a watering system. But if you have only half a dozen plants, the most efficient method is a slow drizzle from a garden hose. To prevent runoff, build a low earthen dam around the drip line of the plant (approximately the same diameter as the plant's upper parts.) Let the hose run slowly for about a half hour on each plant.

Know when and how much

Some estimates say roses perform well with 1 inch of water per week. However, this doesn't take into account the temperature, soil type (water moves quicker through sandy soils), the size of the plants, and other factors.

The best way to determine how much and how often to water is to check soil moisture. Push a hollow metal tube into the soil about 1 foot deep and check the condition of the extracted soil. The 6 inches of the soil in the bottom of the tube—representing the 6- to 12-inch levels—should be moist but not dripping wet. If this area of soil is dry, water deeply. Avoid waiting until your plants tell you they need water by wilting or dropping their leaves.

Avoid overhead watering

Some gardeners prefer to water with an overhead sprinkler. Although many plants can be covered in a short time, this method carries two big drawbacks for roses: It encourages black spot fungus spores to germinate, and it wets and spoils the blooms. If you must water with a sprinkler, do it early in the morning so the foliage has a chance to dry quickly in the sun.

Another option is to apply a fungicidal spray shortly after overhead watering because watering tends to cause the leaf stomata (pores) to open, allowing the spray to be absorbed.

Bed layouts dictate choices

If you have individual plants strategically placed in the landscape, an aboveground hose is probably the most efficient way to water. However, if you have large beds of roses or mixed plants, you'll want a watering system that can serve as large an area as possible.

It's best to water the soil of the entire bed, not just at the base of the plants, to encourage root systems to expand and give the plant better access to food and water.

When beds are linear, use a rigid plastic pipe laid above or below the ground to carry water. Emitters of various kinds can be attached to the pipe to disperse water to plants.

For an irregular layout, use flexible tubing or soaker hoses fitted with emitters to reach all areas. Leaky hoses can be used, but they should be laid out to ensure maximum coverage. The emitters—nozzles, tubes, pinholes—should deliver water in a fine spray or slow drizzle to cover the most area and to prevent runoff. To prevent black spot germination, water should not touch lower foliage.

For container gardens, use thin, flexible tubing with one or two emitters per pot.

How will it look?

Watering systems include hoses, pipes, or a combination of both, which can be located above or below ground level. Aboveground pipes are relatively easy to maintain and can be moved or removed when working in the beds, but they can look awkward among plants and flowers. Underground piping is generally not visible but is difficult to repair if you sever it with a shovel while working in the beds.

Other considerations

The length of the tubing and emitters depends on water pressure. Emitters at the end of the run should function as well as those at the beginning. If needed, add a device to increase water pressure on outside faucets. Other time- and labor-saving tools include automatic timers and liquid fertilizer dispensers.

Mulching, Feeding, and Fertilizing

The proper care and feeding of your roses helps them weather the seasons and return faithfully each year.

Mulch—the material added to the planting area surface to retain water—helps keep roses moist. Water evaporates quickly from soil in hot weather, and mulch slows this process.

Why mulch?

Mulch has many purposes. It suppresses weeds, adds organic material to the soil, hides the appearance of an aboveground watering system, gives beds a pleasing overall appearance, and serves as the base for winter protection.

Vegetable gardeners often use black or clear plastic mulch to boost the soil temperature around tomato plants, and landscape fabric does a great job of weed suppression, but neither of these materials is recommended for mulching a rose bed. Organic mulch is preferred because it serves a variety of purposes well.

Mulch deep

Add 3 to 4 inches of organic materials to the soil surface every year. The list of good choices includes:

Pine needles The most common rose mulch used in areas with pine forests, pine needles are available and inexpensive, do not support weed seed germination, and add soil nutrients.

Hardwood chips This mulch has the same advantages as pine needles. The environmentally friendly Earth-Kind program at Texas A&M uses this material.

Shredded or chipped bark Although bark can work well, beware of the source. Logs are often moved and held in salt water prior to milling. The retained salt in the bark is unhealthy for roses and other plants.

Manure and compost Although manure and compost feed and improve the soil, weed-suppression ability is low because weeds can germinate both below and in the mulch. They also retain water somewhat less well than other materials.

opposite, above Wood chips, bark, straw, and pine needles, left to right, are all excellent organic mulch choices. ***opposite, below*** An annual topdressing of compost adds nutrients that roses need.

Feed your soil before fertilizing

Feeding and fertilizing your roses are actually two separate but complementary practices.

First, feed the soil with a regular supply of organic matter when planting, followed by mulching and topdressing existing beds. Organic material nourishes the soil bacteria and other microorganisms that break down minerals and other nutrients into forms that can be used by plants.

Fertilizer contains the minerals or elements necessary for plant growth and development. The three most important macronutrients are nitrogen, phosphorus, and potassium. Micronutrients—elements needed in small amounts—include calcium, sulfur, magnesium, boron, chlorine, manganese, iron, zinc, copper, molybdenum, and selenium.

Fertilizers must be labeled with the percentage of the three macronutrients. The numbers 6-4-8 on a label, for example, mean the product contains 6 percent nitrogen, 4 percent phosphorus, and 8 percent potassium. The letters are also referred to as N-P-K, the scientific abbreviations for those elements. The remaining 82 percent of the fertilizer is filler or carrier material.

When to fertilize

Organic fertilizers are best applied early in the season, since they remain in the soil for longer periods than inorganic products. However, they can be applied at any time. More is not better—apply as recommended on the label.

Inorganic fertilizers are best applied later in the spring when the soil warms up. Depending on the length of your growing season, two to three applications of dry inorganic fertilizer should be enough. Many gardeners add small amounts of liquid or water-soluble fertilizer to their fungicidal spray.

Mulching, Feeding, and Fertilizing

Organic and inorganic fertilizers do the same job but have significant differences. Organic fertilizers are derived from plants or animals that contain macronutrients and micronutrients. Examples of plant-derived fertilizers are compost, alfalfa meal, seaweed meal, and cottonseed meal. Animal-derived fertilizers include manure, blood meal, bonemeal, fish meal or extract, and feather meal. Some fertilizers can contain both organic and chemical components.

Because there are no consistent standards for processing organic fertilizers, the N-P-K (nitrogen-phosphorus-potassium) analysis can differ among products. For example, bone meal, an organic source of phosphorus, may have an analysis of 4-12-0 from one supplier and 2-14-0 from another. Commercial organic products usually contain a blend of vegetable and animal components to produce a balanced fertilizer. Carefully read the label to check the contents as well as the N-P-K analysis.

Plants can't tell the difference

When choosing between an organic and an inorganic product, consider:

Roses can't tell the difference between organic or synthesized nitrogen, minerals, or elements. Once soil microorganisms convert the nitrogen into a form the plants can use, it's all the same to them.

You do not need a fertilizer specially formulated for roses. Roses need a balanced (or mostly balanced) fertilizer such as a 20-20-20 liquid or 6-6-4 granular product.

High-nitrogen fertilizers such as a 22-2-2 lawn fertilizer are not recommended for roses unless the roses show nitrogen deficiency.

Organic benefits and drawbacks

Organic fertilizers are relatively low in nutrients when compared with inorganic fertilizers, but they have several advantages:

Remain in the soil longer and don't leach out with rain or overwatering.

Release nutrients slowly over an extended period of time.

Help improve soil structure.

Can mobilize existing soil nutrients. For example, alfalfa meal or pellets contain the chemical triacontanol, an alcohol-based hormone that acts as a catalyst to increase nutrient uptake and promote more vigorous plant growth.

The biggest disadvantage of organic fertilizers is the high cost. You can make your own inexpensive organic meal fertilizer mix from bulk meals bought at a feed store.

Experienced rosarians depend heavily upon alfalfa meal or pellets, also available at nurseries or feed and grain stores. Spread the pellets on rose beds a couple times a year or apply an alfalfa tea to revitalize any slow-growing or problem plants.

To make alfalfa tea, fill a 33-gallon trash can or other large container nearly full of water. Wrap one or two 5-gallon amounts of alfalfa in a burlap or permeable plastic sack and submerge in the water. Let this mixture steep for five to seven days (or until you can no longer stand the odor.) Apply about 1 gallon of the tea to the roots of each big rose, a half-gallon for miniatures. The alfalfa contains a hormone that helps the plant take up more nutrients.

Inorganic benefits and drawbacks

Inorganic fertilizers, sold in granular and liquid form, are mined or synthetically manufactured. Most offer a balance of N-P-K, but some are weighted heavily to specific elements.

The advantage: They're quick acting because the nutrients are readily available to the plant. The disadvantage: If overused, or applied before the soil warms up enough to activate the microorganisms that break them down, inorganic fertilizers can leach through the soil and foul nearby waterways.

When using inorganic fertilizers:

Wait until temperatures reach about 60°F before applying so soil microorganisms are active enough to use the fertilizer.

Water beds well before applying.

Apply either liquid or granular fertilizer in moderation. Frequent small doses are better than one or two big ones.

Avoid getting granular fertilizer on wet foliage because it can burn the leaves.

Scratch a dry fertilizer into the soil, then water the beds again.

How to get your money's worth

When purchasing a fertilizer, whether organic or inorganic, get the greatest amount of active ingredients for your money. With different N-P-K analyses, dry weights, and prices among products, this can be hard to determine.

Here's a simple formula: Divide the price per pound of the product by the total percentage of N-P-K. For example, a 6-8-6 product selling for $9.99 for 1.8 pounds costs $5.55 per pound. Divide 5.55 by .20, the total percentage of N-P-K, for a cost of $27.75 per pound of actual fertilizer.

By comparing the true cost of macronutrients between products, you can determine which offers the best value, regardless of label names and claims.

left Alfalfa pellets release an alcohol containing triacontanol, which acts as a growth stimulant for roses. You can buy alfalfa pellets in feed and grain stores as well as in some well-stocked nurseries. ***above*** A slow-release chemical fertilizer may need to be applied only once each growing season. ***below*** Look for balanced N-P-K numbers on fertilizers for roses. This means that the numbers will be approximately the same value.

Pests

Everyone loves roses, including a host of diseases, insects, and animals.

Although pest damage may not seriously affect plant health, it may make your rose garden look unattractive. A few pests kill plants entirely. Take an Integrated Pest Management (IPM) approach to control these threats. Although chemical pesticides take time to apply, cost money, and carry risks to the environment, they can serve as the last resort in certain cases.

Integrated Pest Management

IPM combines cultural, physical, biological, and chemical tools to minimize economic, environmental, and health risks. The levels, in order of use, are:

1. **Establish** acceptable pest levels.
2. **Take** preventive cultural measures.
3. **Monitor** pests.
4. **Add** physical controls.
5. **Use** biological/natural controls.
6. **Apply** chemical controls.

How IPM works with aphids

As an example, consider aphids, a common pest in nearly all rose gardens, and follow the six-step process.

Establish acceptable pest levels: Some people cannot accept any aphids on their roses, but others tolerate them.

Take preventive cultural measures: Aphids seem less attracted to Old Garden Roses and some shrub roses than to hybrid teas, floribundas, and miniatures.

Monitor pests: Pay attention to your roses and look for the presence of aphids or other pests.

Add physical controls: Crush aphids with your fingers (gloves are optional) or wash them off plants with water.

Use biological/natural controls: Biological controls take a variety of forms. For aphids, this includes adding insect predators such as green lacewings or ladybugs, spraying insecticidal soaps, and applying jojoba oil insecticide.

Apply chemical controls: Use an insecticide.

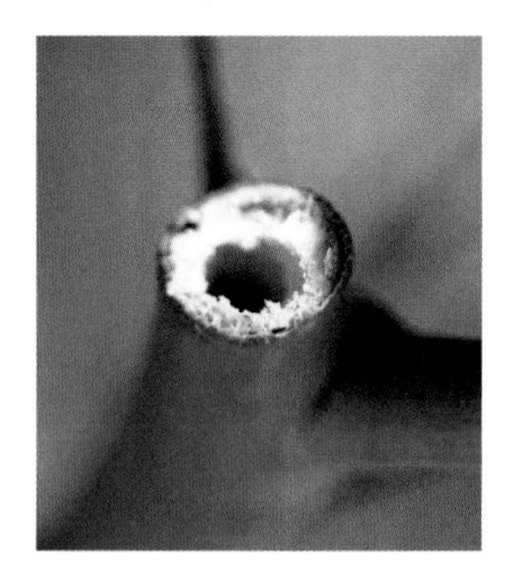

Cane Borer

Many insects, including sawflies, carpenter bees, and some wasps, bore a hole into the end of a dead rose cane or one that's been pruned too high above a bud or leaf axil. Cane borers do not kill the cane; the cane is already dead or dying before the borers enter to lay their eggs. Canes and leaves turn brown and rot. It can be difficult to find either the original insect or larvae.

Damage: Holes appear in the pithy center of canes.

Signs: Difficult-to-see larvae become small caterpillars.

Prevention and management: Though many sources suggest painting or coating newly pruned canes with a sealing substance, it's a waste of time. Simply prune dead or dying canes that show evidence of cane borers. Some wasps lay their eggs on cut canes. The eggs hatch into caterpillars that burrow into the cane pith. Because the wasps feed on aphids, controlling aphids may also encourage the wasps to find other nesting sites with a more reliable source of food.

Japanese Beetle

Japanese beetles are prevalent and destructive in every state east of the Mississippi River. Infestations are also noted in California, Iowa, Missouri, and Nebraska. Beetle larvae appear as white soil-borne grubs. Adult beetles typically emerge in midsummer.

Damage: Leaves are chewed between the veins, creating a lacy appearance.

Signs: Metallic-green-and-bronze ½-inch-long beetles with a white fringe near their wings appear.

Prevention and management: Grubs can be treated with milky spore (*Bacillus popilliae*) or with parasitic nematodes. Insecticides containing imidacloprid can also be effective against grubs. For adult beetles, hand picking is the most popular remedy. Drop them in a bucket of soapy water, since crushing and leaving them in place emits a pheromone that attracts more beetles. Mechanical traps attract more beetles than they kill. Several chemical insecticides show effectiveness against adult beetles. Most Japanese beetles overwinter in turfgrass, so treat your lawn.

Leafhopper

Leafhoppers suck the sap out of leaves. The name comes from the insects' habit of hopping off leaves when the plant is touched.

Damage: Foliage is white-stippled or puckered.

Signs: Slender, wedge-shape insects about ½ inch long are usually green, yellow, or brown. Usually found on the undersides of leaves, they run sideways and jump when the plant is touched.

Prevention and management: Clean up plant debris in fall to prevent leafhoppers from overwintering. Ladybugs, damselwings, and lacewings consume leafhopper eggs and larvae. Organic insecticides such as neem oil and pyrethrins can be effective against leafhoppers. Wash them off leaves with a strong spray of water directed to the undersides of leaves, but do this in the morning so leaves can dry quickly, which prevents fungal problems.

Leaf Roller

Leaf rollers, essentially caterpillars, can be spotted when you inspect curled, rolled-up leaves. They feed on foliage and buds at the end of rose shoots.

Damage: Leaves and buds appear chewed and curled.

Signs: Green caterpillars, ½ to ¾ inch long and hatched from the larvae of small moths, are found inside rolled leaves, often bound with silken webbing.

Prevention and management: Since leaf rollers in the United States often infest canna plants, remove cannas from rose gardens. Mechanically control leaf rollers by cutting off and disposing of infected leaves. Organic controls include neem oil, pyrethrins, and *Bacillus thuringiensis* (also called Bt). Predators, such as lacewing larvae, assassin bugs, tachinid flies, and wasp parasites will dine on leafroller larvae or eggs. Inspect plants in late winter or early spring for egg masses that are about the size of a thumbprint, laid on smooth wood. Large infestations may require chemical products.

Midge

A tiny fly, *Dasineura rhodophaga*, lays its eggs on the tips of growing stems. After hatching, the larvae feed on the buds and stems, then drop to the ground to pupate in loose soil inside a silken cocoon.

Damage: Stem tips turn black, giving a burnt appearance.

Signs: Adult rose midges resemble mosquitoes in shape and appearance, growing about 1 to 2 millimeters long. Full-grown larvae, sometimes reddish, reach nearly 2 millimeters long.

Prevention and management: Mechanical and biological controls are generally ineffective against midges, although you can lightly cultivate the soil to destroy the cocoons. Apply the chemical diazinon to the soil to prevent ground pupation and overwintering as a preventive approach. Most commercial insecticides are effective when applied to new foliage.

Raspberry Cane Borer

This slender, ½-inch-long beetle doesn't confine itself to raspberries. It punctures tender young rose canes and girdles them under the bark before laying its eggs.

Damage: The insect is seldom seen, but you'll know the damage is there when you see a wilting cane tip. The adult borers lay their eggs one season. The larvae then burrow in and overwinter in the cane, emerging as adults the following spring.

Signs: The raspberry cane borer is mainly black with horns and long antennae. The cylindrical, legless larvae are white, reaching about ¾ inch long.

Prevention and management: The best treatment is to prune the cane a few inches below the wilted area. Since the life cycle of the borer is two years, prompt removal of wilted canes is important. When you see the insects, apply an organic or chemical insecticide effective against borers.

Pests

Rose Slugs

Rose slugs are the larval stage of sawflies. They are not actually slugs, but earned their name because they resemble slugs when curled up at rest. They should not be confused with leaf rollers.

Damage: Rose slugs feed on leaf tissues and chew holes in the leaves, eventually leaving only the skeleton of the veins showing.

Signs: These pests look like small pale green slugs up to ¾ inch long, usually found on the undersides of leaves. Depending on the species of sawfly, the larvae may exude a slimy substance (like slugs), while others are hairy.

Prevention and management: For small outbreaks, use forceful water streams or handpick slugs off leaves. For larger infestations, neem oil, insecticidal soap, and horticultural oil have proved effective. *Bacillus thuringiensis* will not work because these are sawfly larvae, not butterfly or moth larvae. Most chemical insecticides also work on rose slugs.

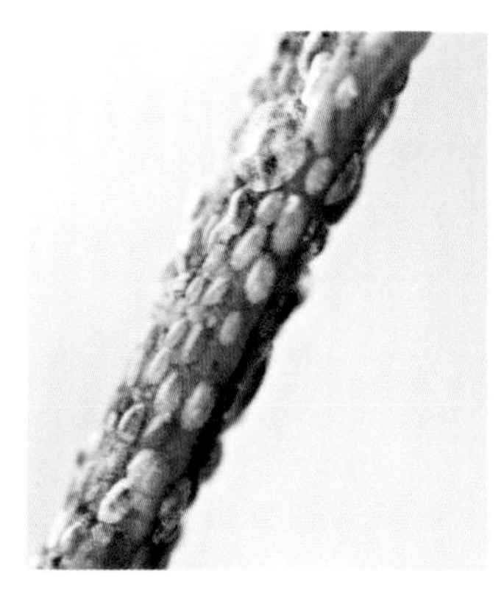

Scales

Rose scales are an infrequent and generally low-level pest that can be caused by a variety of insects. They feed on plant tissue and form a crusty shell over their bodies for protection, giving them their name.

Damage: The symptoms of rose scale are bumpy, discolored, and occasionally distorted canes, although leaves may be affected as well.

Signs: Female scales are nearly circular, flat, white, and tiny. Males are much smaller, with narrow and elongated shapes. These insects suck the sap from the plant.

Prevention and management: The best treatment is to prune out the infected areas. Spray the bare canes with a lime-sulfur horticultural oil mix—the usual components in what is known as dormant spray—as you put the plants to bed for the winter and again in the spring to suffocate scales. Insecticidal soap can also help. Cut out and destroy any old, badly infested canes. Some ladybugs and parasitic wasps attack scales.

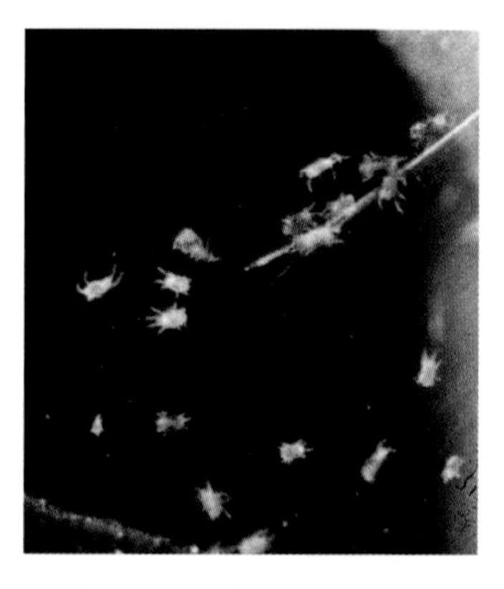

Spider Mites

Technically arachnids rather than insects, spider mites are minuscule pests that appear during hot, dry weather. They come up from the soil and appear first on the undersides of the lower leaves of a plant.

Damage: Spider mites suck the juices out of the leaves, causing discoloration and leaf drop. These pests are especially troublesome for miniature roses because they grow so low to the ground.

Signs: Minute specks the size of pepper grains are hard to see unless you tap them off the plant onto a sheet of white paper, where they will start to crawl around.

Prevention and management: Washing the undersides of the rose leaves with a hose or watering wand is effective against spider mites but must be done repeatedly. Natural predators such as ladybugs and minute pirate bugs can also have good results. To be effective, chemical products must contain a miticide rather than simply an insecticide.

Thrips

Thrips are small insects whose presence is hard to detect until the damage appears.

Damage: Thrips symptoms appear as brown streaks or spots on rose petals, most evident on white or yellow blooms. Foliage may be flecked with yellow.

Signs: Tiny yellow or brown insects are seen when a deformed or streaked flower is pulled apart and shaken over a piece of white paper.

Prevention and management: Severe thrips infestations can be fought with predator nematodes and predator mites as well as biological products containing the fungus *Beauveria bassiana*. As with other insect pests, most commercial insecticides are effective. In recent years, a particularly pernicious species known as chilli thrips has appeared in the southwestern United States. Unlike flower thrips, this species feeds on leaves and other plant tissue, and seems especially resistant to biological controls. Insecticides containing either acephate or imidacloprid as the active ingredient have proved most effective against chilli thrips.

Deer

Deer, a problem across the country, regard rose foliage and buds as prime delicacies.

Damage/signs: Canes and flowers show damage from chewing.

Prevention and management: Only two methods repel deer: a sturdy fence at least 8 feet high and an aggressive guard dog. Other remedies, either homemade or commercial, have limited success. Homemade controls include deodorant soap, human hair, egg white or pepper sprays, and a host of others. Commercial repellent products for deer often contain predator urine, dried porcine or bovine blood, or foliage sprays with unpleasant tastes such as capsaicin (pepper). These must be reapplied on a regular basis to maintain effectiveness. Rotate product use so deer don't become accustomed to just one repellent. Netting over a strong frame can also be used to keep out deer.

Rabbits and Other Chewing Animals

Rabbits, voles, and armadillos often bedevil roses.

Damage/signs: Canes and flowers show damage from chewing.

Prevention and management: Commercial repellent products for rabbits and rodents often contain predator urine, dried porcine or bovine blood, or foliage sprays with unpleasant tastes such as capsaicin (pepper). These must be reapplied on a regular basis to maintain effectiveness. Rotate product use so pests don't become accustomed to just one repellent. Rabbits tend to nibble on roses during the winter. To protect plants, encircle rose bushes with netting or chicken wire; bury the lower few inches in the ground to prevent burrowing by voles and other critters.

PROTECT YOUR ROSES

Protect roses from the chewing teeth of rodents and the scraping antlers of deer with chicken wire. The stems of standard roses are especially vulnerable. Watch for animal tracks in snowy weather to see whether pests are in your area. Rabbit and deer tracks are easy to spot in snow. Another thing to look for is animal scat that may appear in your garden.

Diseases

Some diseases are merely annoying, but others pose a more serious threat to rose health.

Steps to take against disease

Unlike insect pests, you can take completely organic cultural and mechanical steps to lessen the impact of fungal diseases on roses:

Purchase disease-resistant varieties. No variety is totally free from all fungal diseases, but some are more resistant than others.

Avoid crowding plants to maximize air circulation. This deters the germination of disease spores.

Prune each plant enough to open it to air circulation and sunshine. Continually remove unproductive wood.

Practice good sanitation. Keep the ground free of infected leaves; frequently spray your pruning shears with a disinfectant.

Avoid overhead watering and watering late in the evening to prevent fungal diseases.

Never increase the dilution rate of any fungicidal product; protect the environment and your personal safety.

Commercial products

The American Rose Society endorses several commercial products. Three of the most frequently used products are:

Bayer Advanced All-in-One Rose & Flower Care

Ortho RosePride Insect, Disease & Mite Control

Immunox Plus Insect & Disease Control

Greencure, a potassium bicarbonate-based fungicide, cures and prevents powdery mildew, black spot, downy mildew, blights, molds, and other plant diseases.

Anthracnose

Often confused with black spot, anthracnose is a less virulent fungal disease promoted and spread by water on the foliage. Unlike black spot, the tiny ($^1/_8$- to $^1/_{16}$-inch) spots of purplish black seldom cause severe defoliation.

Damage: Distinct dead spots appear on stems and leaves. Dead spots are often yellow first, then turn black. They have a water-spot appearance and are often depressed or sunken.

Prevention and management: Anthracnose is relatively easy to control. Mulch to limit disease spread. Avoid overhead watering. Properly space plants for good air circulation. At end-of-season cleanup, completely remove all plant material; keep it out of the compost to avoid overwintering disease. Most of the organic and chemical fungicides effective against black spot work equally well against anthracnose, including organic fungicides containing potassium bicarbonate.

Black Spot

Black spot, the second most damaging rose disease (downy mildew is the most damaging), is caused by the fungus *Diplocarpon rosae*, with more than 200 known strains. It thrives in wet or humid areas of the country.

Damage: Symptoms include dark rounded spots with feathered edges, along with yellowing of the leaves. Leaf drop is not rapid but persistent. If left untreated, black spot defoliates most rose plants by the end of the growing season. Defoliated plants cannot feed themselves so they go into winter in a weakened state.

Prevention and management: Most home remedies for black spot include baking soda (sodium bicarbonate). Studies show a more effective organic fungicide is potassium bicarbonate, the principal ingredient in various commercial products. Both organic and chemical fungicides prevent rather than cure black spot. Apply regularly beginning when the first leaves form on the plant. To cure an infestation, increase the frequency of application to every three to four days for two weeks to break the reproductive cycle of spore germination.

Crown Gall

Crown gall appears as a bumpy, woody, or corky growth on the crown of budded plants (hence the name) but may also appear on roots and canes. It is caused by a soil-borne bacteria that enters plants through cuts or lesions in the epidermal layer.

Damage: Galls weaken rose bushes, slow their growth, and turn leaves yellow.

Prevention and management: Once crown gall invades a plant there is no cure. Its growth and appearance can be curtailed by cutting off the galls, then treating the affected area with a spray of diluted chlorine bleach. Disinfect pruning shears after each cut by dipping them in a solution of 1 part chlorine bleach and 9 parts water. Healthy, vigorous plants are little affected by crown gall, but numerous galls cause more severe problems. For severe or repeated occurrences, preplanting dips such as Galltrol can help. Destroy severely affected plants.

Downy Mildew

Downy mildew, the most damaging rose disease, resembles neither down nor mildew. Instead, it is often confused with black spot. Downy lesions are usually less regular in shape than black spot markings.

Damage: Downy purple-black blotches appear on the upper sides of leaves, restricted by the leaf veins. The disease causes rapid defoliation of the plant, and it can quickly spread to neighboring bushes.

Prevention and management: Downy mildew is weather-specific. It needs a humidity of at least 85 percent and temperatures below 80°F to develop and can often be found on the West Coast. Most fungicides have little to no effect on preventing or eradicating downy mildew. Once conditions change, the disease disappears but it can do serious damage to a rose garden in the meantime. If you suspect the presence of downy mildew, contact an expert as quickly as possible. Downy mildew can be treated with specific fungicides such as Aliette or Subdue.

Powdery Mildew

Powdery mildew, a fungus, is easy to diagnose. It resembles white powder on new foliage and emerging buds. Its spread is stimulated by warm days and cool nights.

Damage: White patches on leaves look like someone dusted them with flour. Light infestations are ugly but generally harmless, while severe ones twist and stunt leaf growth and development.

Prevention and management: Recipes for homemade treatments abound. One widely available organic commercial product is E-Rase, a contact fungicide made from 97.5 percent jojoba oil. Neem oil has also been used successfully on powdery mildew, while several chemical fungicides are also very effective in controlling it. Promote good air circulation with proper spacing. Remove all affected leaves from the area.

Rust

Rose rust is caused by several fungus species. Wind spreads the orange fungal spores, and moisture allows the spores to enter the leaf tissues. Eventually, spots develop directly on the upper sides of leaves.

Damage: Orange to yellow-brown spots or pustules up to ¼ inch wide appear first on the undersides of rose leaves. If left untreated, rust deforms the leaves and causes leaf drop. Twigs may be attacked. Severely infected plants will be weakened by rust.

Prevention and management: Some rose varieties are particularly susceptible to rust and should be replaced if rust persists year after year. Neem oil can be effective; most chemical fungicides prevent rust. Remove and destroy affected leaves or twigs.

left In regions with cold winters, most of the canes can die back to the ground. Fresh, new growth appears in spring. Remove old, dead wood. ***above*** Use a shallow (less than 45-degree) angle when removing old or new wood. ***below*** Prune to an outward-facing eye or shoot so the new limb will grow in the direction you want.

Pruning

Pruning terrifies most beginning gardeners and even some rose growers who wrongly believe that incorrect pruning stunts or kills a rose.

Pruning does not add vigor or subtract from a rose bush; it merely redirects it. Roses pruned lightly, or not at all, still continue to grow and produce blooms. Roses that are pruned heavily—down to the ground after a severe winter kills all the canes—will regrow and bloom, though later in the season.

Why prune?

There are three basic reasons to prune roses:

To encourage the plant to grow the type of blooms it was bred to grow. Gardeners do not ask a polyantha to grow and bloom like a climber, nor should they expect a rambler to grow and bloom like a hybrid tea. Choose rose varieties for specific purposes, then prune to fulfill those purposes.

To help protect the plant from problems. Susceptibility to diseases and other pests can be greatly reduced with proper pruning practices. Removing damaged and dead wood that can harbor insects or disease and opening crowded bushes to promote air circulation improves plant health and long-term performance.

To shape the bush into an attractive garden plant. Some rose varieties are sprawling and some are leggy. Some grow all their canes on one side of the plant, while others send them out into the lawn or into surrounding bushes. Your roses should grow where you want them to be, not where they are inclined to wander. Careful pruning corrects plant habit problems.

Pruning—cutting canes and leaves off roses—is nearly a year-round activity. In late winter or early spring, do the first pruning to cut out winter damage on last year's growth. Later in the spring, it's time to improve upon the original pruning by cutting out blind shoots and canes that show late dieback.

After each bloom cycle, remove spent blossoms to prepare the plant for its next bloom. In the fall, tender roses can be "headed back" to prevent them from being rocked by autumn winds and to apply winter protection. Experienced rose growers never let their pruning shears gather cobwebs.

Rose pruning basics

The basics of rose pruning are fairly simple and straightforward:

Use sharp bypass pruning shears. Loppers and saws of various sizes can be used for large canes or hard-to-reach places.

Make your pruning cut at a shallow (less than 45 degrees) angle approximately ¼ inch above a bud or leaf scar (the moon-shape mark left on the cane where a leaf has come off) with the slope away from the bud.

Sterilize your pruning shears frequently with a weak bleach solution or a commercial product.

Remove dead, diseased, very thin, and/or spindly canes from all types of roses.

To improve air circulation, which helps plant health and allows room to grow, follow these three rules:

Prune to an outward-facing eye.

Open up the center of the bush.

Cut out crossing canes or any canes touching each other.

However, some of these rules may not apply in all situations. For example, if a cane grows outward at a sharp angle, prune it to an inside eye. That allows the cane to grow inside toward the center of the bush to support new growth, gives the bush a pleasing shape, and keeps it within the bounds you set for it.

Rather than worrying about how to prune your roses perfectly, just do it. Keep a pruning log. List the cane lengths and diameters, number of canes left on the plant, and time of pruning. If the plant's habit and blooms fail to meet your expectations, prune it differently the following year or make corrections during this year's growing season.

Pruning

Don't worry about making a pruning mistake. Roses easily adapt to the kinds of pruning cuts you make, and you learn from the ensuing growth how your cuts made the rose respond. Done properly, pruning improves performance.

Correctional pruning

Correctional pruning should be done throughout the growing season but is most needed in the weeks after the initial spring pruning. Late winter damage and other dieback or problems on canes can be removed at this time. By now, the plant will tell you where it wants to grow.

Weak or spindly shoots at the top of a cane accompanied by much stronger growth lower down are signs that you need to reprune lower. Blind shoots—canes with growing tips killed by the weather or by midges—should be pruned in spring. If the shoot is small, it can be pruned out completely; if it is more advanced and the wood has begun to harden, prune it back to a suitable bud.

Throughout the year, small twiggy shoots emerge on most plants, often low on the canes or in the middle of the bush. Any shoot or cane without a growing tip terminating in a bud or bloom will be the first to get black spot and should be cut out or pruned back.

Pruning for supportive canes

After pruning out winter-damaged canes, prune out weak or small canes, leaving supportive canes. Supportive canes feed the blooms and hold up blooms and their stems.

Small, thin canes produce small blooms. For large blooms on a hybrid tea, for example, keep larger, healthy canes that can produce large stems. Seldom, if ever, does a cane larger in diameter grow from a smaller one. Some gardeners leave no cane skinnier than their thumb (a real rule of thumb) on their first pruning of hybrid teas, knowing this ensures large flowers.

Many roses need physical support. Climbers and large shrubs need trellises or arbors to hold them up, old roses with thin canes need staking to keep them from flopping over, and even heavy bloomers like floribundas may need support to keep them from collapsing during rainy periods. Pruning to inside eyes trains canes to grow in a direction that helps support the plant.

Give miniatures a haircut

Because of their small size and bushy habit, pruning miniatures in a traditional manner can be time-consuming and stressful. If you grow them mostly for landscape color, consider the haircut method: grasp the canes with a gloved hand, pull them together into a bunch, and cut all of them off at the same level.

How to prune climbers

Think of the long canes coming from the base of climbers (basal canes) as a rack or a skeleton on which blooms grow. To get as heavy a bloom as possible, let these canes grow to their full length and train them onto a supportive structure, spreading them out as much as possible.

A basal cane grown one year should bloom the following year on lateral canes growing from it. For repeat bloom, lateral canes should be deadheaded in the summer. In the spring, laterals should be pruned according to the techniques mentioned above. After three to four years, when the laterals on a basal cane stop producing well, the basal cane should be completely removed.

Climbers and other long-caned roses are quite vigorous once established. New canes should be constantly growing from the base to replace old, nonproductive ones. Basal canes that jut into walkways or grow in places you don't want them are better cut out completely than merely shortened.

REJUVENATE UNTAMED ROSES

If you inherit roses left unpruned for many years, try this trick to get them back into a manageable shape and size. Prune half the bush moderately hard one year and the other half the following year. This way the rose will bloom both years while you establish its proper shape and size.

opposite, left Deadhead climbers and remove any canes growing in the wrong direction. ***opposite, above*** Prune at less than a 45-degree angle when making cuts above an outward-facing bud. ***opposite, middle*** The thin, crossing, and dead limbs shown here should be removed. ***opposite, right below*** Prune a cane with winter damage at ground level to promote new growth at its base.

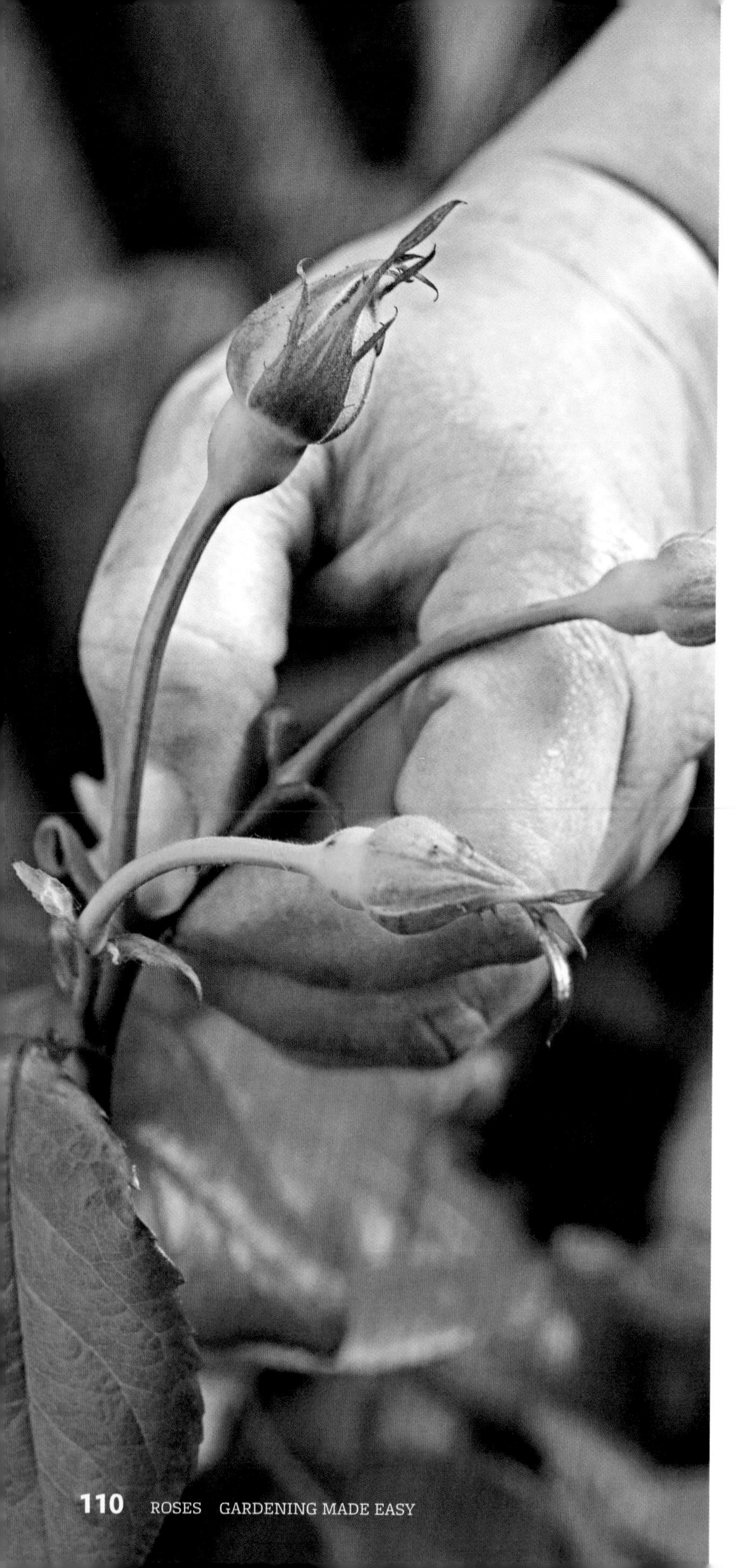

Seasonal Tips

Deadheading and disbudding blooms promote more and bigger flowers. Some pruning chores are best done at specific times of the growing season.

Deadheading

Deadheading is the term for removing spent blooms to promote the quickest possible rebloom. If not deadheaded, the calyxes—rounded portions just below the blooms—begin to form seeds. Seed production robs energy from bloom production, so prompt deadheading is important.

The rule for deadheading hybrid teas is to cut a stem back to the second leaf from the top having at least five leaflets. (In rose terminology, a leaf is the entire growth coming off a stem, while a leaflet is each of the individual portions.) However, this rule can be broken. The five-leaflet advice gives you a cane big enough to grow a new rose of sufficient size and quality, but you may deadhead higher or lower.

An alternate method of deadheading hybrid teas used by some rose growers in late summer or early fall is to simply snap off the bloom and calyx rather than cutting back the cane. This practice leaves more foliage to continue feeding the plant and contributes to better plant growth. The result is more blooms with shorter stems—something you may not want from hybrid teas.

Floribundas and other roses that bloom in sprays should be deadheaded anywhere below the entire cluster.

Shrubs produce flowers from the new growth, so deadhead only the flower and its short stem to encourage rebloom.

left Hybrid teas grow bigger single flowers when they are disbudded. Remove all but the bud at the terminal end of the stem by pinching or pruning.

Disbudding

Disbudding, practiced throughout the year, is another way to make your roses do what you want. For large individual blooms on hybrid teas, grandifloras, or other types of roses, leave the terminal bud—the one that comes out first at the top of the stem—in place, and remove all of the others as early as possible. This diverts all of the plant's energy to the terminal.

To achieve a uniform cluster on floribundas or other spray roses, do the opposite: remove the terminal as early as possible. This allows the other buds to develop into blooms at the same time and with sufficient space. Waiting until the terminal bud blooms and then taking it out results in a hole in the middle of the spray.

Seasonal pruning

Most roses need little or no pruning their first two to three years. Spend that time learning their growth and bloom habits. Knowing these, you'll be able to do a better pruning job when they mature. Pruning principles remain the same, but how they are specifically applied can change from one variety to the next, even within the same rose family.

Spring and new bush pruning

Appropriate and safe pruning times are different throughout the country, based on longtime weather patterns. Some areas rely on indicators such as "prune when the redbuds bloom" while others use specific dates such as Presidents' Day weekend as starting times. Late pruning is safer than pruning too early.

Dried out or blackened canes are obvious signs of winter damage. The main indicator is the color of the pith in the center of the cane; it should be white to greenish white. The darker brown the pith, the more damage has occurred.

Modern bush roses such as hybrid teas, grandifloras, and floribundas should be pruned to at least very light brown pith, while Old Garden Roses, shrubs, and climbers can be left slightly darker. Monitor your plants and reprune as needed when growth begins to correct any errors.

After spring pruning, spray the remaining canes and the surrounding ground with a fungicide with an added surfactant/sticker-spreader, because disease spores can survive winter.

Fall pruning

Pruning of any kind stimulates more growth. In the fall, you should cut fewer blooms for the house. Stop deadheading and let seed production take over. Forcing your plant to continue to bloom into cold weather, whenever that normally arrives in your area, places it at risk for severe damage from a hard freeze. As temperatures drop, the plants shut themselves down and move food from their leaves and stems into their roots.

There's one pruning exception: Cut tall modern roses—hybrid teas and grandifloras—to about 4 feet tall to prevent them from whipping in the wind. This process is often called heading back.

HOW TO DEADHEAD A SHRUB ROSE

Many shrub roses are bred to cleanly drop their petals and the seedheads that form. To improve the look of the rose and to keep it from expending energy creating a seedhead, follow these simple deadheading tips:

1 WHERE TO PRUNE Look for the bare sepals left behind after the petals fall and the green seedheads that form below them. Prune at the base of the seedhead stem or just lop off the seedhead, being careful not to clip surrounding areas.

2 AFTER DEADHEADING The new, red growth indicates where the next crop of flowers will come from.

PRUNE NEW GROWTH FIRST

When pruning after a hard winter, prune new growth first. These are the canes most apt to be damaged, and often must be taken out completely. If you cut out the old ones first, then find that the new ones are damaged or killed, you'll have to start from scratch with a new plant.

left Stop deadheading roses in the fall. This lets the rose produce colorful hips and go dormant instead of putting its energy into flower production. ***above*** Use a plastic collar around roses to hold layers of leaves and soil around the tender bases. ***below*** A rose cone provides some winter protection from damaging winds and frost.

Fall and Winter Maintenance

Severely cold weather can kill the canes of most rose varieties. An even bigger danger is the death of the crown or bud union of a grafted plant such as a hybrid tea. When this happens, the desired variety dies, leaving just the rootstock. Tender roses such as hybrid teas and grandifloras benefit from winter protection in all but the warmest regions (Zones 9 and warmer).

Fall bed preparation

To prepare rose beds for winter, clean up and remove any leaves, petals, and other plant material on the ground to prevent diseases from being carried into the following year. Refrain from pulling leaves off the bushes until after a hard frost when they can be snapped off easily. Removing them too early can tear the stems.

Stop fertilizing plants to discourage top growth. Any tall, freestanding plants should be pruned (also called "heading back") to about 4 feet to prevent them from whipping in the wind and disturbing the root structure.

Before applying winter protection, it's a good idea to spray the base of your plants with a lime-sulfur dormant oil to eliminate any insects that might try to overwinter there.

What to use for protection

The types and amounts of winter protection applied depend upon region as well as location and microclimate.

The best protection for tender roses in the coldest areas of the United States is the "Minnesota Tip" method. Carefully dig up the roots on one side of a rose bush. On the opposite side, dig a 3½-foot-long trench about 12 to 14 inches deep. Prune stems to 3 feet and gently tie them together. Carefully tip the rose and the dug-up roots into the trench, being careful not to damage the graft union. Mound the entire trench and root area with 12 inches of soil, then cover the mound with 12 to 18 inches of straw or bags of dry leaves. In spring, remove the layers gradually as weather warms. Reset the rose in an upright position and water thoroughly.

For protection in other cold areas, rose cones, rigid foam cones, cylinders, or wire cages filled with leaves may be used to protect hybrid teas, grandifloras, and floribundas. Plants are trimmed to 1 or 2 feet tall to fit inside the structures.

If you live in USDA Zone 7 or warmer (see Zone map on page 115), place insulating material such as soil, compost, leaves, or grass clippings around the crowns and lower canes of your plants. In addition, 4 to 6 inches of soil or other organic material mounded on top of the crown provides enough protection.

Let plants breathe

The purpose of winter protection is to insulate, not incubate, your plants. Protective material should be porous enough to allow air to penetrate and moisture to evaporate.

Using soil to cover plant crowns (also called "hilling up") generally means you need to remove the soil in the spring. A much easier approach is to use an organic material such as oak leaves, well-aged manure, or compost that can be worked into the soil the following spring.

Check the USDA Zone map (page 115) and speak with a Consulting Rosarian about the type of protection appropriate for your area.

Can I use plastic to protect my roses?

ANSWER: No. Avoid wrapping a rose with plastic for the winter. Plastic heats up in winter sun, causing the rose to grow and making it more susceptible to winterkill when the temperature drops again.

Rose Hardiness

Determining winter hardiness in roses depends on several variables.

Winter hardiness in roses is a difficult, if not impossible, quality to determine for any given variety. Many variables go into hardiness issues:

How was the plant propagated—from a strong or weak bud?

How was the plant dug, stored, and shipped before purchase?

How well has the rose been treated during the growing season?

Is the rose located in a garden microclimate that is warmer or colder than the zone indicates?

Are there other stressful conditions, such as freeze-thaw cycles or drying winds?

It's difficult and economically unfeasible to do a scientifically valid hardiness test on modern rose varieties such as hybrid teas.

This leaves gardeners in very cold areas with three options:

Grow modern rose varieties on their own roots.

Plant roses known to be winter-hardy, such as shrubs and Old Garden Roses.

Seek advice about which roses seem to best weather the conditions in your region.

ROSES FOR HOT AREAS

Heat stress can be a problem for gardeners in hot areas. Water continually and heavily. Ask local Consulting Rosarians for advice about heat-tolerant varieties or use Earth-Kind roses. Consider this list from a Consulting Rosarian in Arizona, which contains three roses also good for northern climates: Hot Princess, Veterans' Honor, and Butter Cream.

HYBRID TEA
Gemini
Hot Princess
Let Freedom Ring
Marilyn Monroe
St. Patrick *(shown)*
Veterans' Honor

FLORIBUNDA
Fabulous! *(shown)*
Julia Child
Lavaglut
Sexy Rexy

MINIATURE
Baby Grand *(shown)*
Bees Knees
Fairhope
Miss Flippens

MINIFLORA
Butter Cream *(shown)*

ROSES FOR COLD AREAS

If you live in a northern region, consider growing one of these hardy varieties with adequate winter protection suggested by a Consulting Rosarian in Minnesota:

HYBRID TEA
Elina
Hot Princess
Moonstone
Secret (*shown*)
Veterans' Honor

FLORIBUNDA
Eyepaint
Hannah Gordon
Iceberg (*shown*)
Playboy
Poulsen's Pearl

MINIATURE
Hot Tamale (*shown*)
Irresistible
Little Artist
Magic Carrousel

MINIFLORA
Butter Cream
Leading Lady
Memphis King (*shown*)
Tiffany Lynn

The United States Department of Agriculture Plant Hardiness Zone Map

The USDA developed a map based on the lowest recorded temperatures across North America. To find your hardiness zone, match the color marking of your area to the key.

RANGE OF AVERAGE ANNUAL MINIMUM TEMPERATURES FOR EACH ZONE

- Zone 2: -50 to -40° F (-45 to -40°C)
- Zone 3: -40 to -30° F (-39 to -35°C)
- Zone 4: -30 to -20° F (-34 to -29°C)
- Zone 5: -20 to -10° F (-29 to -23°C)
- Zone 6: -10 to 0° F (-23 to -18°C)
- Zone 7: 0 to 10° F (-18 to -12°C)
- Zone 8: 10 to 20° F (-12 to -7°C)
- Zone 9: 20 to 30° F (-7 to -1°C)
- Zone 10: 30 to 40° F (-1 to 4°C)

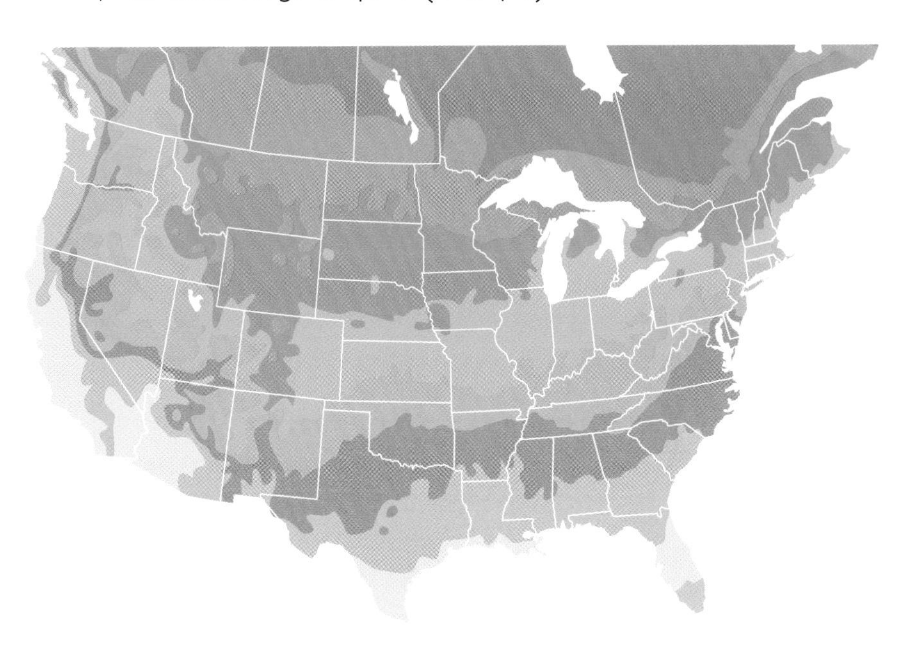

Rose Care Calendar

Northwest

Though the climate here is mild, gardeners often battle diseases caused by excess moisture and too many cool, sunless days. Place roses in as much sun as the yard offers, provide good air circulation that can be enhanced with lots of pruning, and choose varieties resistant to fungal diseases. If you desire perfection, be prepared to spray and otherwise coddle your plants.

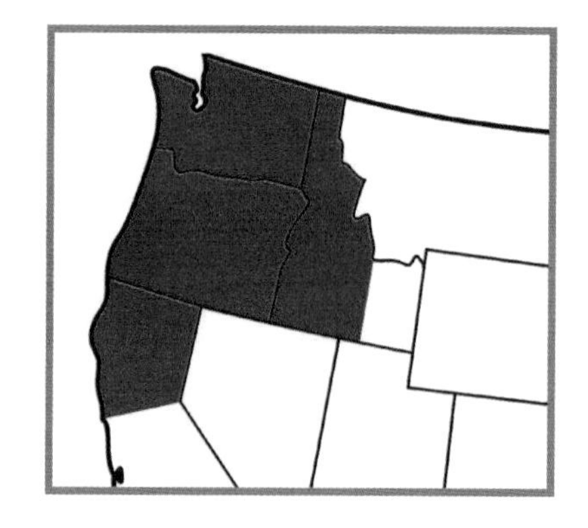

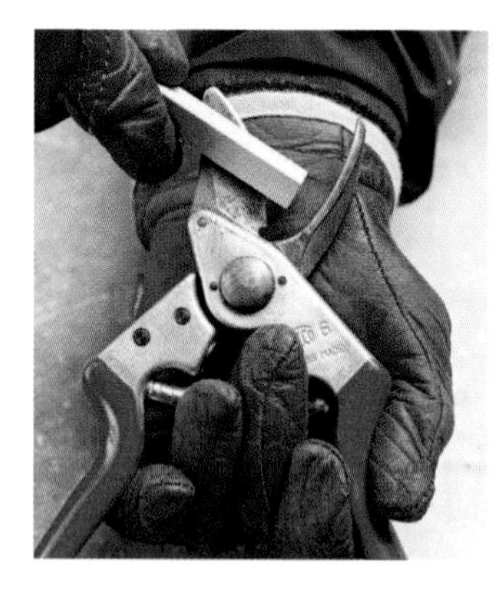

January

Transplant roses as needed.

Sharpen tools.

February

Remove winter protection.

Prune around Presidents' Day weekend in mild areas.

Spray pruned roses with fungicide.

March

Purchase and plant bare-root roses.

Start spray program when leaves appear.

Weed throughout season as needed.

April

Improve initial pruning.

Apply organic fertilizer, if using.

Spray for insects as needed.

May

Apply inorganic fertilizer, if using.

Apply mulch.

Prune blind shoots (stems with no flower buds) and twiggy growth.

June

Continue insect and disease control programs.

Begin watering as needed.

July

Water as needed.

Deadhead as needed.

Fertilize with inorganic fertilizer, fish emulsion, or alfalfa tea.

August

Water as needed.

Maintain insect and disease control programs.

Deadhead as needed.

September

Water as needed.

Lighten up on deadheading and cutting for bouquets.

Fertilize lightly.

October

Maintain disease-control program.

Stop fertilizing and deadheading.

Order plants online or from nursery catalogs.

November

Prune to shorten tall plants.

Clean up beds.

Spray canes and ground with dormant spray.

December

Apply winter protection.

Transplant roses as needed.

Rose Care Calendar

Midwest and Plains

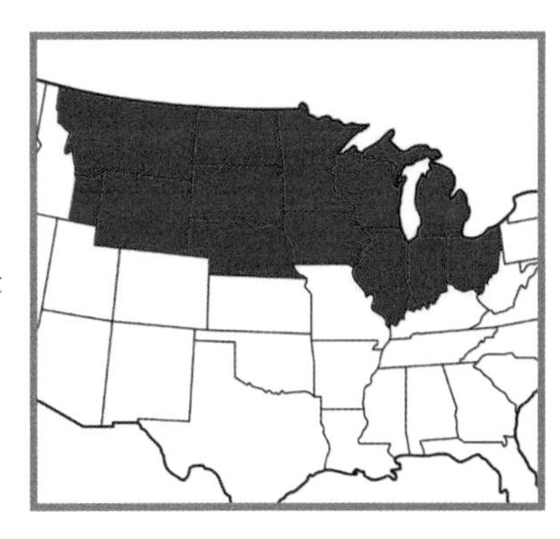

This region of extremes—with cold, windy winters and hot, humid summers—offers a relatively short window of time to enjoy growing roses, making them all the more precious. Grow own-root hybrid teas, grandifloras, and floribundas for better hardiness. Shrubs, species, and Old Garden Roses are good choices here. In the very coldest areas, winter protection is the most important chore you can undertake for your roses.

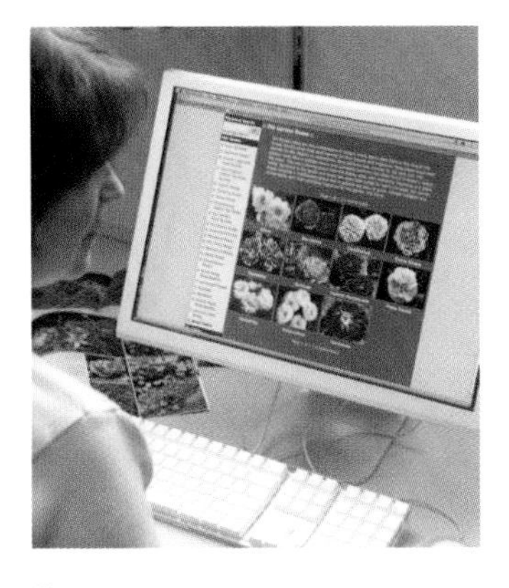

January

Sharpen tools.

Check winter protection.

Order mail-order roses.

February

Purchase spray materials.

Check winter protection.

March

Water roses if there has been no snow cover and the ground is not frozen.

April

Remove winter protection after threat of killing frost is gone.

Prune and apply fungicidal spray.

Plant potted and bare-root roses if possible in your area.

Transplant roses as needed.

May

Start fungicidal spray program when leaves first appear.

Fertilize.

Apply mulch.

Spray for insects as needed.

June

Water and weed.

Remove blind shoots and twiggy growth.

July

Water.

Fertilize.

Apply fish emulsion or alfalfa tea to underperforming plants.

Continue spray program.

Deadhead as needed.

August

Water as needed.

Continue spray program.

Deadhead as needed.

September

Deadhead lightly.

Stop fertilizing.

Water as needed.

October

Stop pruning and deadheading.

Acquire winter protection materials.

Stop spraying.

Clean up beds, removing any diseased leaves or stems.

November

Cut back tall roses to accommodate winter protection program.

Spray with a dormant spray.

Apply winter protection, such as Minnesota Tip method, (shown above and explained on page 113).

December

Read a good book about roses.

Rose Care Calendar

Northeast

Roses peak here in June, slow from heat in midsummer, then bounce back with more blooms during cooler fall temperatures. As in other northern climates, providing winter protection from cold and drying winds is one of the most important tasks facing rose gardeners in the Northeast.

January

Sharpen tools.

Check for loss of winter protection.

February

Purchase spray materials.

Check winter protection.

Water roses if no snow cover.

March

Purchase potted roses.

Remove winter protection.

Prune and spray with fungicide.

Transplant roses as needed.

Water roses if there has been no snow cover.

April

Start fungicidal spray program.

Spray for insects as needed.

Fertilize with organic fertilizer.

Apply mulch.

May

Improve on initial pruning.

Fertilize.

Begin watering as needed.

June

Weed as needed throughout the season.

Prune blind shoots (stems with no flower buds) and twiggy growth.

Continue spray program.

July

Water as needed.

Deadhead as needed.

Treat spindly plants with fish emulsion or alfalfa tea.

Fertilize.

Cut bouquets for the house.

August

Continue spray program.

Deadhead as needed.

Water as needed.

September

Fertilize for the last time.

Deadhead less.

Continue spray program.

October

Discontinue spraying and deadheading.

Prune to shorten tall plants.

Clean up plant debris.

Order mail-order roses.

November

Water.

Spray with dormant spray.

Apply winter protection.

December

Plan rose purchases for the next year.

Rose Care Calendar

Southeast

Roses bloom most of the year in these warm areas, although mountain regions experience a shorter season. Hot, humid conditions that promote diseases require gardeners to provide good air circulation and avoid overhead watering. Plan to use a fungicidal spray program to keep roses looking their best throughout the long growing season.

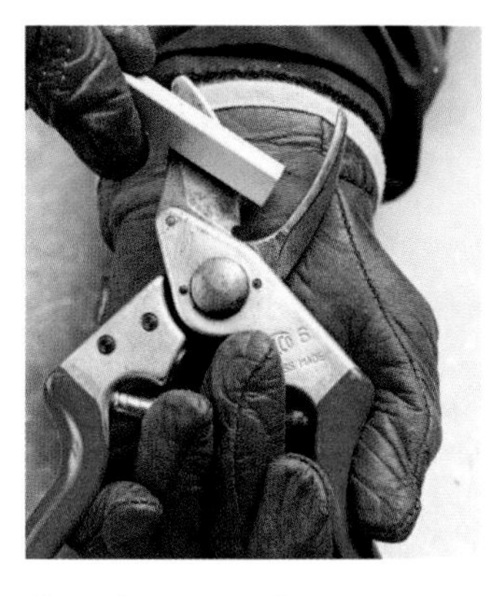

January

Prune in warmer areas.

Spray pruned roses with a fungicide.

Transplant roses if soil and weather permit.

February

Prune, spray, and transplant in cooler areas.

Purchase potted roses if available.

March

Prune, spray, and transplant in colder areas.

Apply mulch.

Apply organic fertilizer.

Water as needed.

April

Start fungicidal spraying when leaves first appear.

Begin insecticidal spraying as needed.

Improve on initial pruning.

May

Weed as needed throughout season.

Prune blind shoots (stems with no flower buds) and twiggy growth.

Deadhead as needed.

June

Fertilize.

Water as needed.

Continue spray program.

July

Apply fish emulsion or alfalfa tea.

Deadhead as needed.

Water as needed.

August

Continue spray program.

Water as needed.

Fertilize.

September

Continue spraying, watering, and deadheading.

Order mail-order roses.

October

Cease fertilizing in colder areas and prepare winter protection.

Begin light deadheading.

Maintain watering and spraying in warmer areas.

November

Prune to shorten tall plants.

Clean up plant debris.

Spray with dormant spray.

Apply winter protection in colder areas.

December

Sharpen tools.

Review cultural practices and plant performance.

Rose Care Calendar

South Central and Lower Midwest

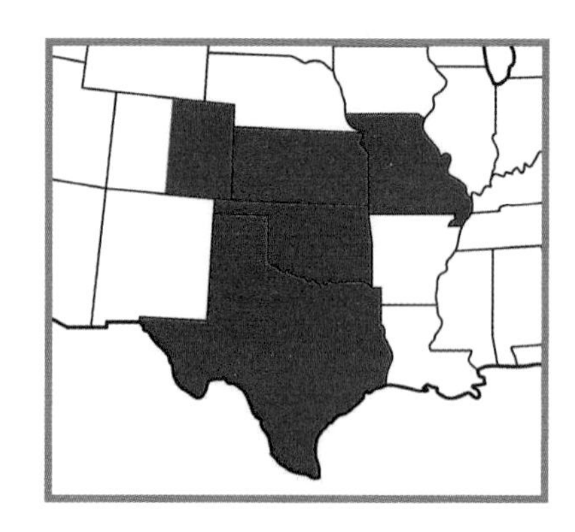

Gardeners here focus on protecting roses during the summer. Buy heat-tolerant varieties and place roses where they get six hours of sunshine in the morning hours while shielding them from harsher afternoon sun. Though roses like at least 1 inch of water per week, don't overwater. In areas where temperatures drop in winter, some protection is still needed.

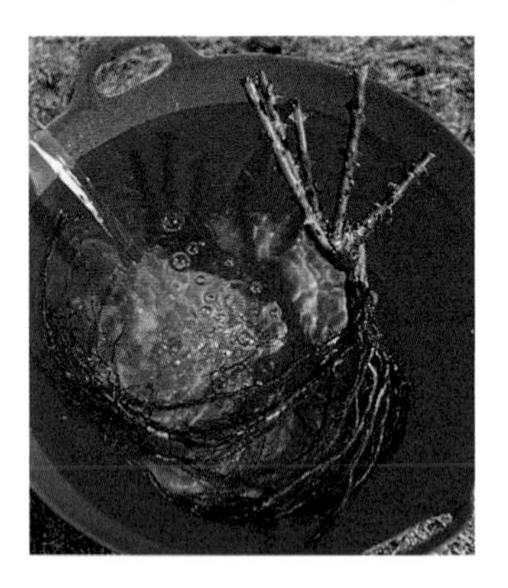

January

Sharpen tools.

Begin pruning in warmer areas.

February

Prune at appropriate time for your zone.

Purchase roses.

Plant potted and bare-root roses as weather warms.

March

Remove winter protection and prune in colder areas.

Transplant roses as needed.

Start fungicidal spray program when leaves first appear.

April

Improve on initial pruning.

Spray for insects as needed.

Fertilize.

Apply mulch.

May

Water and weed.

Prune blind shoots (stems with no flower buds) and twiggy growth.

June

Continue spray program.

Water as needed.

Deadhead as needed.

Cut bouquets for the house.

July

Fertilize with liquid, organic, or inorganic fertilizer.

Apply fish emulsion or alfalfa tea to underperforming plants.

Water as needed.

August

Continue spray program.

Water as needed.

Deadhead as needed.

September

Fertilize for the last time this year.

Continue spray program.

Water as needed.

October

Deadhead lightly.

Prepare winter protection, if needed.

Order mail-order roses.

November

Clean up beds.

Prune to shorten tall plants.

Apply dormant spray.

Apply winter protection, if needed.

December

Transplant roses as needed if ground is workable.

Southwest and Southern California

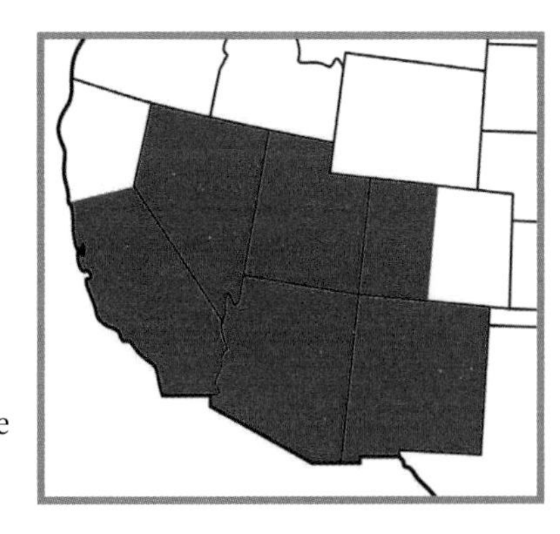

Caring for roses in this temperate region is nearly a year-round activity. Roses love the nearly constant sunshine. Gardeners here should provide more consistent, deep watering and protective organic mulch than in some other parts of the country.

January

Prune roses.

Spray pruned roses with fungicide.

Plant bare-root roses.

Purchase and plant potted roses.

Transplant roses as needed.

February

Start fungicidal spray program when leaves appear.

Apply organic fertilizer.

Apply inorganic fertilizer.

Begin watering as needed.

March

Spray for insects as needed.

Improve on initial pruning.

Apply mulch.

April

Prune blind shoots (stems with no flower buds) and twiggy growth.

Weed throughout season as needed.

May

Continue spray programs.

Continue watering, increasing frequency as weather warms.

Deadhead as needed.

June

Fertilize.

Treat wimpy plants with fish emulsion or alfalfa tea.

Water.

Cut bouquets for the house.

July

Continue spray programs as needed.

Deadhead as needed.

Water.

August

Fertilize with organic, inorganic, or liquid fertilizers.

Water.

Continue spray program as needed.

Deadhead as needed.

September

Spray as needed.

Water as needed.

Deadhead as needed.

October

Stop deadheading.

Stop fertilizing.

Cut fewer bouquets.

Order roses from mail-order nursery sources.

November

Prune to shorten tall plants.

Clean up beds.

Apply dormant spray.

December

Transplant roses as needed.

Sharpen tools.

CHAPTER SIX

Rose Lifestyle

Roses are more than just gorgeous flowers in your garden. Use them in bouquets, recipes, and crafts.

Bountiful Bouquets

One of the joys of having of a rose garden is access to fresh flowers for bouquets. Roses are beautiful as single-flower bouquets or mixed with other cut flowers.

Everyone loves a bouquet of roses. While one-bloom-per-stem hybrid teas and grandifloras are usually considered best for cutting, don't overlook floribundas and other spray roses such as shrubs and climbers. Their blooms can also have a long vase life, and one floriferous stem can create an entire bouquet.

Most Old Garden Roses have a relatively short vase life compared with modern roses, which should last about a week with proper cutting and conditioning. Shrub roses can be used, but cutting lengthy stems removes the next buds; instead, float only the blossoms on water.

How to cut roses

Although taking a special cutting vase to the garden may look romantic, it's not recommended. No matter how quickly the cut stem drops into the water, air hits the cut and immediately seals off the capillaries, eliminating or seriously impeding water uptake.

To ensure a reasonable cut life for roses, recut the stem underwater. Make a slanted cut about 1 inch up the stem, keep it underwater for about 5 to 10 seconds, then transfer the stem to a vase or other container. Add nothing to the water used for cutting because its sole purpose is to open the stem so water and nutrients can be freely taken up.

How to fill a vase

Once a rose is cut underwater, lift it up and place it in a vase of very warm, almost hot, water. The heat helps harden off the bloom. Vase water has two purposes: to feed the bloom just as it would be fed on the plant and to suppress any bacteria that could shut down the flow of nutrient-bearing water to the bloom.

For even longer cut-flower life, place the vase of roses in warm to hot water in the refrigerator for approximately one hour; this significantly increases the life of a cut flower. Vegetables and other foods in the refrigerator will not affect the bloom in this short time period. Strip foliage off any portion of the stem that will stay underwater, because the foliage naturally carries bacteria that can multiply rapidly in water.

Ways to lengthen vase life

Add a floral preservative to the vase water for best results. Brands such as Floralife, Chrysal, and other products can be bought inexpensively from a florist or floral supply house. Homemade preservatives work, although not as well as professional products.

Vase water, with new preservative added, should be changed at least every other day. If a stem works its way out and its blooms wilt, recut the stem underwater and place it back in the vase. It will usually rehydrate and freshen up.

When cut roses are not being actively admired, place them in a dark, cool area. Heat and light cause the blooms to continue to develop, hastening the eventual wilt and petal drop.

BHG TEST GARDEN TIP

SNAP OFF THORNS

Though thorns can stabilize a stem in a bud vase, they generally get in the way when arranging a group of roses in a large vase. To remove unwanted thorns, push them sideways (perpendicular to the length of the cane), and they should snap right off. This is easier and quicker than using a commercial thorn stripper and does not disturb the outer stem.

opposite, above Fresh-cut garden roses can be packed into formal containers or something as casual as a galvanized pail. ***opposite, below left*** When selecting roses for bouquets, choose a variety of colors and flower forms. ***opposite, below right*** Roses will last longer if you cut their stems underwater.

left Rose Petal Ice Cream ***above*** Rosy Cooler ***below*** Pick a bouquet of roses, then use petals for recipes.

Cooking with Rose Petals

Pretty rose petals add a unique, subtle flavor to ice cream and a dreamy appeal that's perfect for outdoor gatherings. Remember: Never use pesticides on any plant you plan to eat. All roses are edible, with the flavor more pronounced in darker varieties. Be sure to remove the bitter white portion of the petals.

Rose Petal Ice Cream

Harvest a basket of rose petals and whip up a creamy summer treat that tastes as delicious as your rose garden looks.

PREP 30 minutes CHILL overnight FREEZE according to manufacturer's directions plus 4 hours

- 1½ cups whipping cream
- 1½ cups milk
- ⅔ cup sugar
- 3 egg yolks
- 1 teaspoon vanilla
- 2 cups rose petals (such as rugosa rose)
- 2 tablespoons chopped rose-scented geranium leaves

1. In a medium saucepan stir together cream, milk, and sugar. Heat over medium heat until sugar is dissolved and mixture is just starting to simmer. Do not allow to boil. Whisk the egg yolks lightly in a small bowl; gradually whisk in about 1 cup of the milk mixture. Pour the egg yolk mixture back into the saucepan. Cook, stirring constantly, over medium heat for 6 to 8 minutes or until mixture thickens and coats the back of a metal spoon. Remove from heat and stir in vanilla. Immediately place in a large bowl of ice water and stir for 2 minutes to cool slightly. Stir in rose petals and geranium leaves. Transfer to a storage container; cover and chill overnight.
2. Strain the custard mixture through a fine-mesh sieve; discard solids. Freeze in a 2-quart ice cream freezer according to manufacturer's directions. Transfer to an airtight storage container and freeze for 4 hours before serving.
Makes 6 (½-cup) servings.

Rosy Cooler

Try different roses each time you make this light, cooling drink and discover which ones have the most aromatic and pleasing flavors.

PREP 30 minutes CHILL overnight FREEZE according to manufacturer's directions plus 4 hours

- 4 cups rose petals, plus more for garnishing (optional), such as Cecile Brunner, Double Delight, Gertrude Jekyll, Mister Lincoln, Perfume Delight, or Zephirine Drouhin
- 1 bottle dry white, blush, or sparkling wine
- ¼ cup vodka
- 1 cup fresh raspberries plus, more for garnish (optional)
- Ice cubes
- Sparkling water (optional)
- Mint sprigs (optional)

1. Cut out the yellow or white centers at the base of the rose petals to avoid any bitter taste.
2. In a 2-quart glass bowl combine the rose petals, wine, vodka, and raspberries; cover and chill for 2 hours. The color of the rose petals and the number of raspberries you use will affect the cooler's pink hue.
3. Before serving, strain the wine mixture; discard petals and raspberries. Serve over ice. If desired, top with a splash of sparkling water and garnish with additional berries, rose petals, or mint sprigs. Makes 6 (½-cup) servings.

Cooking with Rose Petals

Rose and Berry Summer Salad

Add rosy flavor and soft color to summer salads. Rose petals add an elegance that transforms a simple salad into a special occasion.

START TO FINISH 25 minutes

- 7 ounces soft sheep's milk cheese or Brie cheese
- 6 cups mixed baby greens with baby red lettuce leaves or salad greens such as red romaine, red oak leaf, or other red lettuce leaves
- ¼ cup snipped rose petals or other assorted edible flowers
- 8 to 12 ounces smoked white fish, smoked black cod (sablefish), or smoked salmon, bones removed and cut into 6 pieces
- ¼ cup snipped fresh dill
- ¼ cup salad oil
- ¼ cup champagne vinegar or white wine vinegar
- 1 teaspoon sugar
- ½ teaspoon ground cardamom
- ½ teaspoon coarsely ground black pepper
- Sea salt or salt and freshly ground black pepper
- 3 cups raspberries or blackberries

1. Cut cheese into thin wedges. In a large bowl toss greens and rose petals.
2. On 6 salad plates arrange cheese, fish, and mixed greens. Sprinkle with dill.
3. For dressing, in a small screw-top jar combine oil, vinegar, sugar, cardamom, and coarsely ground pepper. Cover tightly and shake until well combined. Season dressing with sea salt and freshly ground black pepper. Drizzle dressing over fish and greens. Serve with fresh berries. Makes 6 servings.

COOKING WITH ROSE HIPS

Rose hips develop after the flower fades. Heirloom roses, such as rugosas, hybrid musks, and species, as well as wild varieties, produce the largest hips. Harvest hips when they're fully colored (red, orange, or purplish) and ripe. Richer in vitamin C than oranges, rose hips have become a valued ingredient in vitamin supplements. They also contain vitamins A, B, E, and K. Harvest these delectably tart and nutrient-rich seedpods and use them fresh or dried to make jam, jelly, tea, or syrup. Or leave the rose hips on the plants and savor their bright beauty throughout the winter, as long as birds don't eat them all.

Candied Rose Petals

Add natural beauty and sweet flavor to baked goods with candied rose petals. Transform simple cookies, cakes, and cupcakes into garden-inspired goodies for special brunches or desserts.

START TO FINISH 30 minutes

- 2 teaspoons meringue powder
- ¼ cup water
- Superfine sugar
- Rose petals, whole Miniature roses, or rosebuds

1. Combine 2 teaspoons of meringue powder (available at kitchen supply stores) and the water in a clean, dry 8-ounce custard cup. Stir with a fork or wire whisk until the powder dissolves. Set aside.
2. Line a cookie sheet with waxed paper. Sprinkle it with a thin layer of superfine sugar. Gently pick petals from roses that have just begun to open. Also use rosebuds or whole miniature roses.
3. Rinse rose petals with cold water. Blot them with paper towels and lay them out to finish drying. Use a small, clean paintbrush, such as an artist's brush, to lightly coat the petals or rosebuds with meringue mixture.
4. Sprinkle sugar over the petals to coat them evenly. Shake off excess sugar. Place petals on the pan and let them dry overnight in a cool, airy place. If the petals are not used immediately, store them in a covered tin in the refrigerator for up to 3 weeks.

Crafting with Roses

Rose flowers, petals, and hips can be used in crafting projects that are decorative and fragrant.

Fresh and dried roses make beautiful and fragrant materials for gifts and home decor. Place sachets in closets and drawers to impart their scent among sheets, towels, and clothing. Create wearable rose jewelry. And build gorgeous bouquet centerpieces for special occasions.

Rose-Wreathed Pillar Candle

Create a romantic ambience at a garden party or wedding with these enchanting, rose-encircled candles.

What You Need

- Floral-foam wreath form
- Short-stemmed roses
- Rosebuds
- Long pearl-head pins

Instructions

1. The secret to suspending the wreath of roses on the candle is to use a floral-foam wreath form as the base for the floral arrangement. Soak the wreath in water; then insert short-stemmed roses, beginning with larger blossoms and filling in the bare spots with rosebuds until the top and outer edges are covered.

2. Secure the wreath to the candle with long pearl-head pins. You will need to use a lot of pins around the top and bottom because the wreath will be quite heavy.

3. Fill in around the candle with more rosebuds if needed.

BHG TEST GARDEN TIP

GROW YOUR OWN WEDDING BOUQUET

One of the most expensive aspects of a wedding is the flowers. If you plan ahead, you can grow your own bridal bouquet and centerpieces by planting rose bushes that flower in the same color scheme as your wedding. Use flowers from your garden and supplement with florist flowers if necessary.

Crafting with Roses

Rose Sachets

Blend the subtle perfume of dried rose petals with aromatic spices and essential oils. When making sachets, begin with exquisitely fragrant roses.

What You Need

- 1 large glass or ceramic bowl
- 8 cups dried rose petals, such as Blanc Double de Coubert, Double Delight, Fragrant Cloud, Madame Alfred Carriere, and Sombreuil
- 1 ounce ground cinnamon
- 1 ounce ground mace
- ½ ounce ground cloves
- 12 tonka beans (powdered in coffee grinder or spice mill)
- Essential oils of rose and musk
- 1 1-gallon wide-mouth glass jar
- Fabric
- Ribbon

Instructions

1. In a large glass or ceramic bowl combine the rose petals, spices, and tonka beans. Add 20 drops each of the rose and musk essential oils. Stir well.

2. Place the mix in a 1-gallon wide-mouth glass jar. Store the jar in a dark place for 3 weeks to allow the sachet mix to age. Shake the jar daily to blend the contents.

3. Make sachets by placing ¼ cup of the mix in the center of a 6-inch square of fabric. (Use scraps of cotton, linen, or other breathable cloth. Cut the fabric with pinking shears for a decorative edge.)

4. Draw up the corners of the fabric to form a pouch. Tie a 12-inch length of ribbon around the gathered neck of the pouch. Repeat for each square. This recipe makes a dozen sachets.

Rose Beads

Create unique beads for jewelry or swags for a holiday tree using the natural sweet-scented petals of roses.

What You Need

4	cups dried rose petals
	Coffee or spice mill
	Cast-iron pot
	Bottled rosewater
1	2-quart glass or porcelain bowl
¼	cup flour
	Essential oil of rose
	Large plate or tray
	Carpet thread
	Darning needle
	Coat hanger
	Beading thread

Instructions

1. Dry the rose petals in a warm, dark, airy place until they are brittle. Pulverize the petals in a coffee or spice mill until they're finely powdered.
2. In a cast-iron pot blend the rose petal powder with enough rosewater to make a mash. Simmer on the stove for 30 minutes, stirring often. Add rosewater as needed to prevent scorching.
3. Repeat the simmering process 3 days in a row, leaving the mash in the pot from day to day. The mash will gradually react with the iron and turn black.
4. Place the mash in a glass or porcelain bowl. Blend in the flour to form a dough. If you don't shape the beads right away, cover the dough and store it in the refrigerator for up to 3 days.
5. To shape beads, pinch off bits of dough; roll them between your thumb and forefinger into smooth, pea-size spheres. Dab your fingertips with rose essential oil to intensify the beads' fragrance as you shape them. Set the finished beads on a large plate.
6. String the beads onto 15-inch lengths of carpet thread, knotted at one end, using a darning needle. Push the needle through the center of each bead; slide the bead onto the thread. Tie strands of beads to the bottom of a hanger; knot each strand to secure it.
7. Hang the beads to dry in a warm, dark place. Each day, gently slide the beads up and down each thread to prevent them from sticking to it. Beads dry completely in a week to 10 days.
8. Restring on beading thread in desired length. Attach a clasp or tie the strand with a knot.

CHAPTER SEVEN

Rose Gallery

Browse this showcase for the best of the best varieties in each rose family. There's a size, color, shape, and form to suit every garden.

Hybrid Teas

Hybrid teas are the most popular family of roses in the United States—and perhaps the world.

In the Rose Hall of Fame, created by the national rose societies from 41 countries, nearly 60 percent of the "World's Favorite Rose" Awards have gone to hybrid teas.

Thanks to their large and often fragrant blooms on erect, manageable plants, hybrid teas remain the epitome of roses for many gardeners. Their beauty continues to win fans and accolades even though they're generally the least-hardy roses and require the most care to perform at their best.

For cutting, hybrid teas are ideal, especially when they're kept disbudded. You'll get a larger, more impressive cutting rose when you remove any side buds from each shoot, leaving only the center bud at the end to develop.

Anyone can grow hybrid teas, but gardeners in USDA Zone 7 and colder regions should provide adequate winter protection. Gardeners in Zone 5 and colder areas should consider growing own-root roses for greater potential hardiness.

Because many factors, such as snow cover, wind, and temperature, are involved in the winter hardiness of roses, it's impossible to predict which hybrid teas will survive winter. The bloom size and plant habit for hybrid teas vary greatly and depend on the varieties and where they're grown. In the following gallery of hybrid teas, use this general guide for size references:

BLOOM SIZE

SMALL: Less than 2 inches wide
MEDIUM: 2 to 5 inches wide
LARGE: More than 5 inches wide

PLANT SIZE

SHORT: Less than 4 feet tall
MEDIUM: 4 to 5½ feet tall
TALL: More than 5½ feet tall
UPRIGHT: Generally less than 2½ feet wide
BUSHY: 2½ to 4 feet wide
SPREADING: More than 4 feet wide

Bewitched

BLOOM SIZE, TYPE: Large, classic
FRAGRANCE: Moderate to heavy
GROWTH HABIT: Medium, bushy
DISEASE RESISTANCE: Good
ARS RATING: 7.7
COMMENTS: This clear pink variety dates to 1967. The damask fragrance varies from moderate to heavy, depending on the weather.

Black Magic

BLOOM SIZE, TYPE: Medium, classic
FRAGRANCE: Light
GROWTH HABIT: Tall, bushy
DISEASE RESISTANCE: Good
ARS RATING: 7.7
COMMENTS: Originally a florist's variety, Black Magic made a successful transition to the garden. The deep red blooms with near-black overtones are borne singly and are great for cutting.

Bride's Dream

BLOOM SIZE, TYPE: Medium, classic
FRAGRANCE: Light
GROWTH HABIT: Medium, bushy
DISEASE RESISTANCE: Good
ARS RATING: 8.1
COMMENTS: Beautiful light pink blooms show nice form, developing primarily one to a stem. Plants grow with characteristic hybrid tea-size blooms and good disease resistance.

Brigadoon

BLOOM SIZE, TYPE: Large, classic
FRAGRANCE: Light
GROWTH HABIT: Medium, upright
DISEASE RESISTANCE: Good
ARS RATING: 7.8
COMMENTS: Although this rose is classed as a pink blend, the petal edges of its distinctive blooms can be nearly red at times. They are borne generally in small clusters on clean, upright plants.

Chrysler Imperial

BLOOM SIZE, TYPE: Large, classic
FRAGRANCE: Heavy
GROWTH HABIT: Medium, bushy
DISEASE RESISTANCE: Fair
ARS RATING: 7.8
COMMENTS: A classic red rose with exceptional fragrance, Chrysler Imperial is a good choice for dry areas. In any location, pruning promotes airflow that helps avoid disease problems.

Crystalline

BLOOM SIZE, TYPE: Large, classic
FRAGRANCE: Light
GROWTH HABIT: Medium, bushy
DISEASE RESISTANCE: Good
ARS RATING: 8.0
COMMENTS: The pure white flowers are borne both singly and in small sprays. This variety performs best in warm weather, which promotes blooms with excellent form.

Dainty Bess

BLOOM SIZE, TYPE: Medium, single
FRAGRANCE: Light
GROWTH HABIT: Medium, bushy
DISEASE RESISTANCE: Good
ARS RATING: 8.5
COMMENTS: This winner, introduced in 1925, is the undisputed queen of the single hybrid teas. Light-pink blooms with low petals and prominent red stamens are borne in medium-size sprays.

Double Delight

BLOOM SIZE, TYPE: Large, classic
FRAGRANCE: Heavy
GROWTH HABIT: Medium, bushy
DISEASE RESISTANCE: Good
ARS RATING: 8.4
COMMENTS: One of the most beautiful and fragrant hybrid teas. White blooms growing in small sprays show variable amounts of red edges.

Dublin

BLOOM SIZE, TYPE: Large, classic
FRAGRANCE: Heavy
GROWTH HABIT: Medium, upright
DISEASE RESISTANCE: Good
ARS RATING: 8.2
COMMENTS: Light red blooms with smoky overtones and a raspberry fragrance are borne on vigorous, upright plants. Hot weather produces a redder color and enhances performance.

Electron

BLOOM SIZE, TYPE: Large, classic
FRAGRANCE: Heavy
GROWTH HABIT: Tall, spreading
DISEASE RESISTANCE: Good
ARS RATING: 7.8
COMMENTS: A glorious garden rose! Its only drawbacks are a spreading habit and vicious thorns. Blooms are intense deep pink, very fragrant, and borne singly much of the time.

Elina

BLOOM SIZE, TYPE: Large, classic
FRAGRANCE: Light
GROWTH HABIT: Tall, bushy
DISEASE RESISTANCE: Excellent
ARS RATING: 8.6
COMMENTS: A heavy bloomer with a quick repeat of creamy, light yellow blooms, it is the highest-rated yellow hybrid tea on the market today.

Elizabeth Taylor

BLOOM SIZE, TYPE: Large, classic
FRAGRANCE: Light
GROWTH HABIT: Tall, spreading
DISEASE RESISTANCE: Good
ARS RATING: 8.4
COMMENTS: Vigorous plants grow tall and wide. Elizabeth Taylor's medium pink blooms with darker edges are borne singly or in small sprays. The best blooms are produced in warm weather.

Elle

BLOOM SIZE, TYPE: Large, classic
FRAGRANCE: Heavy
GROWTH HABIT: Medium, bushy
DISEASE RESISTANCE: Good
ARS RATING: 7.7
COMMENTS: Grow Elle for its very fragrant, soft pink blooms with golden yellow at their bases. The blooms grow larger in cool weather, which produces more intense colors.

Falling in Love

BLOOM SIZE, TYPE: Large, classic
FRAGRANCE: Medium
GROWTH HABIT: Medium, bushy
DISEASE RESISTANCE: Good
ARS RATING: 7.9
COMMENTS: Warm pink blooms with lighter petal edges and a near-white underside make an intriguing combination. Abundant flowers carry a pleasing fragrance.

Firefighter

BLOOM SIZE, TYPE: Large, classic
FRAGRANCE: Heavy
GROWTH HABIT: Medium, bushy
DISEASE RESISTANCE: Good
ARS RATING: 7.7
COMMENTS: A deep red rose with great form and exceptional fragrance, Firefighter is the first in a series of Remember Me roses.

Folklore

BLOOM SIZE, TYPE: Medium, classic
FRAGRANCE: Medium
GROWTH HABIT: Tall, bushy
DISEASE RESISTANCE: Good
ARS RATING: 8.2
COMMENTS: Tall, vigorous plants that are slightly mildew-prone bear orange-pink blooms with a golden yellow underside. A heavy bloomer with a good repeat, it needs disbudding because it tends to bloom in sprays.

Fragrant Cloud

BLOOM SIZE, TYPE: Large, classic
FRAGRANCE: Heavy
GROWTH HABIT: Medium, bushy
DISEASE RESISTANCE: Fair
ARS RATING: 8.1
COMMENTS: Arguably the most fragrant hybrid tea, this variety bears light red, slightly orangey blooms in profusion. A must for any rose garden.

Frederic Mistral

BLOOM SIZE, TYPE: Large, classic
FRAGRANCE: Heavy
GROWTH HABIT: Medium, bushy
DISEASE RESISTANCE: Good
ARS RATING: 7.9
COMMENTS: Light pink blooms with deep pink centers and petal undersides grace this rose. Extremely fragrant.

Garden Party

BLOOM SIZE, TYPE: Large, classic
FRAGRANCE: Light
GROWTH HABIT: Medium, upright
DISEASE RESISTANCE: Good
ARS RATING: 7.9
COMMENTS: This progeny of Peace has large creamy-white blooms with touches of pink around the petals' edges. For 50 years, it's been a great performer in the garden.

Gemini

BLOOM SIZE, TYPE: Large, classic
FRAGRANCE: Light
GROWTH HABIT: Medium, upright
DISEASE RESISTANCE: Excellent
ARS RATING: 8.2
COMMENTS: Weather determines the intensity of pink markings on the light pink blooms. The flowers of this extremely popular variety are produced mostly singly and are ideal for cutting.

Ingrid Bergman

BLOOM SIZE, TYPE: Large, classic
FRAGRANCE: Light
GROWTH HABIT: Medium, bushy
DISEASE RESISTANCE: Good
ARS RATING: 7.8
COMMENTS: This vigorous, hardy variety hails from the Poulsen nursery in Denmark. Medium red blooms are very large and produced in abundance.

Just Joey

BLOOM SIZE, TYPE: Large, informal
FRAGRANCE: Heavy
GROWTH HABIT: Medium, spreading
DISEASE RESISTANCE: Good
ARS RATING: 7.9
COMMENTS: One of the few hybrid teas in this color, Just Joey has buff-amber blooms that carry a strong fragrance. Medium, somewhat spreading plants have good disease resistance.

Kardinal

BLOOM SIZE, TYPE: Medium, classic
FRAGRANCE: Light
GROWTH HABIT: Medium, upright
DISEASE RESISTANCE: Good
ARS RATING: 8.5
COMMENTS: Bred for use by florists, this rose also works well in a garden. The medium red blooms, borne mostly singly, have incredible substance and are great for cutting.

Keepsake

BLOOM SIZE, TYPE: Large, classic
FRAGRANCE: Light
GROWTH HABIT: Medium, bushy
DISEASE RESISTANCE: Good
ARS RATING: 8.0
COMMENTS: Beautiful, large blooms in shades of pink make it a winner, particularly in cool weather. Plants are robust with good disease resistance.

Let Freedom Ring

BLOOM SIZE, TYPE: Large, classic
FRAGRANCE: None
GROWTH HABIT: Tall, bushy
DISEASE RESISTANCE: Good
ARS RATING: 7.9
COMMENTS: Bred by an American amateur hybridizer, Ernest Earman, this light red variety bears classic shape blooms on tall, bushy plants.

Liebeszauber

BLOOM SIZE, TYPE: Large, classic
FRAGRANCE: Medium
GROWTH HABIT: Tall, spreading
DISEASE RESISTANCE: Excellent
ARS RATING: 8.0
COMMENTS: This extremely vigorous plant's name means "love's magic" in German. Large, deep red blooms are produced in large sprays, so constant disbudding is needed for best results.

Louise Estes

BLOOM SIZE, TYPE: Large, classic
FRAGRANCE: Medium
GROWTH HABIT: Medium, bushy
DISEASE RESISTANCE: Good
ARS RATING: 8.3
COMMENTS: With deep pink blooms, lighter petal edges, and great classic form, this rose could be considered a warm-weather version of Keepsake. Plants are vigorous and disease resistant.

Love and Peace

BLOOM SIZE, TYPE: Large, classic
FRAGRANCE: Light
GROWTH HABIT: Medium, upright
DISEASE RESISTANCE: Good
ARS RATING: 7.8
COMMENTS: An offspring of Peace, this lovely rose grows yellow blooms with splashes of orange, pink, and light red. Most blooms are borne one to a stem.

Lynn Anderson

BLOOM SIZE, TYPE: Large, classic
FRAGRANCE: Light
GROWTH HABIT: Tall, upright
DISEASE RESISTANCE: Fair
ARS RATING: 7.5
COMMENTS: Named for the country singer, Lynn Anderson grows small sprays of white to light pink blooms with deep pink or cerise petal edges. Plants need black-spot protection in rainy areas.

Marilyn Monroe

BLOOM SIZE, TYPE: Large, classic
FRAGRANCE: Light
GROWTH HABIT: Medium, bushy
DISEASE RESISTANCE: Excellent
ARS RATING: 7.9
COMMENTS: Large, soft apricot blooms with impeccable form and substance are borne mostly singly on robust, very thorny plants with great disease resistance.

The McCartney Rose

BLOOM SIZE, TYPE: Large, classic
FRAGRANCE: Heavy
GROWTH HABIT: Medium, bushy
DISEASE RESISTANCE: Fair
ARS RATING: 7.9
COMMENTS: Named for entertainer Paul McCartney, this rose has won the most trial awards. Medium pink blooms are highly fragrant.

Memorial Day

BLOOM SIZE, TYPE: Large
FRAGRANCE: Heavy
GROWTH HABIT: Medium, spreading
DISEASE RESISTANCE: Good
ARS RATING: 7.7
COMMENTS: Large, soft pink blooms carry a heavy damask fragrance. Plants prefer warm weather for heavy and quick repeat bloom.

Midas Touch

BLOOM SIZE, TYPE: Large, classic
FRAGRANCE: Light
GROWTH HABIT: Medium, bushy
DISEASE RESISTANCE: Good
ARS RATING: 7.5
COMMENTS: Solid yellow, unfading blooms open quickly. They are borne mostly one per stem on very disease-resistant plants.

Mister Lincoln

BLOOM SIZE, TYPE: Large, classic
FRAGRANCE: Heavy
GROWTH HABIT: Tall, bushy
DISEASE RESISTANCE: Fair
ARS RATING: 8.3
COMMENTS: Velvety red blooms with incredible fragrance make this rose a must for any cutting garden. Plants are somewhat disease-prone.

Moonstone

BLOOM SIZE, TYPE: Large, classic
FRAGRANCE: Light
GROWTH HABIT: Medium, upright
DISEASE RESISTANCE: Excellent
ARS RATING: 8.2
COMMENTS: Off-white blooms with pink petal edges and a pink center produce an attractive garden display. The flowers show great form but need warm weather to do well.

New Zealand

BLOOM SIZE, TYPE: Large, classic
FRAGRANCE: Heavy
GROWTH HABIT: Medium, bushy
DISEASE RESISTANCE: Excellent
ARS RATING: 7.9
COMMENTS: One of the few roses that combines excellent disease resistance with great fragrance, New Zealand's light pink blooms do best in cool weather. Plants have good repeat bloom habits.

Olympiad

BLOOM SIZE, TYPE: Large, classic
FRAGRANCE: None
GROWTH HABIT: Medium, bushy
DISEASE RESISTANCE: Excellent
ARS RATING: 8.6
COMMENTS: The best red hybrid tea for disease resistance, this variety, which commemorates the Los Angeles Olympics of 1984, regrettably has little to no scent. Plants produce classic blooms.

Opening Night

BLOOM SIZE, TYPE: Large, classic
FRAGRANCE: Light
GROWTH HABIT: Medium, bushy
DISEASE RESISTANCE: Good
ARS RATING: 7.8
COMMENTS: Cooler weather brings out the best color—deep, vivid red. Blooms display great form and distinctive ruffled petal edges. Plants are very productive and have good disease resistance.

Peace

BLOOM SIZE, TYPE: Large, classic
FRAGRANCE: Light
GROWTH HABIT: Tall, spreading
DISEASE RESISTANCE: Excellent
ARS RATING: 8.1
COMMENTS: A 65-year-old winner. Blooms should be vibrant yellow and pink. If you can find a plant that resembles the original Peace, get it.

Perfect Moment

BLOOM SIZE, TYPE: Large, classic
FRAGRANCE: Light
GROWTH HABIT: Medium, bushy
DISEASE RESISTANCE: Fair
ARS RATING: 7.8
COMMENTS: With yellow at the base of its petals and red at the edges, Perfect Moment makes an eye-catching addition to the garden.

Pristine

BLOOM SIZE, TYPE: Large, classic
FRAGRANCE: Light
GROWTH HABIT: Medium, bushy
DISEASE RESISTANCE: Good
ARS RATING: 8.6
COMMENTS: Despite their tendency to open very quickly, Pristine's white blooms with delicate pink brushings are considered among the most beautiful. The bushes grow strong and vigorous.

Rosemary Harkness

BLOOM SIZE, TYPE: Large, informal
FRAGRANCE: Heavy
GROWTH HABIT: Medium, bushy
DISEASE RESISTANCE: Excellent
ARS RATING: 8.0
COMMENTS: This rose should be more widely known and grown. Blooms are a mix of orange, salmon, and pink. Great disease resistance.

Savoy Hotel

BLOOM SIZE, TYPE: Large, classic
FRAGRANCE: Light
GROWTH HABIT: Tall, bushy
DISEASE RESISTANCE: Excellent
ARS RATING: 7.8
COMMENTS: The quintessential cool-weather hybrid tea, Savoy Hotel produces great quantities of light pink, classical-form blooms on tall, disease-resistant plants.

Secret

BLOOM SIZE, TYPE: Large, classic
FRAGRANCE: Heavy
GROWTH HABIT: Medium, bushy
DISEASE RESISTANCE: Good
ARS RATING: 7.9
COMMENTS: A great hybrid tea for a fragrance garden, this offspring of Pristine shows deeper pink brushings than its parent, with longer-lasting blooms and strong plants.

Sheer Elegance

BLOOM SIZE, TYPE: Large, classic
FRAGRANCE: Light
GROWTH HABIT: Medium, bushy
DISEASE RESISTANCE: Good
ARS RATING: 7.8
COMMENTS: Classic blooms of salmon pink that hold their form make Sheer Elegance a must for the cutting garden. The plant is of average size for a hybrid tea, with good disease resistance.

Silver Jubilee

BLOOM SIZE, TYPE: Medium, classic
FRAGRANCE: Light
GROWTH HABIT: Tall, upright
DISEASE RESISTANCE: Excellent
ARS RATING: 8.6
COMMENTS: Blooms that blend pink, salmon, and amber are borne on exceptionally disease-resistant plants. The flowers form sprays. This variety does best in cool weather.

St. Patrick

BLOOM SIZE, TYPE: Large, classic
FRAGRANCE: Light
GROWTH HABIT: Medium, bushy
DISEASE RESISTANCE: Good
ARS RATING: 8.0
COMMENTS: Green-tinged buds open to yellow blooms with the faintest hints of green on strong, vigorous plants. St. Patrick performs exceptionally well in hot weather.

Stephens' Big Purple

BLOOM SIZE, TYPE: Medium, informal
FRAGRANCE: Heavy
GROWTH HABIT: Medium, upright
DISEASE RESISTANCE: Good
ARS RATING: 7.5
COMMENTS: The color of this very fragrant rose from New Zealand can vary from raspberry pink-purple to deep violet-purple. Most of the flowers are borne singly. Despite the many petals, the blooms still open well in cool weather.

Sunset Celebration

BLOOM SIZE, TYPE: Large, classic
FRAGRANCE: Light
GROWTH HABIT: Tall, bushy
DISEASE RESISTANCE: Excellent
ARS RATING: 7.8
COMMENTS: This United Kingdom import was named for the 100th anniversary of *Sunset* magazine. Strong, very vigorous plants with great disease resistance produce profuse, well-formed buff-amber blooms.

Tahitian Sunset

BLOOM SIZE, TYPE: Large, classic
FRAGRANCE: Heavy
GROWTH HABIT: Medium, bushy
DISEASE RESISTANCE: Good
ARS RATING: 7.7
COMMENTS: Strongly fragrant, blooms in a changing blend of pink and apricot grow on vigorous, productive plants.

Tiffany

BLOOM SIZE, TYPE: Large, classic
FRAGRANCE: Heavy
GROWTH HABIT: Medium, upright
DISEASE RESISTANCE: Good
ARS RATING: 7.9
COMMENTS: An oldie but a goodie, this classic bears light-pink blooms with yellow at the petals' base. The flowers are exceptionally fragrant but need warm weather to perform at their best.

Touch of Class

BLOOM SIZE, TYPE: Large, classic
FRAGRANCE: Light
GROWTH HABIT: Tall, bushy
DISEASE RESISTANCE: Good
ARS RATING: 8.9
COMMENTS: One of ARS's highest-rated hybrid teas, Touch of Class bears soft salmon-pink blooms that nearly always grow one per stem, making them ideal for cutting.

Veterans' Honor

BLOOM SIZE, TYPE: Large, classic
FRAGRANCE: Light
GROWTH HABIT: Medium, bushy
DISEASE RESISTANCE: Good
ARS RATING: 8.1
COMMENTS: Very large, solid red blooms with classic form are produced in abundance on strong, disease-resistant plants.

Voodoo

BLOOM SIZE, TYPE: Large, classic
FRAGRANCE: Moderate
GROWTH HABIT: Tall, upright
DISEASE RESISTANCE: Excellent
ARS RATING: 7.5
COMMENTS: The blooms on this variety are basically orange but contain shades of amber, pink, and yellow depending upon the weather. Plants are exceptionally disease resistant.

Grandifloras

Grandifloras, at least ideally, are a perfect combination of hybrid teas and floribundas: plants with large blooms produced both individually and in sprays.

The first grandiflora, Queen Elizabeth, displays the prototype characteristics of this class: large, tall, rugged disease-resistant plants that produce both sprays and one-per-stem blooms.

Grandifloras are consistent rebloomers that can be disbudded and enjoyed as single blooms, similar to hybrid teas, or cut and brought into the house as complete bouquets, like floribundas. Many varieties bear classic blooms; others have more informal flowers.

Although the grandiflora class wasn't established until 1955, older varieties such as Buccaneer are called grandifloras today. That's because the American Rose Society, which is in charge of rose classification, often retroactively classifies older varieties once a new family has been approved. The grandiflora class is not recognized in Europe or other rose-growing countries outside the United States and Canada.

Tall, rugged roses such as Fragrant Plum or Gold Medal (the highest rated grandiflora) are ideal for the backgrounds of rose or mixed gardens. Shorter varieties, including Tournament of Roses, can be placed in the foreground. Pay attention to the size you select: Some grandifloras can reach 8 feet tall or more.

Fragrant varieties such as Maria Shriver and Melody Parfumée should be planted where they can be easily smelled and enjoyed.

BLOOM SIZE

SMALL: Less than 2 inches wide
MEDIUM: 2 to 5 inches wide
LARGE: More than 5 inches wide

PLANT SIZE

SHORT: Less than 4 feet tall
MEDIUM: 4 to 5½ feet tall
TALL: More than 5½ feet tall

PLANT HABIT

UPRIGHT: Generally less than 2½ feet wide
BUSHY: 2½ to 4 feet wide
SPREADING: More than 4 feet wide

About Face

BLOOM SIZE, TYPE: Large, informal
FRAGRANCE: Light
GROWTH HABIT: Tall, upright
DISEASE RESISTANCE: Good
ARS RATING: 7.7
COMMENTS: The blooms of About Face are primarily orange, with shadings of pink and salmon. They are informal in shape and are borne mostly singly on strong, upright plants.

Candelabra

BLOOM SIZE, TYPE: Medium, classic
FRAGRANCE: Light
GROWTH HABIT: Medium, bushy
DISEASE RESISTANCE: Good
ARS RATING: 7.6
COMMENTS: Candelabra, a moderate-size plant for a grandiflora, carries warm orange blooms that open to show beautiful golden stamens. Flowers are borne mostly in large, open clusters.

Caribbean

BLOOM SIZE, TYPE: Medium, classic
FRAGRANCE: Light
GROWTH HABIT: Medium, bushy
DISEASE RESISTANCE: Good
ARS RATING: 7.6
COMMENTS: Apricot to orange blooms with yellow at the base of the petals and touches of pink make Caribbean's flowers especially attractive. They grow both singly and in clusters on plants of manageable size.

Cherry Parfait

BLOOM SIZE, TYPE: Large, informal
FRAGRANCE: Light
GROWTH HABIT: Short, bushy
DISEASE RESISTANCE: Good
ARS RATING: 7.9
COMMENTS: White to light yellow blooms with cerise petal edges make Cherry Parfait an eye-catching rose. The flowers grow in medium-size clusters on short, compact plants.

Crimson Bouquet

BLOOM SIZE, TYPE: Large, classic
FRAGRANCE: Medium
GROWTH HABIT: Medium, bushy
DISEASE RESISTANCE: Excellent
ARS RATING: 7.9
COMMENTS: Crimson Bouquet showcases large red blooms, held singly and in small clusters, on medium-size bushes that have great disease resistance.

Dream Come True

BLOOM SIZE, TYPE: Large, classic
FRAGRANCE: Light
GROWTH HABIT: Tall, upright
DISEASE RESISTANCE: Good
ARS RATING: 7.5
COMMENTS: Hybridized by amateur John Pottschmidt, this variety has gorgeous yellow blooms shot with orange and cerise pink. They grow mostly singly on tall, robust plants.

Earth Song

BLOOM SIZE, TYPE: Large, informal
FRAGRANCE: Heavy
GROWTH HABIT: Medium, bushy
DISEASE RESISTANCE: Good
ARS RATING: 8.2
COMMENTS: This very hardy rose, part of the Griffith Buck series, produces medium to deep pink blooms that open quickly to show golden stamens. They are borne singly and in small sprays.

Fame!

BLOOM SIZE, TYPE: Large, classic
FRAGRANCE: Medium
GROWTH HABIT: Tall, spreading
DISEASE RESISTANCE: Excellent
ARS RATING: 8.1
COMMENTS: Hot pink blooms with great classic form are borne in profusion, mostly singly, on large, vigorous, very disease-resistant plants.

Fragrant Plum

BLOOM SIZE, TYPE: Large, classic
FRAGRANCE: Heavy
GROWTH HABIT: Tall, bushy
DISEASE RESISTANCE: Good
ARS RATING: 7.7
COMMENTS: Very fragrant lavender blooms with more deeply hued petal edges make this a great rose for cutting. The flowers grow mostly in small sprays on tall, robust plants.

Gold Medal

BLOOM SIZE, TYPE: Large, classic
FRAGRANCE: Light
GROWTH HABIT: Tall, bushy
DISEASE RESISTANCE: Good
ARS RATING: 8.4
COMMENTS: This is the highest rated grandiflora. Gold Medal earns its name with deep golden blooms with pink petal edges that grow singly or in small sprays. Plants are tall and very productive.

Honey Dijon

BLOOM SIZE, TYPE: Large, classic
FRAGRANCE: Medium
GROWTH HABIT: Medium, bushy
DISEASE RESISTANCE: Good
ARS RATING: 7.5
COMMENTS: The unusual tan to mustard blooms exhibit good form and grow in sprays on strong plants. Honey Dijon was hybridized by amateur James Sproul.

Maria Shriver

BLOOM SIZE, TYPE: Large, classic
FRAGRANCE: Heavy
GROWTH HABIT: Medium, bushy
DISEASE RESISTANCE: Good
ARS RATING: 7.5
COMMENTS: Named for the former first lady of California, this variety has very fragrant, pure white blooms of classic form borne in medium to large sprays.

Melody Parfumée

BLOOM SIZE, TYPE: Large, classic
FRAGRANCE: Heavy
GROWTH HABIT: Medium, bushy
DISEASE RESISTANCE: Good
ARS RATING: 7.7
COMMENTS: Medium lavender to purple blooms in large, loose sprays make this a very attractive garden rose. The flowers are exceptionally fragrant, and the plant is a fast repeat bloomer.

Octoberfest

BLOOM SIZE, TYPE: Medium, classic
FRAGRANCE: Medium
GROWTH HABIT: Tall, upright
DISEASE RESISTANCE: Excellent
ARS RATING: 7.5
COMMENTS: Classic orange blooms with yellow and pink overtones are carried on very upright, disease-resistant plants. The flowers form in well-arrayed sprays.

Prominent

BLOOM SIZE, TYPE: Medium, classic
FRAGRANCE: Light
GROWTH HABIT: Medium, bushy
DISEASE RESISTANCE: Good
ARS RATING: 7.5
COMMENTS: Bright orange-red blooms with classic form are borne in small sprays on very healthy plants. Prominent is somewhat short for a grandiflora, but it's very productive with blooms.

Queen Elizabeth

BLOOM SIZE, TYPE: Large, informal
FRAGRANCE: Light
GROWTH HABIT: Tall, bushy
DISEASE RESISTANCE: Excellent
ARS RATING: 7.9
COMMENTS: Queen Elizabeth is the epitome of the grandiflora class, with very tall, robust plants and medium pink blooms formed singly and in sprays. It does not like hard pruning; let it grow tall.

Radiant Perfume

BLOOM SIZE, TYPE: Large, classic
FRAGRANCE: Medium to heavy
GROWTH HABIT: Medium, bushy
DISEASE RESISTANCE: Good
ARS RATING: 7.5
COMMENTS: Solid yellow blooms with an enticing fragrance grace this variety. The flowers grow singly and in small sprays, opening quickly on robust plants.

Reba McIntyre

BLOOM SIZE, TYPE: Large, classic
FRAGRANCE: Light
GROWTH HABIT: Medium, bushy
DISEASE RESISTANCE: Good
ARS RATING: 7.7
COMMENTS: Named after the country singer, this New Zealand variety has red-orange blooms with a nice, light fragrance. They are carried singly and in sprays on tidy, compact plants.

Rejoice

BLOOM SIZE, TYPE: Medium, classic
FRAGRANCE: Medium
GROWTH HABIT: Medium, spreading
DISEASE RESISTANCE: Fair
ARS RATING: 8.0
COMMENTS: Rejoice, from amateur breeder Thomas McMillan, was the first rose to win a Gold Medal at the American Rose Society's trial grounds in Shreveport, Louisiana, in 1985. Soft pink blooms with brushings of salmon and amber are borne in large sprays.

Strike It Rich

BLOOM SIZE, TYPE: Large, classic
FRAGRANCE: Heavy
GROWTH HABIT: Tall, bushy
DISEASE RESISTANCE: Good
ARS RATING: 7.9
COMMENTS: Large sprays of golden yellow flowers with pink overtones are carried on tall, robust plants. This excellent rose is a solid garden performer.

Tournament of Roses

BLOOM SIZE, TYPE: Large, classic
FRAGRANCE: Light
GROWTH HABIT: Short, bushy
DISEASE RESISTANCE: Excellent
ARS RATING: 8.2
COMMENTS: Beautiful blooms with deep pink centers and lighter petal edges form in medium-size sprays. Plants grow only 3 to 4 feet tall with excellent disease resistance.

Wild Blue Yonder

BLOOM SIZE, TYPE: Large, informal
FRAGRANCE: Heavy
GROWTH HABIT: Medium, bushy
DISEASE RESISTANCE: Good
ARS RATING: 7.7
COMMENTS: Medium purple, very fragrant blooms with reddish edges form in large clusters. It's one of several fine purple roses bred by Weeks Roses in recent years.

Floribundas

Floribundas are the quintessential spray rose. They were created in the early 20th century as a cross between hybrid teas and polyanthas.

Floribunda roses range from short to tall, bloom sizes vary from small polyantha-like flowers to virtual hybrid teas, and bloom forms are more variable than any other rose family, ranging from five-petal singles to many-petal flowers.

To picture an ideal spray, imagine arranging roses or other flowers in a vase. You would give each bloom room to display itself without crowding the others, but leave no holes or gaps in the bouquet. You would place all the blooms at the same level, with a flat or slightly rounded top to the bouquet. Finally, you would arrange the stems so the bouquet was nearly round rather than lopsided or angular. This bouquet describes what an ideal floribunda spray should look like.

While hybrid teas are usually considered the best for cut roses, floribundas offer the same combination of colors, fragrances, and forms, but on just one or two stems rather than many. Varying sizes and heavy bloom habit make floribundas ideal for many landscape uses.

Consider growing single roses with alluring stamens. Also beautiful are semidoubles (about 10 to 20 petals per flower) that quickly open to reveal their stamens as the blooms age.

Floribundas with an "excellent" rating for disease resistance are the easiest to care for, but the rest are also worth growing because of other stellar traits.

BLOOM SIZE

SMALL: Less than 2 inches wide
MEDIUM: 2 to 4 inches wide
LARGE: More than 4 inches wide

PLANT SIZE

SHORT: Smaller than 4 feet tall
MEDIUM: 4 to 5½ feet tall
TALL: More than 5½ feet tall
UPRIGHT: Generally less than 2½ feet wide
BUSHY: 2½ to 4 feet wide
SPREADING: More than 4 feet wide

Angel Face

BLOOM SIZE, TYPE: Large, classic
FRAGRANCE: Heavy
GROWTH HABIT: Medium, bushy
DISEASE RESISTANCE: Fair
ARS RATING: 7.7
COMMENTS: Angel Face is one of the most fragrant floribundas. Large purple blooms grow on strong plants.

Apricot Nectar

BLOOM SIZE, TYPE: Large, classic
FRAGRANCE: Heavy
GROWTH HABIT: Medium, bushy
DISEASE RESISTANCE: Good
ARS RATING: 8.0
COMMENTS: This fragrant variety bears large, buff-apricot blooms on medium-size plants.

Bella Rosa

BLOOM SIZE, TYPE: Small
FRAGRANCE: Light
GROWTH HABIT: Short, bushy
DISEASE RESISTANCE: Excellent
ARS RATING: 7.8
COMMENTS: Bella Rosa could well have been classed as a polyantha. Low-growing, disease-resistant plants carry small pink blooms borne in large clusters.

Betty Boop

BLOOM SIZE, TYPE: Medium, semidouble
FRAGRANCE: Medium
GROWTH HABIT: Medium, bushy
DISEASE RESISTANCE: Good
ARS RATING: 8.0
COMMENTS: White blooms with cerise edges and yellow bases are carried in small sprays. This rose was named for the animated cartoon character.

Betty Prior

BLOOM SIZE, TYPE: Medium, single
FRAGRANCE: Light
GROWTH HABIT: Tall, bushy
DISEASE RESISTANCE: Fair
ARS RATING: 8.2
COMMENTS: Large sprays of single medium pink blooms are borne in profusion. The tall plants are somewhat prone to black spot.

Bill Warriner

BLOOM SIZE, TYPE: Medium, classic
FRAGRANCE: Light
GROWTH HABIT: Medium, bushy
DISEASE RESISTANCE: Good
ARS RATING: 7.8
COMMENTS: Salmon pink blooms with classic form grace this variety, named for a longtime hybridizer at the Jackson & Perkins Company. Blooms open quickly to show attractive stamens.

Black Cherry

BLOOM SIZE, TYPE: Medium, classic
FRAGRANCE: Light
GROWTH HABIT: Medium, bushy
DISEASE RESISTANCE: Good
ARS RATING: 7.5
COMMENTS: Medium-size, manageable plants bear large clusters of solid red blooms with a light, fruity fragrance.

Blueberry Hill

BLOOM SIZE, TYPE: Large, semidouble
FRAGRANCE: Medium
GROWTH HABIT: Medium, spreading
DISEASE RESISTANCE: Good
ARS RATING: 7.8
COMMENTS: Large, light purple blooms set in medium-size sprays are nicely fragrant and open quickly to show their stamens.

Bolero

BLOOM SIZE, TYPE: Large, informal
FRAGRANCE: Medium
GROWTH HABIT: Medium, spreading
DISEASE RESISTANCE: Good
ARS RATING: 7.6
COMMENTS: This great garden plant carries medium-size sprays of large, fragrant white flowers on somewhat spreading bushes.

Brass Band

BLOOM SIZE, TYPE: Medium, informal
FRAGRANCE: Light
GROWTH HABIT: Medium, upright
DISEASE RESISTANCE: Good
ARS RATING: 7.9
COMMENTS: A real eye-catcher! This rose bears distinctive blooms of orange and yellow in medium-size sprays on strong, upright plants.

Burgundy Iceberg

BLOOM SIZE, TYPE: Medium, informal
FRAGRANCE: Light
GROWTH HABIT: Tall, spreading
DISEASE RESISTANCE: Fair
ARS RATING: 7.6
COMMENTS: Tall, somewhat gangly plants have deep purple, low-petal-count blooms that form in large, loose sprays. It's a color sport of Brilliant Pink Iceberg, which is a sport of Pink Iceberg.

Cathedral

BLOOM SIZE, TYPE: Large, classic
FRAGRANCE: Light
GROWTH HABIT: Medium, bushy
DISEASE RESISTANCE: Good
ARS RATING: 7.8
COMMENTS: Originally named Coventry Cathedral for the church destroyed in WWII, this variety has large yellow-orange blooms with hints of pink. Plants bear small, well-formed clusters of flowers.

Cherish

BLOOM SIZE, TYPE: Medium, classic
FRAGRANCE: Light
GROWTH HABIT: Tall, upright
DISEASE RESISTANCE: Good
ARS RATING: 7.6
COMMENTS: Soft medium pink blooms with classic form are borne both as singles and in small sprays on upright plants.

Chihuly

BLOOM SIZE, TYPE: Large, informal
FRAGRANCE: Light
GROWTH HABIT: Medium, bushy
DISEASE RESISTANCE: Good
ARS RATING: 7.5
COMMENTS: Named after the renowned glass artist Dale Chihuly, these large blooms are an eye-catching mix of reds and yellows, forming in medium-size sprays.

City of London

BLOOM SIZE, TYPE: Medium, semidouble
FRAGRANCE: Heavy
GROWTH HABIT: Tall, spreading
DISEASE RESISTANCE: Fair
ARS RATING: 7.6
COMMENTS: Delicate pink blooms in large, well-arrayed sprays grace this award-winning rose. Long, floppy canes need pruning or support.

Class Act

BLOOM SIZE, TYPE: Large, informal
FRAGRANCE: Light
GROWTH HABIT: Medium, bushy
DISEASE RESISTANCE: Good
ARS RATING: 7.8
COMMENTS: Strong plants with large white blooms that form in good size sprays offer great garden performance. Class Act does well in all areas of the country.

Day Breaker

BLOOM SIZE, TYPE: Medium, classic
FRAGRANCE: Medium
GROWTH HABIT: Medium, bushy
DISEASE RESISTANCE: Good
ARS RATING: 7.9
COMMENTS: The perfect combination: Fragrant, perfectly formed, classic blooms of yellow, amber, and pink form in large, well-arrayed sprays on this variety from England.

Dicky

BLOOM SIZE, TYPE: Medium, semidouble
FRAGRANCE: Light
GROWTH HABIT: Medium, spreading
DISEASE RESISTANCE: Fair
ARS RATING: 8.3
COMMENTS: Beautiful salmon pink blooms form in large clusters on this appealing variety. The canes are on the thin side and need support in rainy areas.

Easy Going

BLOOM SIZE, TYPE: Large, informal
FRAGRANCE: Light
GROWTH HABIT: Medium, bushy
DISEASE RESISTANCE: Excellent
ARS RATING: 8.0
COMMENTS: This rose, a color sport of Livin' Easy, has the same attributes, but it bears blossoms that are yellow-amber in color. Large sprays of blooms are borne on very disease-resistant bushes.

Ebb Tide

BLOOM SIZE, TYPE: Medium, informal
FRAGRANCE: Heavy
GROWTH HABIT: Medium, upright
DISEASE RESISTANCE: Good
ARS RATING: 7.6
COMMENTS: Deep purple, very fragrant flowers with good repeat bloom form in large sprays on medium-size plants.

Escapade

BLOOM SIZE, TYPE: Medium, semidouble
FRAGRANCE: Medium
GROWTH HABIT: Medium, bushy
DISEASE RESISTANCE: Good
ARS RATING: 8.6
COMMENTS: Fragrant silvery-pink blooms form in large, somewhat crowded sprays on strong, highly rated plants. A must for any garden.

Eureka

BLOOM SIZE, TYPE: Large, informal
FRAGRANCE: Light
GROWTH HABIT: Medium, bushy
DISEASE RESISTANCE: Good
ARS RATING: 7.8
COMMENTS: This winner from Germany features sprays of large amber-yellow blooms and very glossy green foliage on medium-size plants.

Europeana

BLOOM SIZE, TYPE: Medium, informal
FRAGRANCE: Light
GROWTH HABIT: Medium, bushy
DISEASE RESISTANCE: Good
ARS RATING: 8.6
COMMENTS: One of the most widely grown floribundas, this variety performs well in all areas of the country. Its deep red blooms grow in large sprays on strong, medium-size plants.

Eyepaint

BLOOM SIZE, TYPE: Small, single
FRAGRANCE: Light
GROWTH HABIT: Tall, spreading
DISEASE RESISTANCE: Excellent
ARS RATING: 8.3
COMMENTS: More of a shrub than a floribunda, Eyepaint is a large, spreading plant that bears abundant single red blooms with white eyes and golden stamens. It serves as a stellar landscape rose.

Fabulous!

BLOOM SIZE, TYPE: Medium, informal
FRAGRANCE: Light
GROWTH HABIT: Medium, upright
DISEASE RESISTANCE: Good
ARS RATING: 7.7
COMMENTS: Often called a white Sexy Rexy (one of its parents), this variety bears large, well-formed sprays of informal white blooms on upright, disease-resistant plants.

First Edition

BLOOM SIZE, TYPE: Small, classic
FRAGRANCE: Light
GROWTH HABIT: Medium, bushy
DISEASE RESISTANCE: Good
ARS RATING: 8.2
COMMENTS: Compact plants bear large clusters of small, classic blooms in shades of orange, amber, and pink.

First Kiss

BLOOM SIZE, TYPE: Medium, semidouble
FRAGRANCE: Light
GROWTH HABIT: Medium, bushy
DISEASE RESISTANCE: Good
ARS RATING: 8.2
COMMENTS: Very soft pink blooms are borne in large, somewhat crowded sprays on this popular variety. Plants have good disease resistance and quick repeat bloom.

Flirtatious

BLOOM SIZE, TYPE: Medium, informal
FRAGRANCE: Medium
GROWTH HABIT: Medium, bushy
DISEASE RESISTANCE: Good
ARS RATING: 7.6
COMMENTS: Blooms start out light yellow before fading to pale pink with yellow overtones as they age. They are borne in large sprays on bushy plants.

Fragrant Delight

BLOOM SIZE, TYPE: Medium, semidouble
FRAGRANCE: Heavy
GROWTH HABIT: Medium, spreading
DISEASE RESISTANCE: Excellent
ARS RATING: 7.9
COMMENTS: These very fragrant flowers appear in an unusual shade of pink-amber in medium-size, somewhat irregular sprays. This highly disease-resistant variety should be more widely known and grown.

Francois Rabelais

BLOOM SIZE, TYPE: Medium, informal
FRAGRANCE: Light
GROWTH HABIT: Medium, spreading
DISEASE RESISTANCE: Good
ARS RATING: 7.5
COMMENTS: Vivid red old-fashioned blooms are the hallmark of this Romantica variety from Meilland of France. They are mildly fragrant and do well in warm weather.

French Lace

BLOOM SIZE, TYPE: Large, classic
FRAGRANCE: Medium
GROWTH HABIT: Medium, bushy
DISEASE RESISTANCE: Good
ARS RATING: 8.1
COMMENTS: It's not quite a floribunda, not quite a hybrid tea. Fragrant creamy-white, perfectly formed hybrid tea-type blooms form in small, crowded sprays on strong plants.

Gene Boerner

BLOOM SIZE, TYPE: Medium, classic
FRAGRANCE: Light
GROWTH HABIT: Medium, bushy
DISEASE RESISTANCE: Good
ARS RATING: 8.3
COMMENTS: These compact plants, named for the longtime Jackson & Perkins hybridizer who popularized floribundas, bear loads of medium pink blooms in large, well-formed sprays.

George Burns

BLOOM SIZE, TYPE: Medium, informal
FRAGRANCE: Medium
GROWTH HABIT: Short, bushy
DISEASE RESISTANCE: Good
ARS RATING: 7.7
COMMENTS: Get a real color blast from the red stripes on light yellow blooms with deep yellow eyes. This low-growing variety bears blooms in small, irregular sprays.

Glad Tidings

BLOOM SIZE, TYPE: Medium, classic
FRAGRANCE: Light
GROWTH HABIT: Medium, bushy
DISEASE RESISTANCE: Good
ARS RATING: 8.1
COMMENTS: Tidy plants are good for landscape use. The medium-size, deep-red classic blooms form in well-arrayed sprays.

Golden Holstein

BLOOM SIZE, TYPE: Medium, semidouble
FRAGRANCE: Light
GROWTH HABIT: Medium, bushy
DISEASE RESISTANCE: Excellent
ARS RATING: 8.2
COMMENTS: Solid yellow blooms with gorgeous golden stamens characterize these strong, bushy plants. The sprays are large and somewhat irregular in size and shape.

Goldmarie

BLOOM SIZE, TYPE: Medium, informal
FRAGRANCE: Light
GROWTH HABIT: Short, bushy
DISEASE RESISTANCE: Good
ARS RATING: 7.5
COMMENTS: Golden yellow blooms occasionally tinged with red grow in small sprays on disease-resistant, somewhat short plants.

Grüss an Aachen

BLOOM SIZE, TYPE: Medium, informal
FRAGRANCE: Light
GROWTH HABIT: Short, bushy
DISEASE RESISTANCE: Good
ARS RATING: 8.3
COMMENTS: This is the first floribunda, introduced in 1911. Short plants bear light, creamy-pink blooms in profusion. Flowers have a heavily petaled, old-fashioned appearance.

Guy de Maupassant

BLOOM SIZE, TYPE: Medium, informal
FRAGRANCE: Heavy
GROWTH HABIT: Tall, bushy
DISEASE RESISTANCE: Good
ARS RATING: 7.7
COMMENTS: This very fragrant pink variety named after the 19th-century French writer bears medium-size sprays of many-petalled blooms. It's one of the Meilland Romantica series.

H. C. Andersen

BLOOM SIZE, TYPE: Medium, informal
FRAGRANCE: Light
GROWTH HABIT: Medium, upright
DISEASE RESISTANCE: Good
ARS RATING: 8.0
COMMENTS: This tough, hardy variety from Denmark, named for storyteller Hans Christian Andersen, has deep red blooms in large but irregular sprays.

Hannah Gordon

BLOOM SIZE, TYPE: Large, informal
FRAGRANCE: Light
GROWTH HABIT: Tall, spreading
DISEASE RESISTANCE: Excellent
ARS RATING: 8.8
COMMENTS: The highest rated floribunda has large, light pink blooms with deep cerise edges carried in large clusters on strong, thorny, spreading plants. It is sometimes sold as Nicole.

Honey Perfume

BLOOM SIZE, TYPE: Medium, classic
FRAGRANCE: Heavy
GROWTH HABIT: Medium, upright
DISEASE RESISTANCE: Good
ARS RATING: 7.7
COMMENTS: Very fragrant amber-yellow blooms array themselves in small sprays. Tidy plants have good disease resistance.

Hot Cocoa

BLOOM SIZE, TYPE: Medium, informal
FRAGRANCE: Medium
GROWTH HABIT: Medium, spreading
DISEASE RESISTANCE: Excellent
ARS RATING: 7.9
COMMENTS: Intriguing, dusky red blooms are borne in medium-size clusters on very disease-resistant plants.

Iceberg

BLOOM SIZE, TYPE: Medium, semidouble
FRAGRANCE: Light
GROWTH HABIT: Tall, bushy
DISEASE RESISTANCE: Fair
ARS RATING: 8.7
COMMENTS: White semidouble blooms are borne in large, loose sprays on plants somewhat susceptible to black spot.

International Herald Tribune

BLOOM SIZE, TYPE: Medium, semidouble
FRAGRANCE: Medium
GROWTH HABIT: Short, bushy
DISEASE RESISTANCE: Excellent
ARS RATING: 7.9
COMMENTS: Masses of fragrant purple blooms with prominent gold stamens make this a winner in any garden. The relatively short and wide plants are ideal for low borders.

Irish Hope

BLOOM SIZE, TYPE: Large, informal
FRAGRANCE: Medium
GROWTH HABIT: Tall, bushy
DISEASE RESISTANCE: Excellent
ARS RATING: 7.7
COMMENTS: Medium to large, fragrant sprays of soft yellow, informal blooms grow on tall, slightly bushy plants.

Ivory Fashion

BLOOM SIZE, TYPE: Large, classic
FRAGRANCE: Medium
GROWTH HABIT: Medium, bushy
DISEASE RESISTANCE: Good
ARS RATING: 8.3
COMMENTS: With a rating of 8.3 and an introduction more than 50 years ago, this rose must be good. Fragrant large creamy-white blooms are carried on bushy plants.

Johann Strauss

BLOOM SIZE, TYPE: Large, informal
FRAGRANCE: Light
GROWTH HABIT: Medium, bushy
DISEASE RESISTANCE: Good
ARS RATING: 7.8
COMMENTS: Soft pink blooms with yellow overtones grace this rose named for the waltz composer. Lightly fragrant blooms are borne both singly and in small sprays.

Judy Garland

BLOOM SIZE, TYPE: Medium, classic
FRAGRANCE: Medium
GROWTH HABIT: Medium, bushy
DISEASE RESISTANCE: Good
ARS RATING: 7.6
COMMENTS: Judy Garland is an eye-catcher. Bright yellow flowers with orange to red petal edges have a light apple scent and are carried in small sprays on strong plants.

Julia Child

BLOOM SIZE, TYPE: Large, informal
FRAGRANCE: Light
GROWTH HABIT: Medium, bushy
DISEASE RESISTANCE: Excellent
ARS RATING: 8.1
COMMENTS: This rose is one of the most disease-resistant varieties to come from U.S. hybridizers in years. Julia Child bears large, solid yellow blooms that form in small sprays on medium-size plants.

Lavaglut

BLOOM SIZE, TYPE: Small, informal
FRAGRANCE: None
GROWTH HABIT: Medium, bushy
DISEASE RESISTANCE: Good
ARS RATING: 8.7
COMMENTS: Meet the top exhibition floribunda in the U.S. The name, German for “lava glow,” aptly describes the small, deep red, pompon blooms that seem to last forever. Sprays are large and well formed.

Lime Sublime

BLOOM SIZE, TYPE: Medium, classic
FRAGRANCE: Light
GROWTH HABIT: Medium, bushy
DISEASE RESISTANCE: Good
ARS RATING: 7.6
COMMENTS: White with sublime shades of chartreuse, these classic blooms are borne in small sprays on tidy plants.

Little Darling

BLOOM SIZE, TYPE: Small, classic
FRAGRANCE: Light
GROWTH HABIT: Medium, spreading
DISEASE RESISTANCE: Good
ARS RATING: 8.2
COMMENTS: This variety, the parent of many miniatures, carries small classic pink blooms with yellow at the petal base and light pink on the edges. The blooms are borne in large sprays on vigorous plants that belie the name "little."

Livin' Easy

BLOOM SIZE, TYPE: Large, informal
FRAGRANCE: Light
GROWTH HABIT: Medium, bushy
DISEASE RESISTANCE: Excellent
ARS RATING: 8.1
COMMENTS: Extremely large sprays of orange blooms brushed with yellow grow on rugged, highly disease-resistant plants. This outstanding floribunda should be rated even higher.

Margaret Merril

BLOOM SIZE, TYPE: Large, classic
FRAGRANCE: Heavy
GROWTH HABIT: Tall, upright
DISEASE RESISTANCE: Good
ARS RATING: 8.2
COMMENTS: Very fragrant white blooms are borne in medium-size sprays on tall, strong plants that hold up well.

Marina

BLOOM SIZE, TYPE: Medium, semidouble
FRAGRANCE: Medium
GROWTH HABIT: Medium, bushy
DISEASE RESISTANCE: Good
ARS RATING: 7.5
COMMENTS: Bright, solid orange blooms with a yellow base have a nice fragrance and form in moderate-size sprays on bushy plants with dark, glossy foliage.

Marmalade Skies

BLOOM SIZE, TYPE: Medium, informal
FRAGRANCE: None
GROWTH HABIT: Medium, bushy
DISEASE RESISTANCE: Good
ARS RATING: 7.8
COMMENTS: Vivid orange blooms call immediate attention to this variety, originally introduced as Tangerine Dream. The large blooms are carried in small to medium sprays on strong plants.

Moondance

BLOOM SIZE, TYPE: Large, classic
FRAGRANCE: Light
GROWTH HABIT: Tall, upright
DISEASE RESISTANCE: Good
ARS RATING: 7.8
COMMENTS: Large, well-arrayed sprays of pure white blooms with mild fragrance grace this variety. This is a good, high-quality white floribunda.

Nearly Wild

BLOOM SIZE, TYPE: Medium, single
FRAGRANCE: Light
GROWTH HABIT: Short, bushy
DISEASE RESISTANCE: Good
ARS RATING: 7.8
COMMENTS: This golden oldie from 1941 has single pink blooms that resemble Betty Prior, except these have a white eye. They are carried in large clusters on short plants.

Our Lady of Guadalupe

BLOOM SIZE, TYPE: Medium, informal
FRAGRANCE: Light
GROWTH HABIT: Short, bushy
DISEASE RESISTANCE: Good
ARS RATING: 8.0
COMMENTS: Soft pink blooms arrayed in large clusters open quickly and fade to a very pleasing light pink on rather short, bushy plants.

Paprika

BLOOM SIZE, TYPE: Medium, single
FRAGRANCE: Light
GROWTH HABIT: Short, bushy
DISEASE RESISTANCE: Good
ARS RATING: 8.1
COMMENTS: Single-petal, brick red flowers with prominent golden stamens are carried on short, spreading bushes.

Passionate Kisses

BLOOM SIZE, TYPE: Medium, informal
FRAGRANCE: Light
GROWTH HABIT: Medium, bushy
DISEASE RESISTANCE: Good
ARS RATING: 8.2
COMMENTS: Medium pink blooms with silver-pink on the undersides are borne in large sprays. Plants grow to moderate height.

Playboy

BLOOM SIZE, TYPE: Medium, single
FRAGRANCE: Light
GROWTH HABIT: Medium, bushy
DISEASE RESISTANCE: Good
ARS RATING: 8.5
COMMENTS: Vivid red-and-yellow single blooms that never fail to attract the eye characterize this rose. Cut some of the medium-size, well-formed sprays for bouquets.

Playgirl

BLOOM SIZE, TYPE: Medium, single
FRAGRANCE: Light
GROWTH HABIT: Short, bushy
DISEASE RESISTANCE: Excellent
ARS RATING: 8.4
COMMENTS: The offspring of Playboy and Angel Face, Playgirl has deep pink single blooms that grow in large clusters on rather short plants.

Pleasure

BLOOM SIZE, TYPE: Large, informal
FRAGRANCE: Light
GROWTH HABIT: Medium, bushy
DISEASE RESISTANCE: Good
ARS RATING: 8.0
COMMENTS: Loads of large, medium pink blooms in small sprays hold their color well. Bushes produce well in all climates.

Preference

BLOOM SIZE, TYPE: Medium, semidouble
FRAGRANCE: Light
GROWTH HABIT: Medium, bushy
DISEASE RESISTANCE: Good
ARS RATING: 7.7
COMMENTS: A rose preferred by many gardeners, Preference has velvety scarlet blooms that open quickly to show beautiful stamens. Flowers are borne on tidy, compact plants.

Pretty Lady

BLOOM SIZE, TYPE: Large, informal
FRAGRANCE: Medium
GROWTH HABIT: Medium, upright
DISEASE RESISTANCE: Excellent
ARS RATING: 8.2
COMMENTS: Bred in the United Kingdom by amateur hybridizer Len Scrivens, this rose bears huge sprays of off-white blooms with creamy-white centers. Plants are upright with good repeat bloom.

Priscilla Burton

BLOOM SIZE, TYPE: Large, semidouble
FRAGRANCE: Medium
GROWTH HABIT: Medium, bushy
DISEASE RESISTANCE: Good
ARS RATING: 8.3
COMMENTS: Rose breeder Sam McGredy calls this a "hand-painted" floribunda. Each light pink flower has slightly different markings of pink to deep red, depending on the weather.

Rainbow Sorbet

BLOOM SIZE, TYPE: Medium, semidouble
FRAGRANCE: Light
GROWTH HABIT: Medium, upright
DISEASE RESISTANCE: Good
ARS RATING: 8.0
COMMENTS: Sometimes described as Playboy with more petals, this rose has yellow blooms with cerise petal edges. The flowers form in medium-size clusters.

Regensberg

BLOOM SIZE, TYPE: Medium, classic
FRAGRANCE: Medium
GROWTH HABIT: Short, bushy
DISEASE RESISTANCE: Excellent
ARS RATING: 7.9
COMMENTS: The flowers of this so-called hand-painted floribunda—because the markings are variable from bloom to bloom—are deep pink with silvery-white undersides.

Royal Occasion

BLOOM SIZE, TYPE: Medium, informal
FRAGRANCE: Light
GROWTH HABIT: Medium, bushy
DISEASE RESISTANCE: Good
ARS RATING: 8.5
COMMENTS: Solid red blooms with distinctive black petal edges grow in medium-size, well-formed sprays. Sometimes sold as Montana.

Sarabande

BLOOM SIZE, TYPE: Medium, semidouble
FRAGRANCE: Light
GROWTH HABIT: Medium, bushy
DISEASE RESISTANCE: Good
ARS RATING: 8.0
COMMENTS: Vivid orange-red blooms with golden stamens maintain the popularity of this 1957 variety. The blooms grow in large, irregular sprays with nice fragrance.

Scentimental

BLOOM SIZE, TYPE: Large, informal
FRAGRANCE: Heavy
GROWTH HABIT: Medium, bushy
DISEASE RESISTANCE: Good
ARS RATING: 7.7
COMMENTS: Large, very fragrant blooms are reminiscent of Old Garden Roses. Red-striped light pink blooms form in small, crowded sprays.

Sexy Rexy

BLOOM SIZE, TYPE: Medium, informal
FRAGRANCE: Light
GROWTH HABIT: Medium, upright
DISEASE RESISTANCE: Good
ARS RATING: 8.7
COMMENTS: Sexy Rexy bears large, perfectly formed sprays of light pink blooms. This floribunda is a must for any rose garden.

Sheila's Perfume

BLOOM SIZE, TYPE: Large, classic
FRAGRANCE: Heavy
GROWTH HABIT: Tall, upright
DISEASE RESISTANCE: Excellent
ARS RATING: 8.2
COMMENTS: This British import has classic large yellow blooms with pink petal edges that resemble both hybrid teas and floribundas. Exceptionally fragrant, they're borne singly and in sprays.

Showbiz

BLOOM SIZE, TYPE: Medium, informal
FRAGRANCE: Light
GROWTH HABIT: Short, spreading
DISEASE RESISTANCE: Good
ARS RATING: 8.3
COMMENTS: Loads of informal medium red blossoms grow in large sprays on short, angular plants.

Simplicity

BLOOM SIZE, TYPE: Medium, semidouble
FRAGRANCE: Light
GROWTH HABIT: Medium, upright
DISEASE RESISTANCE: Good
ARS RATING: 7.6
COMMENTS: This upright, nearly thornless plant with small sprays of pink blooms is touted as a hedge plant but may not be the best choice. In many areas, it flowers well into fall.

Singin' in the Rain

BLOOM SIZE, TYPE: Small, classic
FRAGRANCE: Medium
GROWTH HABIT: Medium, bushy
DISEASE RESISTANCE: Good
ARS RATING: 7.7
COMMENTS: Small hybrid tea-type blooms of buff-amber are attractive when fresh but do not age well. Plants bloom profusely.

Summer Fashion

BLOOM SIZE, TYPE: Large, classic
FRAGRANCE: Medium
GROWTH HABIT: Medium, upright
DISEASE RESISTANCE: Good
ARS RATING: 7.8
COMMENTS: Large, fragrant blooms—hybrid tea look-alikes—are carried in small sprays on strong plants. Yellow centers with pink petal edges remind admirers of the well-known Peace.

Sun Flare

BLOOM SIZE, TYPE: Medium, informal
FRAGRANCE: Light
GROWTH HABIT: Medium, bushy
DISEASE RESISTANCE: Excellent
ARS RATING: 7.8
COMMENTS: Ruffled blooms of medium yellow are carried in large sprays on this productive variety. The plant is very disease resistant and quite manageable in size.

Sunsprite

BLOOM SIZE, TYPE: Large, informal
FRAGRANCE: Heavy
GROWTH HABIT: Medium, bushy
DISEASE RESISTANCE: Excellent
ARS RATING: 8.5
COMMENTS: This variety is a classic. Large, very fragrant deep yellow blooms form medium-size, somewhat crowded sprays on strong plants that repeat bloom quickly.

Sweet Inspiration

BLOOM SIZE, TYPE: Large, semidouble
FRAGRANCE: Light
GROWTH HABIT: Medium, bushy
DISEASE RESISTANCE: Good
ARS RATING: 7.7
COMMENTS: Soft medium pink blooms with yellow at the petal base are borne in good-size sprays. Large flowers open to display gorgeous stamens.

Topsy Turvy

BLOOM SIZE, TYPE: Medium, semidouble
FRAGRANCE: Light
GROWTH HABIT: Short, bushy
DISEASE RESISTANCE: Good
ARS RATING: 7.6
COMMENTS: The blooms, scarlet red with a white underside, have an unusual habit of twisting sideways as they age, providing the name. Topsy Turvy makes a very decorative garden plant.

Trumpeter

BLOOM SIZE, TYPE: Medium, informal
FRAGRANCE: Light
GROWTH HABIT: Short, bushy
DISEASE RESISTANCE: Good
ARS RATING: 8.2
COMMENTS: Fiery orange-red blooms in large clusters grab the eye from a distance on Trumpeter, named to honor Louis Armstrong. Short plants have a heavy bloom and good repeat habit.

Tuscan Sun

BLOOM SIZE, TYPE: Medium, classic
FRAGRANCE: Light
GROWTH HABIT: Medium, upright
DISEASE RESISTANCE: Good
ARS RATING: 7.8
COMMENTS: Warm amber blooms blended with shades of orange, yellow, and pink make Tuscan Sun a stunner. The classic blooms form in good-size sprays.

Victorian Spice

BLOOM SIZE, TYPE: Medium, informal
FRAGRANCE: Heavy
GROWTH HABIT: Tall, bushy
DISEASE RESISTANCE: Good
ARS RATING: 7.5
COMMENTS: Originally named L'Aimant for the Coty perfume, the blooms of this fragrant variety range from light pink to salmon pink, depending on the weather. They are borne in irregular sprays.

White Simplicity

BLOOM SIZE, TYPE: Medium, semidouble
FRAGRANCE: Light
GROWTH HABIT: Medium, upright
DISEASE RESISTANCE: Good
ARS RATING: 7.8
COMMENTS: An offspring rather than a sport of the original pink Simplicity, White Simplicity is rated even higher. Creamy-white blooms show soft yellow centers.

Polyanthas

Polyanthas (Greek for "many petals") are typically short, bushy, extremely floriferous roses.

Ideal for use in low borders, mass plantings, and container gardens, polyanthas sport single, semidouble, or double blooms. They also come in a wide range of colors.

The first polyanthas were bred in the 1870s, predating floribundas by nearly 40 years. Although there have been few new polyanthas introduced in recent years, plenty of good older varieties are still on the market.

An interesting characteristic of this family is its tendency to produce genetic mutations, called sports. More polyanthas have been created from sports than have roses in any other family.

Sports can be color mutations of the blooms (all other characteristics remain the same) or climbing mutations that produce long canes.

Many of the bush polyanthas have climbing forms. These large, mounding plants covered with blooms are ideal for many landscape uses, such as creating hedges, covering small trellises, or filling blank spaces in the garden.

Five of the 21 Earth-Kind roses are polyanthas: La Marne, Mlle Cécile Brünner, Marie Daly, Perle d'Or, and The Fairy. That's a good indication of their garden value because the designation is given only to roses with superior disease tolerance and outstanding landscape performance.

They may be oldies, but polyanthas are definitely goodies.

BLOOM SIZE

LARGE: More than 4 inches wide
MEDIUM: 2 to 4 inches wide
SMALL: Less than 2 inches wide

PLANT SIZE

TALL: More than 4 feet tall
MEDIUM: 2 to 4 feet tall
SHORT: Shorter than 2 feet tall

China Doll

BLOOM SIZE, TYPE: Small, double
FRAGRANCE: Light
PLANT SIZE, HABIT: Short, bushy
DISEASE RESISTANCE: Good
ARS RATING: 8.1
COMMENTS: Soft porcelain-pink blooms with yellow at their bases borne in large trusses grace this variety from 1946. The plant is very disease resistant, growing 1 to 2 feet tall. The canes of the climbing version reach up to 6 feet.

La Marne

BLOOM SIZE, TYPE: Medium, single
FRAGRANCE: Light
PLANT SIZE, HABIT: Tall, bushy
DISEASE RESISTANCE: Excellent
ARS RATING: 8.7
COMMENTS: Blush-white single blooms with deep pink petal edges make this Earth-Kind selection a popular variety. The blooms are carried in large, loose clusters on 6-foot plants, tall for a polyantha.

Mademoiselle Cécile Brünner

BLOOM SIZE, TYPE: Medium, double
FRAGRANCE: Light
PLANT SIZE, HABIT: Medium, bushy
DISEASE RESISTANCE: Excellent
ARS RATING: 8.4
COMMENTS: Often called Cécile Brünner, this rose dates from 1880. Light pink blooms with yellow undertones are lightly fragrant, carried in large clusters. It's an Earth-Kind selection.

Marie Pavié

BLOOM SIZE, TYPE: Small, double
FRAGRANCE: Medium
PLANT SIZE, HABIT: Medium, bushy
DISEASE RESISTANCE: Good
ARS RATING: 8.9
COMMENTS: The bush form of this rose reaches 4 feet tall by 2 feet wide but its climbing sport grows much larger. Fragrant white pompon blooms with pink centers are borne in medium-size trusses.

Perle d'Or

BLOOM SIZE, TYPE: Small, double
FRAGRANCE: Heavy
PLANT SIZE, HABIT: Tall, bushy
DISEASE RESISTANCE: Excellent
ARS RATING: 8.5
COMMENTS: Very fragrant apricot-peach blooms are carried in large clusters on nearly thornless plants reaching about 6 feet. A climbing version of this Earth-Kind selection is available.

The Fairy

BLOOM SIZE, TYPE: Small, double
FRAGRANCE: Light
PLANT SIZE, HABIT: Medium, spreading
DISEASE RESISTANCE: Good
ARS RATING: 8.7
COMMENTS: An Earth-Kind selection, The Fairy is one of the most popular roses in the world. Its small pompon blooms are clear pink, fading to near white. Spreading plants bear glossy green foliage.

Shrubs

Shrubs are the largest and most diverse family in the rose world. The plants can range from short near-miniatures to tall and wide specimens.

Shrub rose blooms range from singles to the very double varieties with more than 40 petals. Gardeners should be particularly aware of the plant's size and habit before purchasing any shrub rose. Many shrub roses have been labeled by their family or breeder so gardeners can easily recognize them.

Where appropriate, the gallery lists whether a rose belongs to one of the best known and most loved types: hybrid musk (plants 6 feet and taller with very good disease resistance); hybrid rugosa (bushes 5 to 7 feet tall with very good disease resistance); hybrid kordesii (large plants with blooms in shades of red and pink); Buck (hardy, medium-size shrubs); Austin (mostly very fragrant, very double blooms); Easy Elegance (bred for hardiness and disease resistance on their own roots); Earth-Kind (water-wise selections made by the Texas AgriLife Extension Service); and Knock Out (hardy, very disease resistant, short to medium size.)

You'll find little difference between large shrubs and climbers. Both need support and training to perform their best. Looking for a rose that will grow in the shade? Most large shrub varieties tolerate partial shade.

Many shrubs offer excellent disease resistance, so they require fewer chemical or organic controls. The petal counts and plant sizes of every shrub variety may vary depending upon climate.

BLOOM FORM

SINGLE: 5 to 8 petals
SEMIDOUBLE: 10 to 20 petals
DOUBLE: 20 to 40 petals
VERY DOUBLE: More than 40 petals

PLANT SIZE

SHORT: Up to 4 feet tall
MEDIUM: 4 to 7 feet tall
TALL: More than 7 feet tall

Abraham Darby

TYPE: Austin
BLOOM SIZE, TYPE: Large, very double
FRAGRANCE: Heavy
PLANT SIZE, HABIT: Tall, spreading
DISEASE RESISTANCE: Good
ARS RATING: 8.0
COMMENTS: Abraham Darby is arguably the best of the Austin roses. The large, fragrant blooms grow in small sprays in shades of pink, salmon, and amber. If you have room for it, get it!

Armada

BLOOM SIZE, TYPE: Small, double
FRAGRANCE: Light
PLANT SIZE, HABIT: Medium, spreading
DISEASE RESISTANCE: Excellent
ARS RATING: 8.4
COMMENTS: Extra-large sprays of pink blooms grow on extremely disease-resistant plants. The canes grow 6 to 7 feet long; add support to keep the heavy blooms from flopping over.

Ballerina

TYPE: Hybrid musk
BLOOM SIZE, TYPE: Small, single
FRAGRANCE: Light
PLANT SIZE, HABIT: Medium, spreading
DISEASE RESISTANCE: Excellent
ARS RATING: 8.7
COMMENTS: At peak bloom, huge sprays of small light-pink blooms cover this superb landscape rose. The bush holds itself up well and can be maintained in a 5x5-foot space.

Belinda's Dream

TYPE: Earth-Kind
BLOOM SIZE, TYPE: Medium, very double
FRAGRANCE: Medium
PLANT SIZE, HABIT: Medium, spreading
DISEASE RESISTANCE: Excellent
ARS RATING: 8.5
COMMENTS: Belinda's Dream, an Earth-Kind selection, needs warm weather to perform well. The pink blooms with many petals are borne in profusion on arching plants.

Belle Story

TYPE: Austin
BLOOM SIZE, TYPE: Large, double
FRAGRANCE: Medium
PLANT SIZE, HABIT: Medium, bushy
DISEASE RESISTANCE: Good
ARS RATING: 8.6
COMMENTS: Clear pink blooms with about 35 petals open to show amber centers and golden stamens.

Blanc Double de Coubert

TYPE: Hybrid rugosa
BLOOM SIZE, TYPE: Medium, semidouble
FRAGRANCE: Heavy
PLANT SIZE, HABIT: Medium, upright
DISEASE RESISTANCE: Excellent
ARS RATING: 8.3
COMMENTS: Strong upright plants bear fragrant blooms. Deadhead for repeat bloom.

Bonica

BLOOM SIZE, TYPE: Small, double
FRAGRANCE: None
PLANT SIZE, HABIT: Medium, spreading
DISEASE RESISTANCE: Good
ARS RATING: 8.4
COMMENTS: Bonica bears large trusses of small light to deep pink blooms. The plant is strong with a spreading habit so may need support.

Buff Beauty

TYPE: Hybrid musk
BLOOM SIZE, TYPE: Medium, informal
FRAGRANCE: Medium
PLANT SIZE, HABIT: Medium to tall, spreading
DISEASE RESISTANCE: Good
ARS RATING: 8.2
COMMENTS: Medium, fragrant buff or apricot pompon blooms are carried in small clusters on tall, wide plants.

Carefree Beauty

TYPE: Buck
BLOOM SIZE, TYPE: Large, semidouble
FRAGRANCE: Heavy
PLANT SIZE, HABIT: Medium, upright
DISEASE RESISTANCE: Excellent
ARS RATING: 8.6
COMMENTS: Carefree Beauty is an Earth-Kind rose and the most widely grown Buck rose. Fragrant pink blooms open to show their stamens.

Champlain

TYPE: Hybrid kordesii
BLOOM SIZE, TYPE: Medium, semidouble
FRAGRANCE: Light
PLANT SIZE, HABIT: Short, bushy
DISEASE RESISTANCE: Good
ARS RATING: 8.5
COMMENTS: Champlain, part of the Explorer series, can be kept to a size of 4 feet wide and tall. Semidouble red blooms are borne in sprays.

Cherries 'n' Cream

BLOOM SIZE, TYPE: Medium, semidouble
FRAGRANCE: Medium
PLANT SIZE, HABIT: Medium, bushy
DISEASE RESISTANCE: Good
ARS RATING: 7.8
COMMENTS: Grow this rose for its clove-scented blooms, which are deep cerise pink with a white underside and touches of white around the petal edges. They're produced in small sprays.

Cocktail

BLOOM SIZE, TYPE: Small, single
FRAGRANCE: Light
PLANT SIZE, HABIT: Tall, bushy
DISEASE RESISTANCE: Good
ARS RATING: 8.4
COMMENTS: Solid red single blooms with large yellow eyes are borne in loose clusters on this French import from 1957. Use Cocktail as a moderate-size shrub or train it as a small climber.

Cornelia

TYPE: Hybrid musk
BLOOM SIZE, TYPE: Medium, double
FRAGRANCE: Medium
PLANT SIZE, HABIT: Medium to tall, bushy
DISEASE RESISTANCE: Good
ARS RATING: 8.7
COMMENTS: Deep pink blooms with yellow shadings fade to light pink on this highly rated rose. Small pompon flowers on large, bushy plants.

Countess Celeste

BLOOM SIZE, TYPE: Medium, very double
FRAGRANCE: Medium
PLANT SIZE, HABIT: Short, bushy
DISEASE RESISTANCE: Excellent
ARS RATING: 7.9
COMMENTS: This low-growing plant from Poulsen's of Denmark could well be considered a floribunda. The very double, coral pink blooms grow in small clusters on bushes that remain shorter than 3 feet.

Country Dancer

TYPE: Buck
BLOOM SIZE, TYPE: Large, semidouble
FRAGRANCE: Medium
PLANT SIZE, HABIT: Medium, bushy
DISEASE RESISTANCE: Good
ARS RATING: 8.6
COMMENTS: Like most Buck roses, Country Dancer is a hardy, medium-size plant with very good disease resistance. The fragrant, large deep pink blooms are carried in small clusters and singly.

Dortmund

TYPE: Hybrid kordesii
BLOOM SIZE, TYPE: Medium, single
FRAGRANCE: None
PLANT SIZE, HABIT: Tall, spreading
DISEASE RESISTANCE: Excellent
ARS RATING: 9.1
COMMENTS: The American Rose Society's highest rated shrub, this disease-free plant is covered with single red blossoms with white eyes and golden stamens.

Double Knock Out

TYPE: Knock Out
BLOOM SIZE, TYPE: Medium, double
FRAGRANCE: Light
PLANT SIZE, HABIT: Short, bushy
DISEASE RESISTANCE: Excellent
ARS RATING: 8.2
COMMENTS: This is from the same cross that produced the original Knock Out, but with cherry red double blooms.

Felicia

TYPE: Hybrid musk
BLOOM SIZE, TYPE: Small, informal
FRAGRANCE: Heavy
PLANT SIZE, HABIT: Tall, bushy
DISEASE RESISTANCE: Excellent
ARS RATING: 8.5
COMMENTS: This hybrid musk bears a strong resemblance to its sister, Cornelia. The plant is larger and its light pink blooms are more fragrant.

Flower Carpet

BLOOM SIZE, TYPE: Small, semidouble
FRAGRANCE: Light
PLANT SIZE, HABIT: Short, bushy
DISEASE RESISTANCE: Excellent
ARS RATING: 7.6
COMMENTS: The first in a family of low-growing plants, this disease-resistant variety has deep pink blooms in small clusters. The plant grows about 2 to 3 feet tall and more than 3 feet wide.

Flower Girl

BLOOM SIZE, TYPE: Small, single
FRAGRANCE: Light
PLANT SIZE, HABIT: Medium, spreading
DISEASE RESISTANCE: Good
ARS RATING: 8.2
COMMENTS: Small, light pink blooms that fade to white are borne in large clusters. With a size of 5 feet tall by 4 feet wide, this very floriferous shrub fits most any landscape.

Flutterbye

BLOOM SIZE, TYPE: Medium, single
FRAGRANCE: Medium
PLANT SIZE, HABIT: Tall, spreading
DISEASE RESISTANCE: Good
ARS RATING: 7.7
COMMENTS: Small yellow single flowers with shades of coral, orange, tangerine, and pink seem to dance in the sun like exotic butterflies. Spicy-scented blooms are carried in large, somewhat irregular clusters.

Fred Loads

BLOOM SIZE, TYPE: Medium, single
FRAGRANCE: Light
PLANT SIZE, HABIT: Tall, upright
DISEASE RESISTANCE: Good
ARS RATING: 8.5
COMMENTS: Brilliant orange blooms in large sprays, very sturdy canes, and a comparatively upright growth habit with canes about 10 feet long characterize this award winner.

Funny Face

TYPE: Easy Elegance
BLOOM SIZE, TYPE: Large, semidouble
FRAGRANCE: Light
PLANT SIZE, HABIT: Short, upright
DISEASE RESISTANCE: Good
ARS RATING: 7.7
COMMENTS: Small plants bear distinctive blooms of deep pink with white edges and yellow eyes. Part of the Easy Elegance series, Funny Face grows on its own roots and deserves a wider audience.

Gartendirektor Otto Linne

BLOOM SIZE, TYPE: Small, double
FRAGRANCE: Light
PLANT SIZE, HABIT: Medium, spreading
DISEASE RESISTANCE: Excellent
ARS RATING: 8.8
COMMENTS: Large clusters of medium pink blooms make this a very popular and highly rated variety. Introduced in 1934 and named for the first garden director in Hamburg, Germany, it is still going strong.

Golden Wings

BLOOM SIZE, TYPE: Large, single
FRAGRANCE: None
PLANT SIZE, HABIT: Medium, bushy
DISEASE RESISTANCE: Excellent
ARS RATING: 8.8
COMMENTS: The large light yellow single blooms with orange-red stamens dazzle in the light. Blooms form in sprays of three to five on strong, angular plants that grow about 5 feet tall and wide.

Grace

TYPE: Austin
BLOOM SIZE, TYPE: Large, very double
FRAGRANCE: Heavy
PLANT SIZE, HABIT: Medium, spreading
DISEASE RESISTANCE: Excellent
ARS RATING: 8.0
COMMENTS: Plants grow about 4 feet tall and wide, with small sprays of fragrant warm buff-apricot blooms that fade to light yellow.

Graham Thomas

TYPE: Austin
BLOOM SIZE, TYPE: Large, double
FRAGRANCE: Medium
PLANT SIZE, HABIT: Tall, spreading
DISEASE RESISTANCE: Good
ARS RATING: 8.2
COMMENTS: Named for the United Kingdom's preeminent rosarian, Graham Thomas boasts fragrant deep yellow blooms growing in clusters on plants that can reach more than 12 feet tall.

Greetings

BLOOM SIZE, TYPE: Small, semidouble
FRAGRANCE: Light
PLANT SIZE, HABIT: Medium, upright
DISEASE RESISTANCE: Excellent
ARS RATING: 8.1
COMMENTS: Greetings carries huge, crowded trusses of small red-purple blooms with white eyes. The plant is a heavy bloomer and a good repeater.

Heart 'n' Soul

BLOOM SIZE, TYPE: Medium, semidouble
FRAGRANCE: Light
PLANT SIZE, HABIT: Medium, bushy
DISEASE RESISTANCE: Good
ARS RATING: 7.7
COMMENTS: This French variety, with white blooms that have a wide and deep cerise edge, produces best in northern gardens. Flowers are borne in medium-size sprays on 5-foot-tall plants.

Henry Hudson

TYPE: Hybrid rugosa
BLOOM SIZE, TYPE: Medium, semidouble
FRAGRANCE: Medium
PLANT SIZE, HABIT: Short, bushy
DISEASE RESISTANCE: Excellent
ARS RATING: 9.0
COMMENTS: A very hardy plant from Canada, this compact Explorer Series rose bears small sprays of white blooms.

Heritage

TYPE: Austin
BLOOM SIZE, TYPE: Medium, double
FRAGRANCE: Heavy
PLANT SIZE, HABIT: Medium, spreading
DISEASE RESISTANCE: Good
ARS RATING: 8.4
COMMENTS: Very fragrant, medium pink blooms in small sprays have a tendency to shatter quickly. The nearly thornless plant grows about 5 feet tall and 4 feet wide.

Home Run

BLOOM SIZE, TYPE: Medium, single
FRAGRANCE: None
PLANT SIZE, HABIT: Short, bushy
DISEASE RESISTANCE: Excellent
ARS RATING: 8.1
COMMENTS: Knock Out is one parent of this low grower that has velvety bright red blooms with prominent yellow stamens produced in small sprays. Grow Home Run for disease resistance.

Hope for Humanity

BLOOM SIZE, TYPE: Small, semidouble
FRAGRANCE: Light
PLANT SIZE, HABIT: Tall, bushy
DISEASE RESISTANCE: Good
ARS RATING: 8.0
COMMENTS: Named to commemorate the 100th anniversary of the Canadian Red Cross, this very hardy plant, good for northern gardens, bears small clusters of deep red, mildly fragrant flowers. It tolerates shade.

Jacqueline du Pré

BLOOM SIZE, TYPE: Large, semidouble
FRAGRANCE: Heavy
PLANT SIZE, HABIT: Medium, bushy
DISEASE RESISTANCE: Good
ARS RATING: 7.9
COMMENTS: Named for the late British cellist, this prolific bloomer carries very fragrant light pink ruffled blooms with reddish pink stamens. Jacqueline du Pré grows about 5 feet tall and wide.

John Cabot

TYPE: Hybrid kordesii
BLOOM SIZE, TYPE: Large, semidouble
FRAGRANCE: Light
PLANT SIZE, HABIT: Medium, spreading
DISEASE RESISTANCE: Excellent
ARS RATING: 8.8
COMMENTS: Red blooms form in small clusters and open quickly to reveal their stamens despite the large number of petals. Massive plants grow about 10 feet wide and tall. A member of the Explorer series.

John Davis

TYPE: Hybrid kordesii
BLOOM SIZE, TYPE: Large, double
FRAGRANCE: Heavy
PLANT SIZE, HABIT: Medium, spreading
DISEASE RESISTANCE: Excellent
ARS RATING: 8.7
COMMENTS: If you're looking for a very fragrant, hardy shrub with medium pink double blooms in large clusters, this is it. John Davis was an English explorer.

Kathleen

TYPE: Hybrid musk
BLOOM SIZE, TYPE: Small, single
FRAGRANCE: None
PLANT SIZE, HABIT: Tall, spreading
DISEASE RESISTANCE: Excellent
ARS RATING: 8.5
COMMENTS: One of the larger plants in the hybrid musk family, Kathleen grows canes that can reach 12 feet or longer.

Knock Out

TYPE: Knock Out, Earth-Kind
BLOOM SIZE, TYPE: Medium, semidouble
FRAGRANCE: None
PLANT SIZE, HABIT: Medium, bushy
DISEASE RESISTANCE: Excellent
ARS RATING: 8.6
COMMENTS: Cerise blooms grow in medium clusters on plants with unparalleled disease resistance. It's the top-selling rose in the world.

Lady Elsie May

BLOOM SIZE, TYPE: Medium, semidouble
FRAGRANCE: Light
PLANT SIZE, HABIT: Medium, bushy
DISEASE RESISTANCE: Excellent
ARS RATING: 8.3
COMMENTS: Lady Elsie May, an import from Germany, grows orange-pink blooms borne in small clusters on compact plants.

Lavender Dream

BLOOM SIZE, TYPE: Small, semidouble
FRAGRANCE: Medium
PLANT SIZE, HABIT: Medium, bushy
DISEASE RESISTANCE: Good
ARS RATING: 8.3
COMMENTS: Light pink blooms with lavender shadings adorn this variety from Holland. Blooms achieve better color in the shade. Plants grow about 6 feet wide and tall.

Leonard Dudley Braithwaite

TYPE: Austin
BLOOM SIZE, TYPE: Medium, very double
FRAGRANCE: Heavy
PLANT SIZE, HABIT: Tall, spreading
DISEASE RESISTANCE: Good
ARS RATING: 7.9
COMMENTS: This rose bears the largest and reddest blooms among the Austin roses. Flowers often grow singly and are ideal for cutting.

Linda Campbell

TYPE: Hybrid rugosa
BLOOM SIZE, TYPE: Medium, semidouble
FRAGRANCE: None
PLANT SIZE, HABIT: Tall, spreading
DISEASE RESISTANCE: Good
ARS RATING: 8.1
COMMENTS: The medium red blooms are borne in tight sprays on canes that grow 6 feet or longer.

Lyda Rose

BLOOM SIZE, TYPE: Small, single
FRAGRANCE: Medium
PLANT SIZE, HABIT: Medium, bushy
DISEASE RESISTANCE: Excellent
ARS RATING: 8.9
COMMENTS: Beautiful small white single blooms edged in lavender-pink cover medium to large bushes. The plant will tolerate shade but needs extra attention to keep it going.

Martha's Vineyard

BLOOM SIZE, TYPE: Small, semidouble
FRAGRANCE: Light
PLANT SIZE, HABIT: Short, bushy
DISEASE RESISTANCE: Good
ARS RATING: 8.3
COMMENTS: Profuse small bright-pink blooms cover this low-growing variety that grows about 4 feet wide and tall. Plants have good disease resistance and lend themselves well to low borders or mass plantings.

Mary Rose

TYPE: Austin
BLOOM SIZE, TYPE: Large, very double
FRAGRANCE: Medium
PLANT SIZE, HABIT: Medium, bushy
DISEASE RESISTANCE: Good
ARS RATING: 8.3
COMMENTS: This Austin rose has medium pink double blooms borne on medium-size plants. It will tolerate some shade.

Molineux

TYPE: Austin
BLOOM SIZE, TYPE: Large, very double
FRAGRANCE: Heavy
PLANT SIZE, HABIT: Medium, bushy
DISEASE RESISTANCE: Good
ARS RATING: 8.0
COMMENTS: Large deep yellow exceptionally fragrant blooms grow on this award-winning offspring of Graham Thomas.

Morden Blush

BLOOM SIZE, TYPE: Medium, double
FRAGRANCE: Light
PLANT SIZE, HABIT: Medium, bushy
DISEASE RESISTANCE: Good
ARS RATING: 8.0
COMMENTS: Morden Blush is one of the cold-hardy Parkland series roses bred at the Morden Research Station in Morden, Manitoba. It bears medium pink double blooms that fade to light pink on the petal edges. Blooms are borne singly and in small sprays.

Morden Centennial

BLOOM SIZE, TYPE: Large, double
FRAGRANCE: Light
PLANT SIZE, HABIT: Medium, spreading
DISEASE RESISTANCE: Good
ARS RATING: 8.4
COMMENTS: This variety bears large hot pink blooms in small clusters and singly. Plants grow 6 feet tall and wide. A member of the Parkland series, this cold-hardy rose was bred at the Morden Research Station in Manitoba.

Oranges 'n' Lemons

BLOOM SIZE, TYPE: Medium, double
FRAGRANCE: Light
PLANT SIZE, HABIT: Medium, spreading
DISEASE RESISTANCE: Good
ARS RATING: 7.6
COMMENTS: Striking, distinctive orange blooms with yellow stripes form in crowded sprays. The plants bear long canes with clusters of flowers at the ends.

Outta the Blue

BLOOM SIZE, TYPE: Large, double
FRAGRANCE: Heavy
PLANT SIZE, HABIT: Medium, bushy
DISEASE RESISTANCE: Good
ARS RATING: 7.9
COMMENTS: Rich magenta blooms with yellow at their bases characterize this manageable plant that reaches about 5 feet tall and wide. Fragrant flowers form in small sprays.

Penelope

TYPE: Hybrid musk
BLOOM SIZE, TYPE: Medium, semidouble
FRAGRANCE: Heavy
PLANT SIZE, HABIT: Large, bushy
DISEASE RESISTANCE: Excellent
ARS RATING: 8.8
COMMENTS: As with most of the hybrid musks, this variety can grow in partial shade. The soft pink blooms show large clusters of stamens on moderately tall, bushy plants.

Pink Meidiland

BLOOM SIZE, TYPE: Small, single
FRAGRANCE: Light
PLANT SIZE, HABIT: Medium, bushy
DISEASE RESISTANCE: Good
ARS RATING: 8.6
COMMENTS: One of a series of prolific, disease-resistant shrubs from Meilland of France, this variety has pink single blooms with white eyes. They are borne in small sprays on bushes about 5 feet tall and wide.

Prairie Princess

TYPE: Buck
BLOOM SIZE, TYPE: Large, semidouble
FRAGRANCE: Light
PLANT SIZE, HABIT: Medium to tall, bushy
DISEASE RESISTANCE: Good
ARS RATING: 8.5
COMMENTS: Coral pink blooms with prominent stamens adorn 6-foot-tall plants that in some areas grow equally wide.

Red Ribbons

BLOOM SIZE, TYPE: Small, semidouble
FRAGRANCE: None
PLANT SIZE, HABIT: Short, spreading
DISEASE RESISTANCE: Excellent
ARS RATING: 8.3
COMMENTS: A true groundcover rose, this German import has deep red blooms with prominent stamens. Flowers form in small clusters on plants that grow about 2½ feet tall and 8 feet wide.

Robusta

BLOOM SIZE, TYPE: Large, single
FRAGRANCE: None
PLANT SIZE, HABIT: Tall, spreading
DISEASE RESISTANCE: Good
ARS RATING: 8.8
COMMENTS: Robust is an understatement for this variety. The plant grows 10 feet tall or taller, the sprays of medium red single blooms are large, and the thorns are large and numerous. A heavy bloomer, it will create a sensation in any garden.

Sally Holmes

BLOOM SIZE, TYPE: Large, single
FRAGRANCE: Light
PLANT SIZE, HABIT: Tall, spreading
DISEASE RESISTANCE: Excellent
ARS RATING: 8.9
COMMENTS: This large, strong plant covers itself with huge sprays of large single blooms that start light pink and fade to white. The sprays are crowded unless they are continually disbudded, but their beauty is well worth the effort.

Sea Foam

TYPE: Earth-Kind
BLOOM SIZE, TYPE: Small, double
FRAGRANCE: Light
PLANT SIZE, HABIT: Medium, very spreading
DISEASE RESISTANCE: Excellent
ARS RATING: 8.2
COMMENTS: Sea Foam is a rampant, low-growing plant that can stretch to 12 feet and longer. It seldom grows taller than 2 feet.

Sparrieshoop

BLOOM SIZE, TYPE: Large, single
FRAGRANCE: Medium
PLANT SIZE, HABIT: Tall, upright
DISEASE RESISTANCE: Good
ARS RATING: 8.2
COMMENTS: Named for a town in Germany, this tall plant has strong canes that hold themselves up well. Light pink blooms with large golden stamens form in medium to large clusters that are great for cutting.

Sunrise Sunset

TYPE: Easy Elegance
BLOOM SIZE, TYPE: Small, semidouble
FRAGRANCE: Light
PLANT SIZE, HABIT: Short, spreading
DISEASE RESISTANCE: Excellent
ARS RATING: 8.2
COMMENTS: Pink-blend blooms with yellow at their bases are borne on short, spreading, dense plants with great disease resistance, perfect for low borders. Colors change over time and vary with the temperature.

Westerland

BLOOM SIZE, TYPE: Large, double
FRAGRANCE: Heavy
PLANT SIZE, HABIT: Tall, spreading
DISEASE RESISTANCE: Good
ARS RATING: 8.2
COMMENTS: Beautiful, wonderfully fragrant golden-apricot blooms are carried in medium to large clusters on plants that can reach 10 feet tall. The plant has good disease resistance and is a heavy bloomer if kept deadheaded.

White Meidiland

BLOOM SIZE, TYPE: Large, double
FRAGRANCE: Light
PLANT SIZE, HABIT: Medium, spreading
DISEASE RESISTANCE: Good
ARS RATING: 8.4
COMMENTS: Medium-size clusters of large white blooms are produced in great quantities on this medium-size plant.

William Baffin

TYPE: Hybrid kordesii
BLOOM SIZE, TYPE: Medium, semidouble
FRAGRANCE: Light
PLANT SIZE, HABIT: Large, bushy
DISEASE RESISTANCE: Excellent
ARS RATING: 8.9
COMMENTS: From the Canadian Explorer series, this rose has deep pink blooms with golden eyes. It is hardy and disease resistant.

Once-Blooming Old Garden Roses

Old Garden Roses have a reputation among gardeners, and even rose growers, of being large, sprawling disease-prone plants that don't flower much, but that's just not so.

It is true that some bloom only once, but they make up for that with a long bloom period of nearly two months. Plus, they flower heavily and are fairly disease resistant.

Hybrid gallicas are the exception to the general disease resistance of this rose family. They often show mildew on the new growth that forms after blooming is over.

Gardeners who don't have time to promptly deadhead roses appreciate once-blooming old roses. They don't need to be deadheaded as promptly because no amount of deadheading will promote more flowers.

Old Garden Roses include any variety that existed before 1867, which is when the first modern rose, a hybrid tea, was introduced. New roses created from older varieties can still be considered "old."

The hundreds of Old Garden Roses today are the remainders of a family that once numbered into the thousands. They survived because of their hardiness, the beauty of their blooms, and, perhaps most important, their heavenly fragrance.

The once-blooming Old Garden Roses profiled in this gallery—most rated higher than 8.0—still offer wonderful garden value today.

BLOOM FORM

SINGLE: 5 to 10 petals
SEMIDOUBLE: 10 to 20 petals
DOUBLE: 20 to 45 petals
VERY DOUBLE: More than 45 petals

PLANT SIZE

SHORT: Less than 3 feet tall
MEDIUM: 3 to 6 feet tall
TALL: More than 6 feet tall

Cabbage Rose

FAMILY: Centifolia
BLOOM SIZE, TYPE: Large, very double
FRAGRANCE: Heavy
PLANT SIZE, HABIT: Tall, spreading
DISEASE RESISTANCE: Good
ARS RATING: 8.3
COMMENTS: Large, very fragrant pink blooms packed with petals tend to nod and hang downward in an old-fashioned, romantic manner. The large plants need support.

Cardinal de Richelieu

FAMILY: Hybrid gallica
BLOOM SIZE, TYPE: Medium, very double
FRAGRANCE: Heavy
PLANT SIZE, HABIT: Medium, bushy
DISEASE RESISTANCE: Good
ARS RATING: 8.0
COMMENTS: Deep purple blooms with outstanding fragrance form in medium-size sprays. It grows 3 to 5 feet tall with thin, sprawling canes.

Celestial

FAMILY: Alba
BLOOM SIZE, TYPE: Large, semidouble
FRAGRANCE: Heavy
PLANT SIZE, HABIT: Tall, spreading
DISEASE RESISTANCE: Excellent
ARS RATING: 8.5
COMMENTS: Light pink blooms with prominent stamens are the hallmark of this variety. Like most albas, the bushy plants grow 6 to 8 feet tall.

Celsiana

FAMILY: Damask
BLOOM SIZE, TYPE: Large, semidouble
FRAGRANCE: Heavy
PLANT SIZE, HABIT: Medium, bushy
DISEASE RESISTANCE: Excellent
ARS RATING: 8.7
COMMENTS: Light pink blooms with a strong fragrance make this one of the most popular damasks. Plants reach about 5 feet tall with thin canes that are weighed down with the bloom.

Charles de Mills

FAMILY: Hybrid gallica
BLOOM SIZE, TYPE: Large, very double
FRAGRANCE: Heavy
PLANT SIZE, HABIT: Medium, bushy
DISEASE RESISTANCE: Good
ARS RATING: 8.4
COMMENTS: Deep purple blooms fade to a raspberry pink and are borne in small clusters on rather tall canes of this great hybrid gallica.

Communis (Common Moss)

FAMILY: Moss
BLOOM SIZE, TYPE: Large, very double
FRAGRANCE: Heavy
PLANT SIZE, HABIT: Medium, bushy
DISEASE RESISTANCE: Good
ARS RATING: 8.3
COMMENTS: Communis reaches about 6 feet and carries pink blooms singly and in small clusters.

Complicata
FAMILY: Hybrid gallica
BLOOM SIZE, TYPE: Large, single
FRAGRANCE: Medium
PLANT SIZE, HABIT: Tall, spreading
DISEASE RESISTANCE: Good
ARS RATING: 8.8
COMMENTS: Pink blooms grown singly and in small sprays exhibit very pronounced stamens. Complicata is one of the few single-petal gallicas.

Crested Moss
FAMILY: Centifolia
BLOOM SIZE, TYPE: Large, double
FRAGRANCE: Heavy
PLANT SIZE, HABIT: Medium, bushy
DISEASE RESISTANCE: Good
ARS RATING: 8.7
COMMENTS: Though the name has "moss" in it, this is a centifolia, the family that spawned moss roses. Fragrant rosy-pink blooms form in small clusters. As with Communis, it's also called Common Moss.

Fantin-Latour
FAMILY: Centifolia
BLOOM SIZE, TYPE: Large, double
FRAGRANCE: Medium
PLANT SIZE, HABIT: Medium, bushy
DISEASE RESISTANCE: Good
ARS RATING: 8.4
COMMENTS: Named for a French artist noted for his flower paintings, this rose bears warm pink blooms in medium-size clusters.

Félicité Parmentier
FAMILY: Alba
BLOOM SIZE, TYPE: Medium, very double
FRAGRANCE: Heavy
PLANT SIZE, HABIT: Medium, bushy
DISEASE RESISTANCE: Excellent
ARS RATING: 8.7
COMMENTS: A manageable-size plant for an alba, this variety has soft pink, very double blooms that grow in small sprays.

Great Maiden's Blush

FAMILY: Alba
BLOOM SIZE, TYPE: Medium, double
FRAGRANCE: Heavy
PLANT SIZE, HABIT: Tall, bushy
DISEASE RESISTANCE: Excellent
ARS RATING: 8.1
COMMENTS: Up to a dozen white blooms with pink-blush overtones form in large sprays. Bushes grow blue-green, very disease-resistant foliage.

Henri Martin

FAMILY: Moss
BLOOM SIZE, TYPE: Medium, semidouble
FRAGRANCE: Heavy
PLANT SIZE, HABIT: Medium, bushy
DISEASE RESISTANCE: Good
ARS RATING: 8.6
COMMENTS: Crimson blooms fade to deep pink on this lightly mossed variety. The flowers are borne in medium-size clusters on bushy, 6-foot-tall plants.

James Mason

FAMILY: Hybrid gallica
BLOOM SIZE, TYPE: Large, semidouble
FRAGRANCE: Medium
PLANT SIZE, HABIT: Tall, bushy
DISEASE RESISTANCE: Excellent
ARS RATING: 7.8
COMMENTS: Introduced in 1982 and named for the British actor, this sprawling rose bears large deep red blooms with golden stamens.

Königin von Dänemark

FAMILY: Alba
BLOOM SIZE, TYPE: Medium, very double
FRAGRANCE: Heavy
PLANT SIZE, HABIT: Medium, bushy
DISEASE RESISTANCE: Excellent
ARS RATING: 8.6
COMMENTS: With the pinkest blooms of all the albas, the "Queen of Denmark" grows about 6 feet tall. Blooms are carried in small clusters.

La Ville de Bruxelles

FAMILY: Damask
BLOOM SIZE, TYPE: Medium, very double
FRAGRANCE: Heavy
PLANT SIZE, HABIT: Medium, bushy
DISEASE RESISTANCE: Excellent
ARS RATING: 8.5
COMMENTS: Salmon pink flowers, heavily petaled and very fragrant, are borne in small sprays on disease-resistant plants up to 5 feet tall. La Ville de Bruxelles is French for "The City of Brussels."

Léda

FAMILY: Damask
BLOOM SIZE, TYPE: Medium, double
FRAGRANCE: Medium
PLANT SIZE, HABIT: Short, bushy
DISEASE RESISTANCE: Good
ARS RATING: 8.3
COMMENTS: Sometimes called Painted Damask, this variety may rebloom, rare for a damask. White blooms with tinges of blush and crimson at the petals' edges grow on compact plants.

Madame Hardy

FAMILY: Damask
BLOOM SIZE, TYPE: Medium, very double
FRAGRANCE: Heavy
PLANT SIZE, HABIT: Tall, bushy
DISEASE RESISTANCE: Excellent
ARS RATING: 8.9
COMMENTS: Pure white blooms with green button eyes are borne in medium-size sprays.

Madame Plantier

FAMILY: Alba
BLOOM SIZE, TYPE: Medium, very double
FRAGRANCE: Heavy
PLANT SIZE, HABIT: Tall, spreading
DISEASE RESISTANCE: Good
ARS RATING: 8.8
COMMENTS: This alba has long, arching canes up to 12 feet long. Creamy-white blooms are borne in clusters on nearly thornless plants.

Madame Zöetmans

FAMILY: Damask
BLOOM SIZE, TYPE: Medium, very double
FRAGRANCE: Medium
PLANT SIZE, HABIT: Medium, bushy
DISEASE RESISTANCE: Excellent
ARS RATING: 8.7
COMMENTS: Often compared with Mme Hardy, this damask has smaller blooms that start light pink and fade to white. They grow singly and in small clusters on smaller plants, about 5 feet tall.

Paul Ricault

FAMILY: Centifolia
BLOOM SIZE, TYPE: Large, double
FRAGRANCE: Heavy
PLANT SIZE, HABIT: Tall, spreading
DISEASE RESISTANCE: Good
ARS RATING: 7.6
COMMENTS: Deep pink, intensely fragrant blooms with lots of petals are borne mostly singly on long-caned arching plants. The flowers have an unusual, appealing crepe-paper appearance.

Tuscany

FAMILY: Hybrid gallica
BLOOM SIZE, TYPE: Large, semidouble
FRAGRANCE: Heavy
PLANT SIZE, HABIT: Medium, bushy
DISEASE RESISTANCE: Good
ARS RATING: 8.5
COMMENTS: Velvety black-crimson blooms with stamens that leap out make this a very popular variety. Plants bear thin canes 4 to 5 feet long.

Veilchenblau

FAMILY: Hybrid multiflora
BLOOM SIZE, TYPE: Small, semidouble
FRAGRANCE: Medium
PLANT SIZE, HABIT: Tall, rambling
DISEASE RESISTANCE: Good
ARS RATING: 8.4
COMMENTS: Consider it a rambler with canes 15 feet long. Large trusses of small purple blooms grow on nearly thornless stems.

Reblooming Old Garden Roses

The world of roses experienced a major change in the early 19th century with the introduction of reblooming roses from China.

These reblooming roses from China were crossed and recrossed by French rose breeders to develop hundreds of reblooming roses. France's moderate climate allowed many new roses, many of which bore French names. This crossbreeding also led to a long list of reblooming families. Chinas, teas, and noisettes do particularly well in warm or hot weather, and they're grown well and extensively in the southern United States. Bourbons, hybrid perpetuals, and Portlands seem to do equally well in all parts of the country.

The reblooming habit of Old Garden Roses can't be compared with modern roses that repeat rapidly. These roses generally have an initial flush that's moderately heavy, followed by lighter, sporadic blooms for the rest of the growing season. To encourage a quicker rebloom, deadhead old flowers immediately.

Color behaves in interesting ways among reblooming Old Garden Roses. A hallmark of the noisette family is a palette of yellows: dark, light, creamy, orange, and more. Chinas have a delightful habit of blooms that deepen in color as they age.

Growth habits among these families vary wildly. The bourbons and noisettes can be considered small climbers and should either be supported or allowed to cascade. Hybrid perpetuals tend to grow tall on fairly sturdy plants. Teas, chinas, and portlands display a variety of growth habits.

BLOOM FORM

SINGLE: 5 to 10 petals
SEMIDOUBLE: 10 to 20 petals
DOUBLE: 20 to 45 petals
VERY DOUBLE: More than 45 petals

PLANT SIZE

SHORT: Less than 3 feet tall
MEDIUM: 3 to 6 feet tall
TALL: More than 6 feet tall

Alister Stella Gray

FAMILY: Noisette
BLOOM SIZE, TYPE: Medium, double
FRAGRANCE: Medium
PLANT SIZE, HABIT: Tall, spreading
DISEASE RESISTANCE: Good
ARS RATING: 8.0
COMMENTS: Pale yellow flowers with amber centers borne in small clusters adorn the long (up to 15 feet) canes of this noisette.

Archduke Charles

FAMILY: China
BLOOM SIZE, TYPE: Medium, double
FRAGRANCE: Light
PLANT SIZE, HABIT: Short to medium, bushy
DISEASE RESISTANCE: Good
ARS RATING: 8.5
COMMENTS: Blooms start out rosy pink and turn crimson as they age. They are produced in small sprays on tidy 5- to 6-foot-tall plants.

Autumn Damask

FAMILY: Damask
BLOOM SIZE, TYPE: Medium, double
FRAGRANCE: Medium
PLANT SIZE, HABIT: Medium, bushy
DISEASE RESISTANCE: Excellent
ARS RATING: 8.2
COMMENTS: Except for Léda, with its occasional late blossoms, this is the only reblooming damask. Warm pink blooms in small clusters grow on bushy plants with thin 5-foot canes.

Baronne Prévost

FAMILY: Hybrid perpetual
BLOOM SIZE, TYPE: Large, double
FRAGRANCE: Medium
PLANT SIZE, HABIT: Medium, upright
DISEASE RESISTANCE: Good
ARS RATING: 8.6
COMMENTS: Deep pink blooms in small sprays adorn sturdy, productive plants with good rebloom. The flowers are carried in small sprays and have a moderate aroma.

Boule de Neige

FAMILY: Bourbon
BLOOM SIZE, TYPE: Medium, very double
FRAGRANCE: Medium
PLANT SIZE, HABIT: Tall, bushy
DISEASE RESISTANCE: Good
ARS RATING: 7.9
COMMENTS: The name ("snowball" in French) describes the globular white blooms, which are moderately fragrant and borne in small sprays.

Comte de Chambord

FAMILY: Portland
BLOOM SIZE, TYPE: Medium, very double
FRAGRANCE: Heavy
PLANT SIZE, HABIT: Medium, upright
DISEASE RESISTANCE: Good
ARS RATING: 8.3
COMMENTS: Perfect for the landscape, this rose grows upright and 2 to 3 feet wide. Fragrant pink blooms grow in sprays and repeat nicely.

Cramoisi Supérieur

FAMILY: China
BLOOM SIZE, TYPE: Small, double
FRAGRANCE: Medium
PLANT SIZE, HABIT: Medium, bushy
DISEASE RESISTANCE: Good
ARS RATING: 8.7
COMMENTS: Small crimson (*cramoisi* in French) blooms with a nice aroma grow in small to medium sprays. Medium-size vigorous plants have a good repeat habit.

Duchesse de Brabant

FAMILY: Tea
BLOOM SIZE, TYPE: Large, double
FRAGRANCE: Heavy
PLANT SIZE, HABIT: Medium to tall, bushy
DISEASE RESISTANCE: Excellent
ARS RATING: 8.6
COMMENTS: A designated Earth-Kind variety, this rather tall tea rose has soft rosy-pink blooms with yellow highlights borne in small sprays. Plants reach more than 8 feet tall in warm areas.

Gloire de Dijon

FAMILY: Climbing tea
BLOOM SIZE, TYPE: Large, very double
FRAGRANCE: Medium
PLANT SIZE, HABIT: Tall, spreading
DISEASE RESISTANCE: Good
ARS RATING: 7.8
COMMENTS: Often wrongly labelled as a noisette, this long-caned rose has buff-pink blooms shaded with orange at the centers.

Jaune Desprez

FAMILY: Noisette
BLOOM SIZE, TYPE: Medium, double
FRAGRANCE: Medium
PLANT SIZE, HABIT: Tall, spreading
DISEASE RESISTANCE: Good
ARS RATING: 7.9
COMMENTS: Coppery yellow-pink blooms with a moderate fruity fragrance are borne in small sprays. Canes grow up to 20 feet long.

La Reine

FAMILY: Hybrid perpetual
BLOOM SIZE, TYPE: Large, very double
FRAGRANCE: Heavy
PLANT SIZE, HABIT: Medium
DISEASE RESISTANCE: Good
ARS RATING: 8.0
COMMENTS: Large rosy-pink blooms with good aroma grace "The Queen," an early member of the hybrid perpetual family from 1842. The bush is a manageable size of about 5 feet.

Louise Odier

FAMILY: Bourbon
BLOOM SIZE, TYPE: Medium, double
FRAGRANCE: Heavy
PLANT SIZE, HABIT: Tall, spreading
DISEASE RESISTANCE: Fair
ARS RATING: 8.4
COMMENTS: Think of this rose as a short climber that reaches 8 to 10 feet. Pink blooms are very fragrant, growing in small sprays. The bush is a heavy bloomer and a good repeater.

Madame Alfred Carrière

FAMILY: Noisette
BLOOM SIZE, TYPE: Medium, double
FRAGRANCE: Heavy
PLANT SIZE, HABIT: Tall, spreading
DISEASE RESISTANCE: Good
ARS RATING: 8.9
COMMENTS: A large rose, this light noisette bears white blooms with hints of pink. Small bloom sprays bear a fruity fragrance.

Madame Ernest Calvat

FAMILY: Bourbon
BLOOM SIZE, TYPE: Large, double
FRAGRANCE: Heavy
PLANT SIZE, HABIT: Medium to tall, spreading
DISEASE RESISTANCE: Good
ARS RATING: 8.1
COMMENTS: Pink blooms are fragrant and have a lighter shade on the outer petals. This variety is a good repeat bloomer.

Madame Isaac Pereire

FAMILY: Bourbon
BLOOM SIZE, TYPE: Large, very double
FRAGRANCE: Heavy
PLANT SIZE, HABIT: Medium to tall, spreading
DISEASE RESISTANCE: Good
ARS RATING: 8.4
COMMENTS: Considered the most fragrant Old Garden Rose with intense raspberry aroma, its deep-pink blooms are cupped and quartered. Bushy plants grow to 8 feet and need support.

Madame Pierre Oger

FAMILY: Bourbon
BLOOM SIZE, TYPE: Very double
FRAGRANCE: Heavy
PLANT SIZE, HABIT: Tall, spreading
DISEASE RESISTANCE: Good
ARS RATING: 8.0
COMMENTS: Fragrant very double blooms have a rosy-lilac underside and a pronounced globular form. This typical bourbon plant, about 8 feet tall, requires some disease protection.

Marchesa Boccella

FAMILY: Hybrid perpetual
BLOOM SIZE, TYPE: Large, very double
FRAGRANCE: Medium
PLANT SIZE, HABIT: Medium, upright
DISEASE RESISTANCE: Excellent
ARS RATING: 9.0
COMMENTS: Large pink blooms grow singly on stems that invite cutting. The 4-foot-tall upright plant has excellent disease resistance.

Marchioness of Lorne

FAMILY: Hybrid perpetual
BLOOM SIZE, TYPE: Large, double
FRAGRANCE: Heavy
PLANT SIZE, HABIT: Medium, upright
DISEASE RESISTANCE: Good
ARS RATING: 8.1
COMMENTS: Deep carmine-pink blooms with outstanding fragrance grow in small sprays on strong, upright plants with good repeat habits.

Mermaid
FAMILY: Hybrid bracteata
BLOOM SIZE, TYPE: Large, single
FRAGRANCE: Medium
PLANT SIZE, HABIT: Tall, spreading
DISEASE RESISTANCE: Excellent
ARS RATING: 8.6
COMMENTS: This species hybrid grows with a rampant—20 foot—habit. The large blooms, borne mostly singly, are pale yellow with deep yellow centers and stamens.

Mrs. B. R. Cant
FAMILY: Tea
BLOOM SIZE, TYPE: Large, double
FRAGRANCE: Medium
PLANT SIZE, HABIT: Tall, bushy
DISEASE RESISTANCE: Good
ARS RATING: 8.9
COMMENTS: A tea rose that grows more than 6 feet tall in warm areas, Mrs. B. R. Cant bears silvery-pink blooms with buff undertones, borne singly and in small clusters.

Mutabilis
FAMILY: China
BLOOM SIZE, TYPE: Medium, single
FRAGRANCE: Light
PLANT SIZE, HABIT: Tall, bushy
DISEASE RESISTANCE: Excellent
ARS RATING: 8.9
COMMENTS: Single blooms start out buff yellow, darken to pink, and finally turn crimson; all colors appear together on this Earth-Kind rose.

Old Blush
FAMILY: China
BLOOM SIZE, TYPE: Medium, double
FRAGRANCE: Medium
PLANT SIZE, HABIT: Medium, bushy
DISEASE RESISTANCE: Good
ARS RATING: 8.7
COMMENTS: Old Blush grows two-tone pink blooms in small clusters. Moderate-size plants can reach 6 feet in warm areas.

Reine des Violettes

FAMILY: Hybrid perpetual
BLOOM SIZE, TYPE: Large, very double
FRAGRANCE: Heavy
PLANT SIZE, HABIT: Tall, spreading
DISEASE RESISTANCE: Excellent
ARS RATING: 8.2
COMMENTS: "Queen of the Violets" has large purple blooms that are considered the bluest of all the old roses. The plant, which needs support, is tall and angular with relatively thin canes.

Rose de Rescht

FAMILY: Portland
BLOOM SIZE, TYPE: Medium, double
FRAGRANCE: Medium
PLANT SIZE, HABIT: Short, bushy
DISEASE RESISTANCE: Excellent
ARS RATING: 8.8
COMMENTS: Cerise pompon blooms grow singly or in small sprays on short, compact plants with very disease-resistant foliage. This is a perfect choice for a small garden or container.

Salet

FAMILY: Moss
BLOOM SIZE, TYPE: Large, double
FRAGRANCE: Medium
PLANT SIZE, HABIT: Medium, upright
DISEASE RESISTANCE: Good
ARS RATING: 8.2
COMMENTS: Salet has clear pink blooms with a lighter underside. They grow in small sprays with well-mossed sepals; good rebloom habit.

Souvenir de la Malmaison

FAMILY: Bourbon
BLOOM SIZE, TYPE: Large, double
FRAGRANCE: Heavy
PLANT SIZE, HABIT: Short, bushy
DISEASE RESISTANCE: Excellent
ARS RATING: 8.7
COMMENTS: Pale pink flowers with rosy centers are carried on plants that seldom grow taller than 3 feet. The blooms are very fragrant.

Stanwell Perpetual

FAMILY: Hybrid spinosissima
BLOOM SIZE, TYPE: Medium, semidouble
FRAGRANCE: Heavy
PLANT SIZE, HABIT: Tall, very bushy
DISEASE RESISTANCE: Excellent
ARS RATING: 8.6
COMMENTS: The canes of this large bushy plant are covered with hundreds of small thorns, and it seems never to be out of bloom. Soft pink flowers fade to white and have exceptional fragrance.

Variegata di Bologna

FAMILY: Bourbon
BLOOM SIZE, TYPE: Large, double
FRAGRANCE: Medium
PLANT SIZE, HABIT: Tall, spreading
DISEASE RESISTANCE: Good
ARS RATING: 8.0
COMMENTS: Fragrant white blooms with red-purple stripes are borne singly and in small clusters. A typical bourbon plant, it grows as tall as 8 feet.

Yolande d'Aragon

FAMILY: Portland
BLOOM SIZE, TYPE: Large, very double
FRAGRANCE: Heavy
PLANT SIZE, HABIT: Medium, bushy
DISEASE RESISTANCE: Good
ARS RATING: 8.4
COMMENTS: Heavily fragrant deep pink blooms adorn strong plants. The flowers are produced singly and in small sprays.

Zéphirine Drouhin

FAMILY: Bourbon
BLOOM SIZE, TYPE: Medium, semidouble
FRAGRANCE: Medium
PLANT SIZE, HABIT: Tall, spreading
DISEASE RESISTANCE: Good
ARS RATING: 8.1
COMMENTS: Nearly thornless canes of this vigorous rose can grow more than 10 feet. Profuse flowers are silvery pink with a nice fragrance.

Species

Species roses are wild roses that naturally interbreed with each other. Most have single blooms, but a few have double and even very double flowers.

Species roses are generally pink or white, but you'll also find some yellows and deep pinks to light reds. Sadly, these beauties do not rebloom, but species roses are great for the garden because they offer more than just flowers. Interesting foliage, bark, thorns, and hips all add elements of shape and color. Grow *Rosa sericea pteracantha* for its showy red thorns and white spring flowers.

It's a misconception that all species roses are very large plants. Many have the size and habit of large shrubs, reaching about 6 to 10 feet tall by 4 to 5 feet wide, but some grow 1 or 2 feet shorter and narrower.

Some species roses grow in several forms. *R. banksiae*, for example, has six variations, each with different bloom colors and forms. The largest rose bush in the world is a *banksiae*, covering more than 8,000 square feet in Tombstone, Arizona.

Approximately a dozen species are native to North America. In the Southeast, you may encounter *R. palustris*, the swamp rose. The species known as the prairie rose, *R. blanda*, is native to the Midwest. From the Pacific Northwest to Alaska, the nootka rose, *R. nutkana*, grows wild.

Because few local nurseries sell species roses, check with mail-order sources.

BLOOM SIZE

SMALL: Less than 2 inches wide
MEDIUM: 2 to 4 inches wide
LARGE: More than 4 inches wide

PLANT SIZE

SHORT: Less than 2 feet tall
MEDIUM: 2 to 4 feet tall
TALL: More than 4 feet tall

Rosa banksiae lutea (Yellow Lady Banks' Rose)

BLOOM SIZE, TYPE: Small, double
FRAGRANCE: Light
PLANT SIZE, HABIT: Large, spreading
DISEASE RESISTANCE: Excellent
ARS RATING: 9.1
COMMENTS: Lady Banks' roses were named for the wife of British plantsman Sir Joseph Banks. This rose has solid yellow double blooms borne in large clusters on plants good for warm-climate gardens.

Rosa gallica versicolor (*Rosa mundi*)

BLOOM SIZE, TYPE: Large, semidouble
FRAGRANCE: Moderate
PLANT SIZE, HABIT: Short, bushy
DISEASE RESISTANCE: Good
ARS RATING: 9.0
COMMENTS: The most popular striped species rose is a sport of *R. gallica officinalis*. White blooms are mottled with medium to deep pink. Nicely fragrant small clusters grace 4-foot-tall plants.

Rosa hugonis

BLOOM SIZE, TYPE: Medium, single
FRAGRANCE: Light
PLANT SIZE, HABIT: Medium, bushy
DISEASE RESISTANCE: Excellent
ARS RATING: 8.6
COMMENTS: Reportedly brought from China by a priest in the late 19th century, this rose is often sold as Father Hugo's rose. Solid yellow single flowers grow on a thorny, disease-resistant plant about 9 feet tall. It produces deep scarlet hips in the fall.

Rosa macrantha

BLOOM SIZE, TYPE: Large, single
FRAGRANCE: Light
PLANT SIZE, HABIT: Large, spreading
DISEASE RESISTANCE: Excellent
ARS RATING: 8.0
COMMENTS: This variety has large delicate pink single blooms that age to pure white. They are borne in small clusters on large, spreading thin-caned plants reaching 15 to 20 feet. *Macrantha* means "large flowered" in Latin.

Rosa rubrifolia (Rosa glauca)

BLOOM SIZE, TYPE: Small, single
FRAGRANCE: Light
PLANT SIZE, HABIT: Medium, bushy
DISEASE RESISTANCE: Excellent
ARS RATING: 8.8
COMMENTS: *Rubrifolia* means "red leaves" but an earlier species name is *Rosa glauca*, meaning "gray." Both refer to the blue-green foliage with pink overtones. Vivid pink single blooms feature white eyes.

Rosa rugosa

BLOOM SIZE, TYPE: Medium, single
FRAGRANCE: Light
PLANT SIZE, HABIT: Medium, bushy
DISEASE RESISTANCE: Excellent
ARS RATING: 9.1
COMMENTS: Purple-red single blooms up to 4 inches wide with golden yellow stamens make this an attractive landscape plant. Hardy plants reach about 6 feet tall. In the fall, large red hips form.

Miniatures

Perfect for containers, miniatures delight with their perfect tiny imitations of hybrid teas and floribundas.

Miniatures are generally hardy and produce profuse quantities of blooms throughout the growing season. Miniatures are good choices to edge borders or to plant as accent specimens in mixed gardens or rose gardens.

These small wonders, like other modern roses, originated from wild Chinese roses. *Rosa chinensis minima* was brought to England in the early 1800s, but hybridizing with this miniature species didn't pick up until the 1930s.

For two decades European breeders dominated the market before American Ralph Moore created Centennial Miss in 1952.

It took a while for miniatures to catch on with the rose-buying public, but their beauty and ability to fit into small spaces have made them extremely popular. Another plus: They're generally hardier than hybrid tea roses.

Although large rose companies, such as Weeks Roses, Jackson & Perkins, and Conard-Pyle, often introduce new miniatures, most new varieties come from nursery growers and amateur breeders seeking new forms and colors.

For the best results, select a miniature rose from a nursery or catalog, not a supermarket or florist. Florist miniatures are designed as indoor plants to be discarded after they finish blooming.

Because the American Rose Society requires petite blooms for rose show judging, a bloom size between 1 to 2 inches is standard for miniatures.

PLANT SIZE

SHORT: Less than 1 foot tall
MEDIUM: 1 to 2½ feet tall
TALL: More than 2½ feet tall

PLANT HABIT

UPRIGHT: Less than 1 foot wide
BUSHY: 1 to 2½ feet wide
SPREADING: More than 2½ feet wide

Acey Deucy

BLOOM FORM: Classic
FRAGRANCE: Light
PLANT SIZE, HABIT: Medium, bushy
DISEASE RESISTANCE: Good
ARS RATING: 7.7
COMMENTS: Medium red blooms that resemble small hybrid teas grow mostly singly on moderate-size plants.

Baby Grand

BLOOM FORM: Informal
FRAGRANCE: Light
PLANT SIZE, HABIT: Medium, bushy
DISEASE RESISTANCE: Excellent
ARS RATING: 8.6
COMMENTS: The multiple blooms that grow in small sprays lend Baby Grand the look of a dwarf Old Garden Rose. Flowers are slightly fragrant, borne on highly disease-resistant plants.

Baby Love

BLOOM FORM: Single
FRAGRANCE: Light
PLANT SIZE, HABIT: Tall, spreading
DISEASE RESISTANCE: Excellent
ARS RATING: 8.0
COMMENTS: Buttercup yellow single blooms grow mostly singly on large, bushy plants. Baby Love is revered for its superb disease resistance.

Bees Knees

BLOOM FORM: Classic
FRAGRANCE: Light
PLANT SIZE, HABIT: Medium, bushy
DISEASE RESISTANCE: Good
ARS RATING: 8.0
COMMENTS: The blooms are a gorgeous combination of white with warm apricot centers and pink petal edges. Flowers are borne in large clusters.

Black Jade

BLOOM FORM: Classic
FRAGRANCE: Light
PLANT SIZE, HABIT: Medium, bushy
DISEASE RESISTANCE: Good
ARS RATING: 8.0
COMMENTS: Probably the darkest rose of any type, Black Jade's deep red blooms contrast with golden stamens. Flowers are borne mostly singly on medium-size plants.

Child's Play

BLOOM FORM: Classic
FRAGRANCE: Medium
PLANT SIZE, HABIT: Medium, upright
DISEASE RESISTANCE: Good
ARS RATING: 8.0
COMMENTS: Porcelain-white flowers with pink petal edges contrast beautifully with deep green foliage. Blooms are borne singly or in small clusters.

Cinderella

BLOOM FORM: Informal
FRAGRANCE: Medium
PLANT SIZE, HABIT: Short
DISEASE RESISTANCE: Good
ARS RATING: 8.1
COMMENTS: This rose has been on the market for more than 50 years, primarily because the short plant covers itself with small white blooms. It's ideal for containers.

Crazy Dottie

BLOOM FORM: Single
FRAGRANCE: Light
PLANT SIZE, HABIT: Medium, bushy
DISEASE RESISTANCE: Good
ARS RATING: 8.0
COMMENTS: Named after a friend of the hybridizer, Crazy Dottie has eye-catching brilliant orange single blooms with copper-yellow centers. They're borne singly and in small sprays.

Cupcake

BLOOM FORM: Classic
FRAGRANCE: Light
PLANT SIZE, HABIT: Medium, bushy
DISEASE RESISTANCE: Excellent
ARS RATING: 8.0
COMMENTS: Clear pink flowers with somewhat darker centers are carried in small clusters. Blooms are long-lasting as cut flowers, growing one per stem and in sprays.

Dancing Flame

BLOOM FORM: Classic
FRAGRANCE: Light
PLANT SIZE, HABIT: Medium, bushy
DISEASE RESISTANCE: Good
ARS RATING: 7.7
COMMENTS: The name suits the golden blooms with red edges. Flowers are carried mostly one per stem.

Giggles

BLOOM FORM: Classic
FRAGRANCE: Light
PLANT SIZE, HABIT: Tall, upright
DISEASE RESISTANCE: Light
ARS RATING: 8.8
COMMENTS: Soft coral pink blooms with classic form boost this rose's rating. The plant is on the tall side, with medium green matte foliage.

Gizmo

BLOOM FORM: Single
FRAGRANCE: None
PLANT SIZE, HABIT: Medium, bushy
DISEASE RESISTANCE: Good
ARS RATING: 7.9
COMMENTS: Small brilliant orange-red blooms form in small clusters on this medium-size plant. It works well in the landscape, but don't count on it for cutting.

Gourmet Popcorn

BLOOM FORM: Informal
FRAGRANCE: Light
PLANT SIZE, HABIT: Medium, spreading
DISEASE RESISTANCE: Excellent
ARS RATING: 8.7
COMMENTS: Blooms resemble a bowl of popcorn with a dollop of butter in the center of each popped kernel. The small blooms liberally cover low-growing, spreading plants.

Grace Seward

BLOOM FORM: Single
FRAGRANCE: Medium
PLANT SIZE, HABIT: Tall, bushy
DISEASE RESISTANCE: Good
ARS RATING: 8.2
COMMENTS: Named after a notable California rosarian, the pure white single flowers of Grace Deward sport very large golden stamens on plants with good repeat bloom.

Green Ice

BLOOM FORM: Double
FRAGRANCE: Light
PLANT SIZE, HABIT: Short, bushy
DISEASE RESISTANCE: Good
ARS RATING: 8.0
COMMENTS: Looking for something a little different for a container? Short, very floriferous plants produce small white blooms touched with pink and green as they develop.

Heartbreaker

BLOOM FORM: Classic
FRAGRANCE: Light
PLANT SIZE, HABIT: Medium, bushy
DISEASE RESISTANCE: Good
ARS RATING: 7.9
COMMENTS: White blooms suffused with pink in varying degrees form in small sprays. Disbudding will produce larger individual flowers.

Hot Tamale

BLOOM FORM: Classic
FRAGRANCE: Light
PLANT SIZE, HABIT: Medium, bushy
DISEASE RESISTANCE: Good
ARS RATING: 8.3
COMMENTS: Golden yellow-orange blooms with glowing pink petal edges make this rose a standout in the garden. Bushy plants bear medium green foliage.

Incognito

BLOOM FORM: Classic
FRAGRANCE: Light
PLANT SIZE, HABIT: Medium, upright
DISEASE RESISTANCE: Good
ARS RATING: 8.0
COMMENTS: Unusual, distinctive violet blooms overlaid with russet brown and a yellow underside are nicely set against the dark green semiglossy foliage.

Irresistible

BLOOM FORM: Classic
FRAGRANCE: Medium, spicy
PLANT SIZE, HABIT: Tall, upright
DISEASE RESISTANCE: Excellent
ARS RATING: 9.0
COMMENTS: One of the top-rated exhibition miniatures, this white beauty with the palest of pink centers also does well in the garden. Cut some for the spicy fragrance.

Jean Kenneally

BLOOM FORM: Classic
FRAGRANCE: Light
PLANT SIZE, HABIT: Tall, upright
DISEASE RESISTANCE: Excellent
ARS RATING: 9.1
COMMENTS: This apricot-pink rose, with the highest ARS rating for a miniature, was named for a beloved California rosarian. Blooms grow mostly singly on long stems that are perfect for cutting.

Jeanne Lajoie

BLOOM FORM: Classic
FRAGRANCE: Medium
PLANT SIZE, HABIT: Tall, spreading
DISEASE RESISTANCE: Fair
ARS RATING: 9.1
COMMENTS: The pink blooms on this climber are true miniatures, but the plant itself grows as a large, spreading mound with canes up to 12 feet long. It requires protection against black spot.

Kristin

BLOOM FORM: Classic
FRAGRANCE: Light
PLANT SIZE, HABIT: Medium, bushy
DISEASE RESISTANCE: Good
ARS RATING: 8.1
COMMENTS: White blooms with yellow centers and deep cerise-pink edges are borne singly and in small clusters. A climbing form is available.

Lemon Drop

BLOOM FORM: Classic
FRAGRANCE: Light
PLANT SIZE, HABIT: Medium, bushy
DISEASE RESISTANCE: Excellent
ARS RATING: 7.8
COMMENTS: Solid yellow roses of any kind are relatively scarce, so this 1999 introduction is a good addition to the family. Blooms are carried in small sprays.

Little Artist

BLOOM FORM: Semidouble
FRAGRANCE: Light
PLANT SIZE, HABIT: Short to medium, bushy
DISEASE RESISTANCE: Good
ARS RATING: 8.4
COMMENTS: This "hand-painted" rose from breeder Sam McGredy grows red blooms with white eyes and deeper red brushings. Blooms are carried primarily in sprays.

Little Jackie

BLOOM FORM: Classic
FRAGRANCE: Moderate
PLANT SIZE, HABIT: Medium, upright
DISEASE RESISTANCE: Good
ARS RATING: 7.9
COMMENTS: Red-orange flowers with yellow undersides grace this variety. The blooms are quite fragrant, borne on sturdy plants with semiglossy foliage.

Magic Carrousel

BLOOM FORM: Classic
FRAGRANCE: Light
PLANT SIZE, HABIT: Medium, bushy
DISEASE RESISTANCE: Good
ARS RATING: 8.5
COMMENTS: Introduced in 1972, Magic Carrousel was one of the first miniatures with light pink to white blooms with red edges. Small blooms grow mostly one per stem. A climbing form is available.

Millie Walters

BLOOM FORM: Classic
FRAGRANCE: Light
PLANT SIZE, HABIT: Short, bushy
DISEASE RESISTANCE: Good
ARS RATING: 8.4
COMMENTS: Deep coral pink blooms grow singly and in small sprays on this plant. The rose is named for a former first lady of the American Rose Society.

Minnie Pearl

BLOOM FORM: Classic
FRAGRANCE: Light
PLANT SIZE, HABIT: Medium, bushy
DISEASE RESISTANCE: Excellent
ARS RATING: 9.0
COMMENTS: This highly rated variety named for the comedienne and country-western singer bears light pink blooms with deep pink undersides. Less intense heat produces better color.

My Sunshine

BLOOM FORM: Single
FRAGRANCE: Medium
PLANT SIZE, HABIT: Medium, bushy
DISEASE RESISTANCE: Excellent
ARS RATING: 8.5
COMMENTS: Large, solid yellow single blooms bear a fairly pronounced fragrance. They grow singly and in small clusters on vigorous plants.

Neon Cowboy

BLOOM FORM: Single
FRAGRANCE: Light
PLANT SIZE, HABIT: Short, bushy
DISEASE RESISTANCE: Excellent
ARS RATING: 8.0
COMMENTS: Neon Cowboy has the habit of a short floribunda, with medium-size sprays on short plants. Red blooms are centered with large yellow eyes.

Party Girl

BLOOM FORM: Classic
FRAGRANCE: Medium, spicy
PLANT SIZE, HABIT: Short to medium, spreading
DISEASE RESISTANCE: Good
ARS RATING: 8.2
COMMENTS: Plant this one close to the front door to enjoy the soft yellow-apricot flowers with lighter petal edges and a spicy fragrance. Blooms grow singly and in small clusters.

Pierrine

BLOOM FORM: Classic
FRAGRANCE: Light
PLANT SIZE, HABIT: Medium, bushy
DISEASE RESISTANCE: Good
ARS RATING: 9.0
COMMENTS: Pierrine's large, coral pink blooms have super exhibition form, accounting for the high rating. They're carried mostly one per stem.

Rainbow's End

BLOOM FORM: Classic
FRAGRANCE: None
PLANT SIZE, HABIT: Medium, bushy
DISEASE RESISTANCE: Good
ARS RATING: 8.7
COMMENTS: A pot of gold edged with rubies describes this well-named variety, which also has a climbing form. Golden petals tipped with red are carried on free-flowering plants.

Red Cascade

BLOOM FORM: Informal
FRAGRANCE: None
PLANT SIZE, HABIT: Tall, spreading
DISEASE RESISTANCE: Good
ARS RATING: 7.6
COMMENTS: Canes can reach 10 feet or longer on this climber. The lax canes can be either supported or left to flop as a groundcover. Solid red blooms are borne mostly in small clusters.

Rise 'n' Shine

BLOOM FORM: Classic
FRAGRANCE: Medium
PLANT SIZE, HABIT: Medium, bushy
DISEASE RESISTANCE: Good
ARS RATING: 8.4
COMMENTS: Ralph Moore bred many good yellow minis in his 101 years, and this is one of them. Solid yellow blooms with good form and a nice fragrance are borne in profusion.

Roller Coaster

BLOOM FORM: Semidouble
FRAGRANCE: Light
PLANT SIZE, HABIT: Tall, spreading
DISEASE RESISTANCE: Good
ARS RATING: 8.2
COMMENTS: Red stripes on white blooms with large clusters of stamens form in clusters. Canes reach 5 to 6 feet. In the fall, stop deadheading to encourage orange hips.

Ruby Pendant

BLOOM FORM: Classic
FRAGRANCE: Light
PLANT SIZE, HABIT: Medium, bushy
DISEASE RESISTANCE: Good
ARS RATING: 8.4
COMMENTS: Reddish purple flowers are borne mostly one per stem. Productive, vigorous plants grow with attractive reddish green foliage.

Ruby Ruby

BLOOM FORM: Classic
FRAGRANCE: Light
PLANT SIZE, HABIT: Medium, bushy
DISEASE RESISTANCE: Excellent
ARS RATING: 8.0
COMMENTS: This very floriferous compact plant is the type Europeans would call a patio rose. Solid red blooms are borne in large sprays on vigorous, slightly spreading plants.

Scentsational

BLOOM FORM: Classic
FRAGRANCE: Heavy
PLANT SIZE, HABIT: Medium, upright
DISEASE RESISTANCE: Fair
ARS RATING: 7.6
COMMENTS: Nicely formed blooms in light purple with pink overtones carry one of the heaviest fragrances found in a miniature. Flowers grow singly and in medium-size clusters.

Simplex

BLOOM FORM: Single
FRAGRANCE: Light
PLANT SIZE, HABIT: Medium, bushy
DISEASE RESISTANCE: Excellent
ARS RATING: 8.4
COMMENTS: The five petals of this white rose do not overlap, as do most singles, but separate slightly to form a perfect star. Vigorous, bushy plants have dark green leathery foliage.

Small Miracle

BLOOM FORM: Classic
FRAGRANCE: Light
PLANT SIZE, HABIT: Medium, bushy
DISEASE RESISTANCE: Good
ARS RATING: 7.9
COMMENTS: Small white blooms are lightly fragrant, borne in small sprays on plants with dark green glossy foliage.

Snow Bride

BLOOM FORM: Classic
FRAGRANCE: Light
PLANT SIZE, HABIT: Medium, bushy
DISEASE RESISTANCE: Good
ARS RATING: 8.5
COMMENTS: This variety from 1982 was the hot exhibition white miniature for many years. Perfectly formed blooms are borne mostly singly on vigorous plants.

Starina

BLOOM FORM: Classic
FRAGRANCE: Medium
PLANT SIZE, HABIT: Medium, bushy
DISEASE RESISTANCE: Excellent
ARS RATING: 8.3
COMMENTS: Introduced in 1965, Starina was the miniature to emulate for many years. Orange-red blooms have good form and notable fragrance. Bushy plants are very disease resistant.

Sun Sprinkles

BLOOM FORM: Classic
FRAGRANCE: Light
PLANT SIZE, HABIT: Medium, bushy
DISEASE RESISTANCE: Excellent
ARS RATING: 7.8
COMMENTS: This variety from Jackson & Perkins is one of very few miniatures to receive an AARS award. The deep yellow blooms are borne in profusion, both singly and in small sprays, on compact, very disease-resistant plants.

Sweet Chariot

BLOOM FORM: Informal
FRAGRANCE: Heavy
PLANT SIZE, HABIT: Medium, spreading
DISEASE RESISTANCE: Good
ARS RATING: 8.4
COMMENTS: The blooms swing low on this short, spreading variety. The lavender-purple very double blooms are borne in large, very fragrant clusters. The bushes feature medium green matte foliage.

Sweet Diana

BLOOM FORM: Classic
FRAGRANCE: Light
PLANT SIZE, HABIT: Medium, bushy
DISEASE RESISTANCE: Good
ARS RATING: 7.8
COMMENTS: Named by breeder Harm Saville for his granddaughter, this deep yellow miniature grows small clusters of blooms on vigorous plants.

Minifloras

Minifloras are the newest family of roses. These petite roses bear adorable blooms that measure 2 to 3 inches in diameter.

In 1999, the American Rose Society established the miniflora class at the request of hybridizers who said that they had to discard many promising seedlings simply because the blooms weren't small enough to be considered miniatures. After the class was created, existing larger miniatures were allowed to move into the miniflora category.

At first, breeders expected that minifloras would include both large classic bloom miniatures and short floribundas. However, the classic bloom miniatures dominate the category, with very few floribunda-type plants registered as minifloras.

Most miniflora breeding comes from rose exhibitors and small-scale hybridizers who exhibit the blooms at rose shows. Of the hundreds of miniflora varieties registered, only a handful come from the three biggest United States rose companies: Jackson & Perkins, Weeks Roses, and Conard-Pyle.

Virtually all miniflora blooms are 2 to 3 inches in diameter. The classic blooms of many resemble little hybrid teas. Since miniatures are in their bloodlines, what's "tall" for a miniflora is anything more than 4 feet.

Grow minifloras where you want to grow hybrid teas but just don't have enough room. Follow the same care instructions, providing plenty of sun, fertilizer, pest control, and winter protection. Repeat bloom is generally better than most of their larger counterparts, and they grow well on their own roots, making hardier bushes. Minifloras can produce dozens of blooms on a single bush.

PLANT SIZE

SHORT: Less than 2 feet tall
MEDIUM: 2 to 4 feet tall
TALL: More than 4 feet tall

PLANT HABIT

UPRIGHT: Less than 18 inches wide
BUSHY: 18 to 30 inches wide
SPREADING: More than 30 inches wide

Abby's Angel

BLOOM FORM: Classic
FRAGRANCE: Light
PLANT SIZE, HABIT: Tall, upright
DISEASE RESISTANCE: Good
ARS RATING: 7.7
COMMENTS: Red edges on deep yellow petals makes a stunning bloom. The flowers grow mostly one per stem on 4-foot-tall plants with dark green semiglossy foliage.

Amy Grant

BLOOM FORM: Classic
FRAGRANCE: Light
PLANT SIZE, HABIT: Short, upright
DISEASE RESISTANCE: Good
ARS RATING: 7.5
COMMENTS: Named for the gospel-country singer, Amy Grant has light pink flowers that show a deep pink center. The plant is rather short for a miniflora. Foliage is dark green and glossy.

Autumn Splendor

BLOOM FORM: Classic
FRAGRANCE: Light
PLANT SIZE, HABIT: Medium, bushy
DISEASE RESISTANCE: Good
ARS RATING: 8.1
COMMENTS: This variety includes the colors of fall foliage: yellow, gold, and orange, with slight touches of red. Blooms are carried singly and in small sprays on vigorous, productive plants.

Butter Cream

BLOOM FORM: Classic
FRAGRANCE: None
PLANT SIZE, HABIT: Medium, upright
DISEASE RESISTANCE: Good
ARS RATING: 7.8
COMMENTS: Soft yellow petals with a deeper yellow reverse grow about 2 inches wide on plants with glossy green foliage and good disease resistance.

Conundrum

BLOOM FORM: Classic
FRAGRANCE: Light
PLANT SIZE, HABIT: Medium, bushy
DISEASE RESISTANCE: Good
ARS RATING: 7.7
COMMENTS: Warm yellow blooms with red edges are a hallmark of this rose from hybridizer Robbie Tucker. The flowers are borne singly on vigorous plants.

Dr John Dickman

BLOOM FORM: Classic
FRAGRANCE: Medium
PLANT SIZE, HABIT: Medium, upright
DISEASE RESISTANCE: Excellent
ARS RATING: 7.8
COMMENTS: Absolutely gorgeous lavender blooms with red edges grace this healthy, upright variety named for a longtime writer and columnist for *American Rose* magazine.

Louisville Lady

BLOOM FORM: Classic
FRAGRANCE: Light
PLANT SIZE, HABIT: Medium, bushy
DISEASE RESISTANCE: Good
ARS RATING: 7.6
COMMENTS: Bright light red blooms with a white underside have a long vase life as cut flowers. The plant has dark green glossy foliage.

Memphis King

BLOOM FORM: Classic
FRAGRANCE: Light
PLANT SIZE, HABIT: Short to medium, bushy
DISEASE RESISTANCE: Good
ARS RATING: 7.7
COMMENTS: Probably named for Elvis, this variety bears solid red blooms on a rather short plant with medium green semiglossy foliage.

Memphis Magic

BLOOM FORM: Classic
FRAGRANCE: Light
PLANT SIZE, HABIT: Medium, upright
DISEASE RESISTANCE: Good
ARS RATING: 7.6
COMMENTS: Deep red blooms can be almost black, with a lighter red underside. Flowers are borne in small sprays on medium-size plants.

Olympic Gold

BLOOM FORM: Classic
FRAGRANCE: Light
PLANT SIZE, HABIT: Medium, bushy
DISEASE RESISTANCE: Good
ARS RATING: 7.7
COMMENTS: This rose dates from 1983 and has been reclassified from a miniature to a miniflora. The deep yellow blooms are produced mostly one per stem on vigorous, bushy plants.

Overnight Scentsation

BLOOM FORM: Classic
FRAGRANCE: Heavy
PLANT SIZE, HABIT: Medium, bushy
DISEASE RESISTANCE: Good
ARS RATING: 7.5
COMMENTS: Grow this miniflora for its exceptional fragrance. Large medium pink blooms grow mostly singly on vigorous plants with semiglossy medium to dark green foliage.

Peach Delight

BLOOM FORM: Classic
FRAGRANCE: Heavy
PLANT SIZE, HABIT: Medium, spreading
DISEASE RESISTANCE: Good
ARS RATING: 7.7
COMMENTS: Large, very fragrant deep apricot to peach beauties grow on arching, spreading plants with good disease resistance.

Rocky Top

BLOOM FORM: Classic
FRAGRANCE: Light
PLANT SIZE, HABIT: Medium, upright
DISEASE RESISTANCE: Good
ARS RATING: 7.6
COMMENTS: Named after a country-bluegrass song, these exhibition blooms vary from orange to coral pink depending upon the weather. The plants have dark green semiglossy foliage.

Sassy Cindy

BLOOM FORM: Classic
FRAGRANCE: Light
PLANT SIZE, HABIT: Medium, upright
DISEASE RESISTANCE: Good
ARS RATING: 7.5
COMMENTS: Dark green semiglossy foliage covers 3-foot plants. The exhibition-form blooms are an eye-catching deep red with a light yellow reverse, borne mostly one per stem.

Solar Flair

BLOOM FORM: Classic
FRAGRANCE: Light
PLANT SIZE, HABIT: Medium, bushy
DISEASE RESISTANCE: Good
ARS RATING: 7.5
COMMENTS: Yellow blooms with red petal edges add flair to this sunny variety. The medium-size plants exhibit dark green glossy foliage.

Spring's a Comin'

BLOOM FORM: Classic
FRAGRANCE: Medium
PLANT SIZE, HABIT: Medium, bushy
DISEASE RESISTANCE: Good
ARS RATING: 7.8
COMMENTS: If light pink is the color of spring, this rose qualifies. White blooms with delicate light pink edges are set off by dark green semiglossy foliage.

Tennessee Sunrise

BLOOM FORM: Classic
FRAGRANCE: Medium
PLANT SIZE, HABIT: Medium, upright
DISEASE RESISTANCE: Good
ARS RATING: 7.8
COMMENTS: Sunrise in Tennessee must be filled with blends of yellows, reds, and orange like the blooms on this miniflora. Medium-size plants have good disease resistance and dark green foliage.

Thanks to Sue

BLOOM FORM: Classic
FRAGRANCE: Medium
PLANT SIZE, HABIT: Medium, spreading
DISEASE RESISTANCE: Good
ARS RATING: 7.7
COMMENTS: Semidouble blooms of solid amber to apricot fade to a soft peachy pink. The flowers, borne mostly singly, have a nice aroma. Plants grow to about 2 feet tall with medium green foliage.

Tiffany Lite

BLOOM FORM: Classic
FRAGRANCE: Light
PLANT SIZE, HABIT: Tall, bushy
DISEASE RESISTANCE: Good
ARS RATING: 7.7
COMMENTS: This white sport of Tiffany Lynn produces double blooms in small sprays. Tiffany Lite has a mild fragrance.

Tiffany Lynn

BLOOM FORM: Classic
FRAGRANCE: Light
PLANT SIZE, HABIT: Tall, bushy
DISEASE RESISTANCE: Good
ARS RATING: 8.1
COMMENTS: Introduced in 1985, this lovely rose has light pink petals suffused with deeper pink, especially at their edges.

Valentine's Day

BLOOM FORM: Informal
FRAGRANCE: Light
PLANT SIZE, HABIT: Large, spreading
DISEASE RESISTANCE: Excellent
ARS RATING: 7.5
COMMENTS: Valentine's Day, a climbing miniflora, bears deep red blooms produced in small clusters on arching plants with canes reaching 10 feet.

Whirlaway

BLOOM FORM: Classic
FRAGRANCE: None
PLANT SIZE, HABIT: Tall, upright
DISEASE RESISTANCE: Good
ARS RATING: 7.7
COMMENTS: Whirlaway was the the horse that won the Triple Crown in 1941. His namesake's pure white blooms are borne on tall plants with long stems that are ideal for cutting.

Climbers and Ramblers

Large-flowered climbers and ramblers provide the most romantic look in any rose garden: a bloom-laden archway welcoming guests.

These vigorous and hardy roses have numerous landscape uses. You can cover and partially hide sheds or adorn fences and pergolas. Long-caned roses also provide loads of cutting blooms for the house.

The American Rose Society in 1999 eliminated the classification name of "rambler" and replaced it with the more accurate "hybrid wichuriana." However, the generic term rambler is still useful when describing very long-caned plants with small flowers and nonrecurrent blooms. Ramblers are useful in certain situations, but few are rated at 7.5 or above, partly because they're not grown frequently enough and rated.

The American Rose Society introduced the large-flowered climber classification in 1940. All of the varieties here are large-flowered climbers except those marked otherwise. Interestingly, some varieties do not grow large flowers, and none of them climb by attaching themselves naturally to structures. Use soft ties to manually attach the canes to supports.

Climbers can take two to three years to establish and produce blooms, so choose carefully. To get as heavy a bloom as possible, allow the canes at the base of the plant to grow to their full length and train them onto a structure, spreading them out.

BLOOM SIZE

SMALL: Less than 2 inches wide
MEDIUM: 2 to 4 inches wide
LARGE: More than 4 inches wide

BLOOM TYPE

SINGLE: 5 to 8 petals
SEMIDOUBLE: 9 to 20 petals
DOUBLE: 21 to 45 petals
VERY DOUBLE: More than 45 petals

CANE LENGTH

SHORT: Less than 10 feet
MEDIUM: 10 to 20 feet
LONG: More than 20 feet

Albéric Barbier

BLOOM SIZE, TYPE: Small, double
FRAGRANCE: Medium
FAMILY, CANE LENGTH: Hybrid wichurana, long
DISEASE RESISTANCE: Good
ARS RATING: 8.0
COMMENTS: One of the few ramblers rated higher than 7.5, this rose has nicely fragrant creamy-white flowers with yellow eyes. They grow singly and in clusters.

Altissimo

BLOOM SIZE, TYPE: Large, single
FRAGRANCE: Light
CANE LENGTH: Medium
DISEASE RESISTANCE: Good
ARS RATING: 8.5
COMMENTS: Large, deep red blooms with golden stamens stand out in the garden. Looks like this make up for the lack of fragrance. Strong canes reach 10 to 12 feet.

America

BLOOM SIZE, TYPE: Medium, double
FRAGRANCE: Heavy
CANE LENGTH: Short to medium
DISEASE RESISTANCE: Good
ARS RATING: 8.3
COMMENTS: The first climber to win an AARS award, America has been extremely popular since 1976. Very fragrant medium pink blooms are borne in small sprays.

American Pillar

BLOOM SIZE, TYPE: Small, single
FRAGRANCE: None
FAMILY, CANE LENGTH: Hybrid wichurana, medium
DISEASE RESISTANCE: Good
ARS RATING: 7.9
COMMENTS: Small carmine-pink blooms with white eyes are carried in large clusters on this old favorite. The plant is a heavy bloomer and will reach up to 20 feet.

Awakening

BLOOM SIZE, TYPE: Large, double
FRAGRANCE: Medium
CANE LENGTH: Medium
DISEASE RESISTANCE: Good
ARS RATING: 8.0
COMMENTS: This sport of New Dawn bears fragrant light-pink blooms with some salmon shading. Plants produce large flowers in small clusters.

Berries 'n' Cream

BLOOM SIZE, TYPE: Large, semidouble
FRAGRANCE: Medium
CANE LENGTH: Medium
DISEASE RESISTANCE: Good
ARS RATING: 7.8
COMMENTS: Are these blooms pink with white stripes or white with pink stripes? In either case, they blend nicely in large sprays on a medium-size plant. The variety originated in Denmark.

Blaze Improved

BLOOM SIZE, TYPE: Large, double
FRAGRANCE: Medium
CANE LENGTH: Medium
DISEASE RESISTANCE: Good
ARS RATING: 8.9
COMMENTS: Bred in the Czech Republic in 1935, this red rose, also known as Demokracie, has better disease resistance than its parent. Blooms are borne in medium-size clusters on strong plants. It's a nice rose, but the rating is somewhat inflated.

Brite Eyes

BLOOM SIZE, TYPE: Medium, semidouble
FRAGRANCE: Light
CANE LENGTH: Short
DISEASE RESISTANCE: Excellent
ARS RATING: 7.9
COMMENTS: Medium pink flowers with white eyes and golden stamens are borne in small clusters on this short climber. Because it's from the hybridizer of Knock Out, it's also very disease resistant.

Compassion

BLOOM SIZE, TYPE: Large, double
FRAGRANCE: Heavy
CANE LENGTH: Medium
DISEASE RESISTANCE: Excellent
ARS RATING: 8.5
COMMENTS: Very fragrant salmon pink hybrid tea-type blooms grow in small clusters on very disease-resistant plants.

Don Juan

BLOOM SIZE, TYPE: Large, double
FRAGRANCE: Heavy
CANE LENGTH: Medium
DISEASE RESISTANCE: Good
ARS RATING: 8.2
COMMENTS: Large velvety red blooms with heavy fragrance make this rose perfect for cut flowers. Plants reach 12 to 14 feet, so consider training the canes horizontally to reach the blooms easily.

Dream Weaver

BLOOM SIZE, TYPE: Medium, double
FRAGRANCE: Light
FAMILY, CANE LENGTH: Climbing floribunda, medium
DISEASE RESISTANCE: Good
ARS RATING: 7.9
COMMENTS: Coral pink blooms form in large clusters on a medium-size climber. The flowers have a light rose fragrance. The foliage grows glossy green.

Dublin Bay

BLOOM SIZE, TYPE: Large, double
FRAGRANCE: Medium
CANE LENGTH: Medium
DISEASE RESISTANCE: Excellent
ARS RATING: 8.6
COMMENTS: This deep red rose carries its blooms both in small sprays and singly. Although not as fragrant as Don Juan, it has better disease resistance and is another great climber for cutting.

Fourth of July

BLOOM SIZE, TYPE: Medium, semidouble
FRAGRANCE: Light
CANE LENGTH: Short to medium
DISEASE RESISTANCE: Good
ARS RATING: 8.1
COMMENTS: Extremely attractive light pink blooms with cerise stripes and golden stamens form in medium-size clusters.

Händel

BLOOM SIZE, TYPE: Large, double
FRAGRANCE: Light
CANE LENGTH: Short to medium
DISEASE RESISTANCE: Good
ARS RATING: 7.9
COMMENTS: This variety, introduced in 1965, was one of the first roses to feature light pink blooms with deeper pink petal edges. Lightly fragrant blooms form in small sprays on plants with strong canes.

Harlekin

BLOOM SIZE, TYPE: Medium, double
FRAGRANCE: Medium
CANE LENGTH: Medium
DISEASE RESISTANCE: Good
ARS RATING: 8.1
COMMENTS: Creamy-white blooms are striped with pink, sometimes on petal edges and sometimes throughout the bloom, depending on the weather. These very attractive flowers form in small clusters on plants that average about 10 feet.

High Society

BLOOM SIZE, TYPE: Large, double
FRAGRANCE: Medium
CANE LENGTH: Medium
DISEASE RESISTANCE: Good
ARS RATING: 7.5
COMMENTS: Fragrant magenta-pink blooms grow in large sprays on this vigorous recent introduction. The plant grows about 15 feet tall with a bloom color found on few roses of this type.

Joseph's Coat

BLOOM SIZE, TYPE: Medium, double
FRAGRANCE: Light
CANE LENGTH: Short to medium
DISEASE RESISTANCE: Good
ARS RATING: 7.5
COMMENTS: This rose lives up to its name. Blooms grow in a blend of yellows, oranges, and reds, forming medium-size sprays.

New Dawn

BLOOM SIZE, TYPE: Medium, double
FRAGRANCE: Medium
CANE LENGTH: Medium to tall
DISEASE RESISTANCE: Good
ARS RATING: 8.6
COMMENTS: New Dawn's soft pink blooms carry a moderate fragrance, forming singly and in small clusters. Although it's an Earth-Kind variety, it is susceptible to black spot in damp climates.

Newport Fairy

BLOOM SIZE, TYPE: Small, single
FRAGRANCE: Light
FAMILY, CANE LENGTH: Hybrid wichurana, medium to long
DISEASE RESISTANCE: Good
ARS RATING: 8.5
COMMENTS: The highest rated of the wichurana ramblers, this variety carries light pink single blooms in very large sprays. Plants grow about 20 feet tall.

Night Owl

BLOOM SIZE, TYPE: Medium, single
FRAGRANCE: Medium
CANE LENGTH: Medium
DISEASE RESISTANCE: Good
ARS RATING: 7.8
COMMENTS: Deep purple single blooms contrast stunningly with golden stamens. The moderately fragrant blooms are borne in large sprays on upright plants reaching about 14 feet.

Pearly Gates

BLOOM SIZE, TYPE: Large, double
FRAGRANCE: Heavy
CANE LENGTH: Medium
DISEASE RESISTANCE: Good
ARS RATING: 7.7
COMMENTS: A color sport of America, this sister variety bears large, fragrant blooms of soft pearl pink with slightly deeper pink centers.

Pierre de Ronsard

BLOOM SIZE, TYPE: Medium, very double
FRAGRANCE: Light
CANE LENGTH: Medium to tall
DISEASE RESISTANCE: Excellent
ARS RATING: 8.2
COMMENTS: This rose, named after a 16th-century French poet, has creamy-white flowers suffused with rich pink, carried in small clusters. In the United States, it's sold under the name Eden.

Polka

BLOOM SIZE, TYPE: Large, very double
FRAGRANCE: Medium
CANE LENGTH: Short to medium
DISEASE RESISTANCE: Good
ARS RATING: 7.8
COMMENTS: This multiple-petaled Romantica rose grows large flowers in shades of apricot and yellow. Small sprays form on strong plants reaching about 12 feet.

Ramblin' Red

BLOOM SIZE, TYPE: Large, double
FRAGRANCE: Light
CANE LENGTH: Short
DISEASE RESISTANCE: Excellent
ARS RATING: 7.8
COMMENTS: Solid cardinal red blooms grow in large sprays on this disease-resistant plant from the breeder of Knock Out.

Rosarium Uetersen

BLOOM SIZE, TYPE: Large, very double
FRAGRANCE: Medium
CANE LENGTH: Short
DISEASE RESISTANCE: Excellent
ARS RATING: 8.5
COMMENTS: More a large shrub than a true climber, this rose from Germany grows about 8 feet tall and wide. Deep pink, fragrant blooms grow in large clusters on disease-resistant plants.

Royal Sunset

BLOOM SIZE, TYPE: Large, semidouble
FRAGRANCE: Heavy
CANE LENGTH: Medium to long
DISEASE RESISTANCE: Good
ARS RATING: 8.9
COMMENTS: The highest rated ARS climber, this 50-year-old variety has gorgeous apricot-pink blooms that grow singly and in small clusters on pliable canes.

Social Climber

BLOOM SIZE, TYPE: Large, double
FRAGRANCE: Medium
CANE LENGTH: Short
DISEASE RESISTANCE: Good
ARS RATING: 7.7
COMMENTS: Social Climber grows only about 6 feet tall with strong branching canes and deep green foliage. The fragrant medium pink blooms are borne singly and in small clusters.

Sombreuil

BLOOM SIZE, TYPE: Large, very double
FRAGRANCE: Heavy
CANE LENGTH: Medium
DISEASE RESISTANCE: Good
ARS RATING: 8.8
COMMENTS: Long classified as a climbing tea, this wonderfully fragrant rose is now a large-flowered climber. Many-petaled pure white blooms grow in small sprays on plants that tolerate shade.

Stairway to Heaven

BLOOM SIZE, TYPE: Medium, double
FRAGRANCE: Light
FAMILY, CANE LENGTH: Climbing floribunda, medium
DISEASE RESISTANCE: Good
ARS RATING: 7.5
COMMENTS: Classed as a climbing floribunda, this rose has medium red blooms with a mild aroma. They form in small clusters on plants that reach 10 to 12 feet.

The Impressionist

BLOOM SIZE, TYPE: Large, very double
FRAGRANCE: Heavy
CANE LENGTH: Medium
DISEASE RESISTANCE: Good
ARS RATING: 8.0
COMMENTS: Varying hues of yellow, amber, and orange adorn this, very fragrant, very double rose. Medium tall, bushy plants grow dark green foliage.

Resources

Rose information is available through many sources. As a rose grower, all you need to do is ask.

The American Rose Society

The American Rose Society also offers free advice to all gardeners through the Consulting Rosarian program. Contract the American Rose Society at P.O. Box 30,000, Shreveport, LA 71130, 800-637-6534. Their website is www.ars.org.

Roses by mail

Roses are available from many online sources:

DAVID AUSTIN ROSES
15059 State Hwy. 64 West, Tyler TX 75704
800-328-8893; www.davidaustinroses.com

HEIRLOOM ROSES
24062 NE Riverside Drive, St. Paul, OR 97137
503-538-1576; www.heirloomroses.com

PICKERING NURSERIES
3043 County Road #2 RR#1
Port Hope, Ontario, Canada L1A 3V5
905-753-2155; www.pickeringnurseries.com

REGAN NURSERY
4268 Decoto Road, Fremont, CA 94555
510-797-3222; www.regannursery.com

ROSEMANIA
4020 Trail Ridge Drive, Franklin, TN 37067
888-600-9665; www.rosemania.com

ROSES UNLIMITED
363 N. Deerwood Drive, Laurens, SC 29360
864-682-7673; www.rosesunlimitedownroot.com

THE ANTIQUE ROSE EMPORIUM
Retail centers in Independence and San Antonio, TX
Order: 9300 Lueckemeyer Road, Brenham, TX 77833
800-441-0002; www.antiqueroseemporium.com

VINTAGE GARDENS
4130 Gravenstein Hwy. North, Sebastopol, CA 95472
707-829-2035; www.vintagegardens.com

Index